A DISTANT
THUNDER

A Clio History Book
New Chapter Press • *New York* • *California*

ANNE TOPHAM

A DISTANT

Intimate
Recollections
of the
Kaiser's Court

THUNDER

Library of Congress Card Catalog Number: 92-60938

ISBN: 0-942257-26-X

This book originally appeared in a somewhat different form as three books: Memories of the Kaiser's Court (London: Methuen, 1914; New York: Dodd, Mead, 1914); Memories of the Fatherland (New York: Dodd, Mead, 1916); and Chronicles of the Prussian Court (London: Hutchison & Co., 1926).

Jacket and interior design by Jacek Przybyszewski
Chapter notes by Stewart Wolpin
Glossary and translations by Antje Purucker Kandell
Edited by Jill Mason
Additional research by Hazel Waldner and Maximilian Crisp

10 9 8 7 6 5 4 3 2 1

First printing: September 1992

Manufactured in the United States of America

ACKNOWLEDGMENTS

The publisher would like to thank Geoff Lennox of the Local Studies Library of the Derbyshire County Council and B. Haigh of the Derby Library for providing the biographical information on Anne Topham, Christoph Münch of the German Consulate in New York for his help with the research, and Cynthia Vartan for her thoughtful gift of many of the illustrations. Additional research assistance was provided by the New Canaan (Connecticut) Library. A final thank you to the Bryn Mawr Book Sale, which sold Ewing Walker a drab and dusty volume, thus unwittingly introducing us to the works of Anne Topham. Further ideas and encouragement were given by Maxine Detlefsen, Tonya Detlefsen, and Shirley Cloyes.

The imperial family in 1896. From the top left, standing, Crown Prince Wilhelm, Victoria Louise, the Emperor, the Empress, Adalbert, Eitel-Frederick, Oskar, Joachim, and August-Wilhelm. At this time, the three older boys—the Crown Prince, Fritz, and Adalbert—were already living at the Kadettenschule in Plön under the tutelage of General von Gontard.

C O N T E N T S

Princess Victoria Louise at the time of her confirmation in 1909 at the age of seventeen. Grown up now, she had no need for further education and her governesses were dismissed.

F O R E W O R D

If I had known that the seven years which I spent at the Prussian Court of Kaiser Wilhelm II were to be among the last of a period of imperial progress and splendor almost unparalleled in modern times—between 1902 and 1909, the German Empire was expanding in every quarter of the globe—I should have noted with even increased interest and attention the various happenings of the time.

In recent years, the German nation and the policies that guide its destinies have been put to the test and the psychology of its people put under the light of a virulent criticism as surely the soul of no race in the records of history has ever been investigated. Beyond chronicling certain experiences, this book makes little attempt to interpret the German national consciousness, a complex and, in some respects, contradictory spirit, rising to heights of sublimity, merging into nauseous sentimentality, often inspired by self-interest, yet anxious to convince itself of the purity of its motives, always preserving a sense of being part of a great whole whose culminating splendor is personified in its ruler, deified by his people to an incredible extent.

The picture of Germany before the Great War, as it appeared to those of us who lived there, is one on which we have fixed our gaze with a desperate hope that the German people are, as we had believed, a simple-hearted, kindly, industrious, and highly cultivated people, living up to the same standard of honor as ourselves and inspired by those ideals which make a nation great. But day by day, the outlines of this picture have become blurred by the horrors and agonies of ruthless warfare such as the modern world has never known.

To those of us who knew Germany fairly well, who have lived intimately with her people, the seeming inconsistency in her conduct, the music and the poetry, the idealism which seems so incongruously allied with an overbearing brutality and diseased egoism, is nevertheless in the nature of an easily accepted and understood attitude of mind.

We see and explain to ourselves some of the reasons that have made the German people what they are: We know they are docile and easily led, of a mind liking to keep company with other minds, kept carefully pruned and only allowed to shoot forth in governmentally approved directions. We know they are a people passionately trained from childhood to believe in the divine destiny of the German race, that their patriotism is as their religion, blind maybe and fanatical, but followed with a faithful sense of duty and the necessity of self-sacrifice, a people that take a certain pride in their lack of refinement, which they regard as verging perilously on effeminacy. They have an intense and inherited hatred for French politesse and subtle wit, and prefer a blunt coarseness, a broad form of humor. In it they see the virility and downright honesty which they imagine to be a purely Teuton characteristic.

Before the horror of the present entirely obliterates the happier memories of bygone times, out of the wreck and welter of dissolving friendships and shattered illusions, one puts forth a timid hand, striving to save some broken fragment, to preserve from the turbid flood of events some shadowy recollection of a saner, happier time, when Germany was at peace and all seemed well with the world.

Anne Topham
Old Farm
Spondon, Derbyshire, England
1916

The Princess Victoria Louise Adelheid Mathilde Charlotte as a ten year old in 1902. She called her curls, created by the laborious efforts of Nana, "the bane of my life."

Frau Wolden, Dancing Mistress
Dr. Zunker, Court Physician
Herr Kaspar, Stable Master
Herr Plintzer, Master of the Horse

Princess Louise, Duchess of Baden, Aunt of the Emperor and Godmother to Princess Victoria Louise (Aunty Baden)

Friends of the Emperor

    Prince Philip von Eulenburg

    Prince Dohna of Schlobitten

    Herr Albert Ballin

    Prince Max Egon von Furstenburg, Marshal of the Court

    Baron Speck von Sternburg, Head Administrator of Rominten Forest

Gentlemen of the Emperor's Suite

    Count Robert von Zedlitz-Trutzschler, Master of the Household

    Major von Scholl

Ladies-in-Waiting

    Countess Therese von Brockdorff, Mistress of the Robes

    Countess Mathilde Keller

    Countess Armgard Stolberg

    Fräulein Clare von Gersdorff

Gentlemen-in-Waiting to the Empress

    Herr von Knesebeck

    Baron von Mirbach

In Service to the Court

    Miss Matcham, English Nurse to the Royal Children

    Fräulein von Thadden, Head Governess 1902–1905

    Fräulein von Saldern, Head Governess 1905–1909

    Anne Topham, English Governess

    Mademoiselle Lauru, French Governess

    Count Blumenthal, Governor to Prince Joachim

    General von Gontard, Governor to the Princes at Plön

    Herr Porger, Tutor to the Royal Children

    Herr Gern, Tutor to the Royal Children

MEMBERS OF THE PRUSSIAN COURT
August 1902–December 1909

The Royal Family
   Emperor Wilhelm II
   Empress Augusta Victoria
   Crown Prince Wilhelm
   Prince Eitel-Frederick (Fritz)
   Prince Adalbert
   Prince Oskar
   Prince August-Wilhelm (Au-Wi)
   Prince Joachim
   Princess Victoria Louise
Frequent Family Visitors
   Princess Frederick Charles of Hesse, Sister of the Emperor (Tante Mosse)
   Princess Sophie of Greece, Sister of the Emperor
   Princes Maximilian and Frederick of Hesse, Cousins to the Royal Children
   Princes George and Alexander of Greece, Cousins to the Royal Children
   Princess May of Glücksburg, Cousin to the Royal Children
   Duchess of Schleswig-Holstein-Sonderburg-Glücksburg, Sister of the Empress
   Princess Feodora of Schleswig-Holstein, Sister of the Empress (Tante Feo)

FIRST IMPRESSIONS

Toward the middle of August 1902, on a hot, dusty, suffocating day, I travelled, the prey of various apprehensions, to the town of Homburg-vor-der-Höhe, where the Prussian Court was in temporary residence. There I had been summoned, to join the court in the capacity of resident English teacher to the nine-year-old Princess Victoria Louise of Prussia, only daughter of Wilhelm II and Augusta Victoria, Emperor and Empress of Germany.

A stormy, eight-hour night passage on the North Sea, during which one is tossed on the waves in a state of acute seasickness, and a long train journey through stifling heat, affect anyone's spiritual buoyancy, and it was with a distinct depression that I descended from the train onto the platform of Homburg station.

I confidently expected that a carriage would be waiting for me, but nothing in the least resembling a royal equipage was to be seen. There was only a row of shabby, open *Droschken* harnessed to weary-looking horses.

As my luggage was plainly addressed to the *Königliches Schloss*—the Royal Palace—the group of officials who surrounded me, all talking in strident tones, were most anxious I should get there as soon as possible. I managed to convey to them my idea that a carriage would probably be coming for me soon. After a few minutes, a porter obligingly went outside the station and looked up the long street for the missing vehicle. He returned sadly shaking his head.

"*Kein Wagen*—no carriage," he murmured with an air of finality. So, in spite of my misgivings, they fell upon my various possessions and put them into the oldest and most decrepit of the Droschken—the only one left—with a horse to correspond, and a driver who struck the last note in deplorable shabbiness and stupidity.

It was not thus—in a wretched Droschke, with my luggage piled drunkenly around me at untidy, ill-fitting angles—that I had dreamed of entering the precincts of royalty.

Up the long *Louisenstrasse* and past the *Kurhaus*—a spa hotel—we rattled over the cobblestones. Down a side-street, I glimpsed a smart brougham with a footman sitting beside the coachman on the box, driving quickly in the direction from which we came. I was convinced that this was the carriage meant for me—and later learned I was correct in that assumption—and wanted to return to the station, but all attempts to convey my meaning to the person whose back obscured my view were unavailing. He shrugged his shoulders, whipped his horse, uttered guttural, incomprehensible ejaculations, and pointed to a large old building in front of us before whose gates a sentry was pacing.

The sentry looked surprised and hesitated; the animal in the shafts crawled through the gate and came to a halt in the midst of a big paved courtyard surrounded by open windows and containing in one corner a flower garden of green turf and climbing geraniums. We were in the royal Homburg *Schloss*.

A sun-bathed silence prevailed. Through a gateway, leading into a second courtyard, a fountain was splashing gently with occasional intermittent hesitations and a pigeon crooned slumberously on the roof. Otherwise, it seemed an absolutely deserted spot.

The driver assumed a round-shouldered, blinking, vacuous attitude of masterly inactivity, and his horse took a nap. I descended from the hateful vehicle and wondered what I ought to do next. There was nothing to indicate before which of the many doors I should be set down.

Between heat, exasperation, and uncertainty, added to the fatigue of travel, I was in a parlous condition, one fume and fret of weariness and desperation. Presently, from under the archway, interposing his bulk between me and the glancing sunlight, a gentleman of stately mien, garbed in a black frockcoat and a tall silk hat, came walking slowly. He wore the aspect of an ambassador. I flung myself into his path, assembled the few fragmentary bits of German that remained with me after the emotions of the day, and said something inarticulate.

The black-coated functionary was not a diplomat—I subsequently learned he was a *Hoffourrier*, a minor official who regulated royal journeys and the small financial house-keeping arrangements of the household—but he had the art of seizing a situation at a glance. He wakened the driver, directed him to a door in the corner, and rang a bell; a rush of gaitered footmen followed; something kaleidoscopic swiftly took place.

I found myself following a servant down a long, cool, bare passage decorated with old prints, up a tiny, winding staircase, and into a pleasant, shady room overlooking the red roofs of Homburg away toward great purple hills silhouetted against a pale lemon sky.

The calm beauty from this high-pitched gabled corner soothed my tired soul. I sank into a funny, old-fashioned chair covered with a blue-spotted chintz that had been out of fashion for at least a hundred and twenty years, and contemplated the fat, square sofa and the rest of the furniture, which was delightfully old—so old that its ugliness had mellowed into something charming.

There was a big mirror fixed over a marble-topped mahogany chest of drawers, in which I caught a glimpse of my haggard face, mahogany chairs covered with the before-mentioned chintz, and a carpet of vivid moss green. All was very plain and comfortable and old-world, spotlessly clean and fresh. Flowers were on the writing table which stood in the embrasure of the window.

Soon I heard a chinking of china outside, and a man in a flowing Russian beard parted in the middle brought in a tray with tea. He bowed politely as he entered the room, the bow without which no well-trained German servant came into the presence of those whom he served, and deftly arranged the tea table. He was clad in plain dark livery, such as was worn by all the *Dienerschaft* in royal employment who were below the rank of footmen.

The sight of the teapot and the taste of the tea eased my concern that this cheerful beverage would be one of the luxuries I would have to renounce permanently on leaving England. "German people all drink coffee, and if they do make tea it's like colored water," I had been assured. That this was true still of the great mass of people my experience was to prove, but the court bought its excellent tea from a large London warehouse and brewed it with due respect to its peculiar needs.

The bedroom in which my luggage had been deposited led out of the sitting room. It contained the same quaint furniture, and a short, squat, solid mahogany bedstead with deep wooden sides, covered with one of those big bags filled with down that one could see hanging out of the windows for an airing every morning at hours permitted by the police.

I washed away the dust of the journey, changed, and began to unpack, wondering if my clothes were right, if I ought to have longer or shorter trains on my dresses, and wishing somebody would come along and explain to me any points that might guide my inexperienced steps.

The departing English teacher whose place I was taking had written me a letter purporting to give advice as to wardrobe and etiquette, but she had recently become engaged, and except an impression that white kid gloves were a chief necessity of life at court, there was little of practical use to be gathered from the vague kindliness of her short note. She wrote that there was practically no etiquette except such as can be "seen at a glance," and left it at that.

A knock came at the door. A voice, a cheerful woman's voice, called my name, and with both hands outstretched in welcome, a tall, middle-aged, smiling person entered, who introduced herself as Countess Mathilde Keller, the lady-in-waiting who had written me of the specific details of my position and my suggested journey. She radiated kindness, was gaiety and charm personified, and knew exactly how I felt—how excited, dubious, tired, and worried—and she laughed it all away while she stood clasping my hand and shaking it at intervals.

"And now," she concluded, "you will dine tonight with Her Majesty at half-past seven."

I started back in horror.

"Yes," she laughed, "it is the best opportunity, because the Emperor is away and it will be very quiet—just a few ladies and gentlemen of the court; it will be quite easy. Her Majesty is so sympathetic—she knows how tired you must be. She will not expect you to be brilliant. But when there is a plunge to be made," she pointed downward toward an unfathomable abyss, "it is better to make it and get it over, isn't it?"

"Will the Princess be there?"

"No, not tonight. She is very excited and wanted to come and see you, but is to wait until tomorrow. She has been talking all day about your coming."

I pondered dubiously in what aspect I presented myself to the thoughts of my unknown pupil.

Before dinner I was solemnly conducted by the Countess to the apartments of the Empress. I wore one long white kid glove; the other was crumpled in my hand with a fan, without which even in the coldest weather no

properly equipped lady could, I learned, be considered fit
to appear before royalty. An elderly footman showed us into
an anteroom furnished in brilliant yellow satin, and there
we sat and waited, chatting in the desultory, half-hearted
manner of people who expect every moment to be inter-
rupted. It was ten minutes before a door leading into an
inner apartment was opened and we were ushered in.

"You will kiss Her Majesty's hand," whispered the
Countess as she passed on in front of me.

The Empress was sitting on a sofa with a stick beside
her: she had sprained her ankle severely some days before.
She received us with a smile and a look which revealed at
once that she herself felt a slight embarrassment.

I suppose the Countess presented me—I have no
definite recollection of it—but at any rate, she disappeared
and left us alone together. I bent and kissed the outstretched
hand and felt that the interview was going to be pleasant,
so eminently kindly was the face that met mine with a
certain shy diffidence.

I sat in a chair and talked easily and without restraint
to a mother about her daughter. It was simple and straight-
forward. We exchanged views on theories of education, on
a child's small idiosyncrasies, on the difficulties of giving her
enough fresh air when so many hours were taken up with
study. We became absorbed in our talk and found that we
had many views in common—always a delightful discovery,
whether the other person be an Empress or a charwoman.

At last, Her Majesty realized that hungry ladies and gentlemen were waiting for her appearance and their dinner;
she rose and walked through several rooms, preceded by a
footman who flung open both leaves of the folding doors.

We emerged into an apartment brightly lit with wax candles, where a subdued buzz of conversation suddenly stopped and the whole company bowed and curtsied at once like a field of corn when the wind passes over it.

That first dinner at the royal table had in it many of the unstable elements of a dream. It passed confusedly through my mind as a series of impressions following each other with such rapidity and lack of cohesion that only the Cubist mind could depict it adequately: an impression that my frock is not quite the right thing, that it is too English and not German enough—it was to be a "high" dress, said the Countess, as we parted, and mine was neckless while the other ladies were clothed right up to the ears and chin— further impressions that I am preternaturally dull and stupid, that the smile I attempt is obviously artificial, that I am an isolated speck of mind surrounded by an incomprehensible ocean of German babbling.

At table I sat between a young, uniformed officer and the departing English teacher. I learned with horror that with her departure the following day, I would be left to grapple singlehandedly with whatever difficulties might arise, without any aid or advice. The German *Obergouvernante*—head governess—Fräulein von Thadden, whom I had expected to find at my side with counsel and guidance, had been in contact with some infectious illness and was in strict quarantine. She would continue to be possibly contagious for the next ten days and was being purified and disinfected somewhere with relations. In the meantime, I was to carry on, as well as my ignorance allowed, the numerous duties of her position as well as my own!

The difficulty of the situation was magnified by the perhaps sympathetic pity of the Germans sitting near me and their encouragement to be "firm" toward my pupil, the transparent hints that she was a remarkably difficult child to manage, and that only a person of unyielding discipline who would exact rigid and unquestioning obedience could have the least chance of coping with her temperament.

"I rather like naughty children," I said, with an effort to throw off the forebodings caused by their remarks. "They have so much more character than good ones. Most people who turn out to be remarkable seem to have been distinguished in their youth for naughtiness." They smiled indulgently, with the air of humoring the whims of a child whose words are not to be taken seriously.

"Grownup people can often be annoying, too," I said as a further contribution to the discussion. They smiled again, immediately changed the subject to something quite unconnected with education, and lapsed into German, leaving me stranded in backwater, where I wondered vaguely if I could possibly keep my eyes open much longer and if it would be *lèse-majesté* if my head suddenly sunk into my dessert.

Mercifully, when we rose from the table, I was dismissed by the Empress to a much-needed repose. I had had no sleep the night before; I had travelled all day through the scorching hours with little to eat or drink in a train that shook and rattled and bumped as only continental trains can. I had been fretted by a Droschke driver, presented to an Empress, and supped at the royal table in private, which is much more alarming than on a ceremonious occasion. So it was a mere wreck and shadow of myself which, guided

9

by the pictures, crawled half-dazed along those interminable passages.

*

I breakfasted in the morning with my English compatriot, who was absorbed in packing and vouchsafed not one single helpful hint as to my future conduct, for which to this day I bear her a grudge. She dismissed the whole business with the airy lightness of one whom it no longer concerned. She showed me a silver dish, a wedding present from Her Majesty, and packed it away, humming.

At about half-past ten, a footman came with a summons to go downstairs. I put on my outdoor things and followed him into the sunny courtyard, through an archway, and along winding sandy paths, until I reached a point where I could see the Empress sitting at a table under some trees near what was called the "English garden"—a garden made, and maintained much as she had left it, by that daughter of George III who married a *Landgraf*—a German prince—of Hesse-Homburg.

Here it was that the Emperor's daughter first came dancing lightly into my life. A grassy bank in front descended so steeply to a tiny lake lying below that the shore was hidden. Suddenly, above this bank, appeared the golden head of a girl of nine or so, dressed in a stiff, starched plain white sailor dress with a blue collar and a straw sailor hat.

In English, her mother called to her, "Come here, Sissy," and with a hop, skip, and a jump, she sprang forward and held out her hand to me with frank friendliness.

A few steps behind her came another flying figure in white—her brother, the Prince Joachim, the youngest of the

Emperor's six sons. And then above the bank emerged the pleasant young officer I had met at supper the night before, Count Blumenthal, the governor to the Prince. Both children began talking in German to the Empress, the girl, as far as my limited knowledge permitted me to judge, emphatically contradicting every word her brother said. They were obviously—well, perhaps it would be an overemphasis to call it quarrelling, but they were certainly not in accord. The governor lingered in the background—lingering in the background becomes a fine art at court—raised his eyebrows, and shook his head with a slight shrug.

"They are always *zanken*—wrangling," he said to me when, after a few minutes, the Empress departed, leaving me to the full enjoyment of my duties.

*

The next few days were busied with initiation into that mysterious inner side of court life of which the public necessarily knows little but imagines many silly things. Chief among those early impressions is that of the Emperor, whom I had not yet seen, as he was absent on one of his numerous journeys.

Distilled through the alembic of his daughter's mind, I soon perceived that the Emperor did not always play the part of a frowning imperial personage of fierce moustaches, corrugated brow, and clenched fist—that he frequently receded from this militant posture and became an ordinary domestic papa who made sportive jokes with his family at the breakfast table and was even occasionally guilty of more atrocious forms of puns.

This phase of Papa's character was painfully brought home to me one day when Victoria Louise amused herself by practicing the schoolboy trick—she was very schoolboyish—of making with her mouth and cheek the pop of a champagne cork and the subsequent gurgle of flowing wine.

"Whoever taught you these unladylike accomplishments?" I asked, in the reproving tones appropriate to an instructor of youth.

"Sh-sh-sh! It was Papa," she answered gleefully, repeating the offending sound with an even more perfect imitation. "He can do it splendidly."

Evidently, when not inspecting regiments and making warlike speeches, Papa unbent to a considerable extent in the bosom of his family. I also learned that Papa didn't like pajamas, and "poor Mamma" seldom had time to get a really proper breakfast because after she had poured out Papa's coffee, served his toast, and ministered to his other wants, she had only time to snatch the merest mouthful for herself before he hurried away to call the dogs and put on his cloak for a brisk early morning walk.

"Come on, come on," he reportedly said with impatience, "how you do dawdle over your food! I've finished long ago," and the whole family had to leave its meal uneaten and start on an hour's tramp through the streets of the town.

Papa was the dominating force in the Princess's life. His ideas, his opinions on men and events were persistently quoted by her: trenchant, fluent criticisms of persons of worldwide fame, astonishing verdicts on men of the hour, issued from her lips in bewildering confidences.

"Papa says that Herr Müller" (the name of course was not Müller) "is a *Schafskopf*—blockhead—and doesn't know what he's talking about," she would say glibly of some well-known politician on whose utterances the world was hanging with bated breath.

Prince Joachim, too, was a faithful reporter of all that he heard his father say, and, as these indiscreet repetitions were not for my ears alone but retailed indiscriminately, I was not surprised, as the years went on, that a good deal leaked into the newspapers.

*

When I arrived at the Prussian Court, I was so ignorant of military matters that I had never seen the goosestep. I was introduced to it by my young pupil, who on the first wet day after my arrival, amused herself for a short time by playing sentry-go-up-and-down the *Turnsaal* with Prince Joachim. Assuming the usual masculine privilege, the Prince constituted himself corporal, giving the word of command, *"Augen rechts, Augen links, Parade-Schritt, Präsentiert das Gewehr!"* Being the only other person present, I was the recipient of more military honors during that half hour than ever again fell my lot.

The goosestep, or *Paradeschritt*, as it is called in Germany, consisted of marching with the knee-joint perfectly straight and produced a curious strutting, stilted, jerking, waddling gait, which, especially when seen from the rear, was to the unaccustomed observer ludicrous, as if the performers were trying to throw away their own feet. It was accompanied by loud stamping, and every day when the court was in Berlin, during the ceremony of changing the guard at one o'clock, the *Hof*, paved with hard round cobblestones, resounded and echoed to martial music and the heavy rhythmic tread of soldier's feet until the windows rattled and the solid walls shook.

*

When I first met the Princess, the chief focus of her life was two ponies which, together with a small victoria uphol- stered in pale blue satin, had been presented to her by the Sultan of Turkey. Those two creatures, Ali and Aladdin, were pale fawn with long white silky manes and tails. When they drew the victoria, which had a diminutive groom perched on a small seat behind, the entourage looked like an exotic circus touring the country roads around Homburg. The Princess drove herself and delighted in flourishing a large whip.

At the time of my arrival, one of the sisters of the Emperor, the Princess Frederick Charles of Hesse, *Tante* Mosse, Victoria Louise called her, was in residence at Kron- berg, a beautiful house built in the old Gothic style. Often, another sister, Princess Sophie, whose husband was then the Crown Prince—and later the King—of Greece, was also visiting with her three sons and two daughters. As Kronberg was within an easy drive of Homburg, and as the Princess of Hesse was the mother of six sons, including two pairs of twins, there was no lack of playfellows for Joachim and Victoria Louise.

At Kronberg, I would watch the white-clad children rushing in and out of the doorways, exploring kitchens, cellars, and attics. In the old Homburg Schloss, they had glorious rainy afternoon games in the upper regions of the castle in whose cobwebby rooms, along with old lumber, were to be found many curiosities—old portraits of dead- and-gone Landgrafs and *Landgravines*—princes and princesses of the old German territories—pictures of the children of the old house attired in the cumbersome finery which in past days hampered unfortunate infancy, pieces of old armor, ancient blunderbusses and rapiers, moth-eaten furniture covered in ragged silk.

Four of that happy band of children were to die tragic, early deaths, but there was not a shadow of approaching fate hanging over them on those sunny afternoons.

I soon developed an unsuspected talent in *Verstecken* —hide-and-seek—especially in the role of seeker. I distributed the thrills with even-handed impartiality, not forgetting that even the child of least originality, who hid in the most obvious place with large portions of his anatomy plainly visible, liked to have a run for his money and enjoyed the hovering discovery best when the seeker was baffled and the wrong cupboard persistently searched.

Our game required the seeker to count slowly up to a hundred with tightly shut eyes, but I compromised this wearisome method by allowing five minutes' "law" and began to count at ninety. These odd five minutes were used to leisurely examine objects which I should otherwise never have seen: to an accompaniment of muffled shrieks, thundering footsteps, and a passing vision of fleeting white legs, short frilly skirts, and smudgy princely features, I was able to study steel engravings of hunting scenes which hung on the walls, engravings which would have made a collector's mouth water.

It was with great indignation that Prince Max, the oldest son of the Princess of Hesse, made the discovery that I did not pass these moments in a state of temporary blindness.

"You must keep your eyes shut all the time," he

objected. (They all spoke English and German equally well but preferred German when talking among themselves, with the exception of the Greek children, who always spoke English.)

I had some difficulty persuading Max that I could honorably keep my eyes fixed on a picture without transgressing the rules of the game.

"But you can see us go by out of the corner of your eye," he said.

"I should hear you in any case."

"Well, you must shut your ears as well; hold your hands over them." He was a conscientious little boy and a past master in argument. But the Princess was no stickler for rules.

"Come along, Max," she cried. "I've got a splendid place. Don't begin to count yet, Topsy." I'd only been there a few days, and she had already found a nickname for me. "Topsy" I remained for the rest of my career.

On the evening of one of these days, my pupil told me an interesting bit of news. "Papa is coming back tomorrow morning," she said, "and then you'll see him. I expect you're looking forward to it very much. I shall tell Papa all about you. You are just like all English people—too thin. Why don't you eat more and try to get fatter?"

"I don't want to get fat," I replied. "And if I did, what would be the use when I have to run about all day after you children? I expect I ran at least ten miles this afternoon when we played hide-and-seek."

"I expect you did. It was a wonderful game, wasn't it? Georgie hid in a bath once and Alexander turned the tap on him. But," returning to an earlier subject, "Papa will want to know all about you, and I will tell him you are very thin. Won't you be pleased to see Papa?''

I said something appropriate and noncommittal, but the fearful joy reserved for the morrow troubled my thoughts. Life seemed already to be sufficiently strenuous.

The Emperor Wilhelm II in his British admiral's uniform. This portrait, signed in English: ''William, Admiral of the Fleet,'' was His Majesty's parting gift to me when I left the service of the imperial family in December 1909.

THE KAISER

I first met the Kaiser, Emperor Wilhelm II, at a picnic in the woods that clothe the lower slopes of the Taunus Mountains. The Empress had driven with the Princess, Prince Joachim, and the usual suite of ladies-in-waiting—Countess Keller, Fräulein Clare von Gersdorff, and one or two others —to meet the Emperor and drink tea in the forest. I rode in the carriage with some of the ladies, who talked with me earnestly about the necessity of being extremely strict with the Princess. Above all, I was cautioned, I was to do all I could to oppose and combat a fatal weakness of the Empress, who, I was warned, had a habit of snatching Victoria Louise away from her studies on the grounds of it being such a lovely day, or that the Princess looked pale, or some such frivolous and inadequate excuse.

I was reminded that the Germans were a serious and highly educated nation, and that they expected from the imperial family an example of hard work and indefatigable effort, which it would be my sacred duty to promote.

Herr Porger, Prince Joachim's tutor, was to be at the Schloss the next day, and the two children would begin regular lessons once more. "All the schools have reopened," said Countess Keller, "but Her Majesty is sure to try to stop Princess from having her lessons because her tutor, Herr Gern, is not here, but you must see to it that Princess has her lessons from eight till twelve."

"But if the Empress—" I began. "Surely I can't go against what the Empress says? It would be difficult—"

"Oh, yes," said the Countess, "it is your duty to see that the Princess has her lessons every day from eight to twelve, the same as all other German children. You will of course be present with your sewing or a book at all the lessons— you have, after all, nothing to teach but your own language—the tutors take care of everything else. But you will see that the Empress does not let any of the lessons *ausfallen*—be cancelled."

I recoiled at the idea of setting my puny desire against maternal authority backed by imperial status as to whether lessons should ausfallen or not. It seemed impossible, absurd. I should inevitably be crushed. It would be a ridiculous position for me; besides—

"That is always the problem," said the Countess, reading my thoughts. "Always these interruptions of studies, the Empress interfering and wanting fresh air, things like that."

"And she is such a naughty girl, too, isn't she?" said Fräulein von Gersdorff. "Very rude to Countess von Brockdorff, not at all fond of her lessons—"

"She speaks English quite well," I offered.

"Yes, better than German!" was the Fräulein's reply. "Of course, she's always had an English nurse, but now she *must* learn German—we want to combat the English influence. It is German and Germany she must know about. She is a German princess."

"Naturally," I murmured, "she must be thoroughly German."

This theory of opposing the Empress was, I discovered, a favorite and continuous attitude of the ladies of the court, who believed they possessed some precious virtue in this show of an inflexible sense of duty and a determination to do the right thing, however disagreeable. This opposition resulted invariably, as might be expected, in the triumph of the Empress and the humiliation of the ladies. I often wondered why they persisted so faithfully in following a line of conduct which created an atmosphere of constant bickering and resulted, as far as they were concerned, in absolute failure. "We have done our best; we have done our part; if it fails, we cannot help it," they used to say.

"My life seems as if it's going to be a constant battle," I sighed to Countess Keller as our long row of carriages pulled up to a spot where the ground under the trees was an unearthly green freckled with sunlight.

Away through the trunks of the pines I could see a long table, around which were seated officers in bright blue, gold, and scarlet uniforms. They were talking; or at least one of them was talking, while the others seemed to listen, throwing in a word of assent here and there.

"When His Majesty has finished talking, you will be introduced," said Fräulein von Gersdorff. "The Empress will present you, so don't go far away."

I stood under the trees, waiting, and watching the footmen, clad in liveries of black and scarlet, place camp stools and arrange cakes and teacups, and hearing gusts of the Emperor's conversation, which, being carried on in German, was unintelligible to me, though there was one word, *kolossal,* which kept emerging from the rumble.

Suddenly the group at the table dispersed, and I became aware of one officer walking away in front of the others. There was a clattering of swords; it did not strike me till afterwards how incongruous was this military attire to the peace of the woods diapered with sun and shadow and drenched in the incense of the pines.

His Majesty turned toward the Empress, Fräulein von Gersdorff signalled to me, and I stepped out of the shadows and came forward. The Emperor looked at me with penetrating, rather quizzical brightness; his keen blue eyes were a violent contrast with the deep sunburn of his face.

"How d'ye do?" he said, and held out his hand. He gripped my hand powerfully and I winced. "Ha!" he exclaimed. "The mailed fist? What?"

"It almost feels like it, Your Majesty," I faltered, glad to get my hand back in my own possession. The Emperor, I learned later, often made this remark about the mailed fist to English people.

Then followed a series of questions: What part of England was I from? The Midlands? Derbyshire? He didn't know much about Derbyshire. I told him that the estates of the Duke of Devonshire were in Derbyshire. "Why is he Duke of Devonshire if his estates lie in Derbyshire?" I was unable to explain the anomaly on the spur of the moment.

"Your topsy-turvy English ways of doing things, I

suppose," said the Emperor with a roar of laughter. I smiled wanly and wished I had studied the history of the Dukes of Devonshire a bit more thoroughly.

Other questions: Had I been in Germany before? (Yes, several years earlier I had travelled the continent with a friend.) Did I speak German? (A bit.) Did I know Homburg? (Only the knowledge of a few days' experience.)

The Empress approached and said tea was ready, and we all sat down at a trestle table under the trees. The Empress poured the tea, assisted by Countess Keller. There were sandwiches and different kinds of cakes. It was simple and pleasant, the shadows of the pine branches dancing with the wind on the tablecloth.

The Emperor took large bites out of his sandwiches and talked incessantly, pausing only from time to time to dip his *Zwieback* into his tea, as is permitted by German custom.

As soon as tea was finished, everybody got back in the waiting carriages. There were six carriages altogether, each with four splendid black Trakehner horses. The first one contained the Emperor and Empress and the two children, the others were filled with the ladies and gentlemen of the suite. We drove in the cool of the evening through the hills, by the fields where the peasants were gathering the harvest, the women with red and green handkerchiefs tied around their heads.

I felt anxious about the events of the day and the thought of the unknown difficulties that lay before me; depressed, too, with the constant remandations to "be firm with the Empress." Tomorrow Herr Porger would begin his lessons, and I would have to begin to be firm. Dreadful thought! How was one firm in a language not one's own with people whose lives ran on such different tracks to that of ordinary mortals?

"Mind, now, tomorrow the lessons begin at eight o'clock, and nothing must interrupt them—nothing!" admonished Countess Keller as I descended from the carriage and into the courtyard of the Schloss.

*

The Emperor was not at all what I had expected him to be. I have tried to recall my impressions of him before and after that day in 1902, the man as I pictured him in my mind, and the man I discovered him to be.

In the first fortnight of my life at the Prussian Court, I discovered the Emperor's intense jealousy of England. It was disillusioning; this man who had so often professed friendship for England was not really friendly at all. A frequent topic of conversation at the royal dinner table was the Boer War. It had recently brought upon the British Empire much humiliation and hatred from the people of the Continent who considered England a mighty oppressor of a weak nation. By the time I arrived in Germany, we had achieved a belated victory, but the conflict dragged on in weary guerilla warfare.

I had no convincing arguments to oppose the Emperor's theory that it was the patent lack of British military knowledge which led to all our disasters. He explained to me carefully, with forcible gesture and absolute conviction, how the campaign in South Africa should have been carried out. He told me of all the mistakes made as if I were personally responsible. That an emperor would discuss with his daughter's English teacher the intricacies of contemporary warfare was surprising and characteristic of the Kaiser, who

even in his blunders, was thus distinguished from the
remoteness of other monarchs who moved like well-
regulated machinery across the vision of the world, keeping
their proper places in the orbit of their respective spheres.
Here was a monarch who turned no merely official face to
the public, who put his own personality, his individual tastes
and manner of thought candidly before it, who seemed to
conceal nothing, who took everyone into his confidence
and was indiscreetly open. This sovereign had the great
charm of a breezy unconventionality. At one leap, Wilhelm
would jump down from his throne and good-humoredly ally
himself with a person who, maybe for the first time, was
coming, shrinking, into the awesome presence of royalty.
It cannot be denied that there is something flattering in
having an emperor give you lessons in military strategy.

In most of his pictures, the Emperor preferred to be
depicted with a stern martial expression, the expression he
assumed when on military duty. This was the look he wore
for the first thirty seconds of any interview; it was then
speedily succeeded by a variety of somewhat exaggerated
humorous facial changes.

If he laughed, which he was sure to do, he laughed with
abandon, throwing back his head, opening his mouth to the
fullest possible extent, shaking his whole body, and stamping with one foot to show his excessive enjoyment of the
joke. It was usually unexpected and, until one became used
to it, disconcerting.

The Emperor illustrated in his features all the emotions
that possessed him, and he had many peculiar mannerisms.
He would continually shake the forefinger of his right hand
in the face of anyone whom he wished to convince, or he

would rock slowly on his toes backwards and forwards. At other times, he jiggled violently on one leg. On some days, he appeared to be more restless in this respect than others, and there were times when he preserved a staid, calm dignity of manner; but his usual natural habit was quick and nervous.

Though a good-looking man, the Emperor was not as handsome as his portraits made him out to be. His nose was thick, his blue eyes hard and cold and shallow—except when they were creased in laughter, and then they shone like steel. His head was well shaped and his hair was brown and plentiful; his lips were thick and red and closed over strong, yellow, well-preserved teeth. He always patronized an American dentist.

His right hand had compensating, overwhelming strength; he always kept his left arm, which was practically useless, resting on his hip. His left hand, the fingers of which were ornamented with several heavy rings and also with an ugly brown mole, was incapable of much movement, being able to hold only small light things such as a glove or paper. That hand held the reins when he rode, but it had no control over his horses, which were specially trained to respond only to knee pressure.

The Emperor looked a fine figure in uniform, but the greatest shock of my life—was my first sight of him in ordinary civilian clothes. His Majesty was almost unrecognizable. I don't know if it was the cut of the clothes or the color, or the shape of the hat he was wearing, a somewhat buccaneering type of Panama, but I was reminded of those gentlemen who come on the stage in loud garments at variety shows and sing songs of mingled comedy and pathos to the applause of the gallery. The clothes looked like a bad disguise.

Many German gentlemen lost much in appearance when out of uniform, but none to the extent that their Emperor did. He no longer had any shred of dignity, and, curiously enough, that charm of manner of which I spoke was also bereft of its influence and merged into what was an offensive, wearisome buffoonery. Wilhelm was wise not to appear before his subjects except in uniform.

*

The Emperor's great desire was to see Germany advance in influence and power, and his peculiar transparency of mind allowed everyone to see that he clearly believed it was to his personal efforts that the progress of his country was due. He reminded me of the fly on the wheel who believes that he makes it go round.

After a military review, the Emperor would make a critique to the assembled generals, telling them what was right and wrong in the maneuvers. This custom was ridiculed in military circles. The generals listened to it with exemplary outward respect and inward boredom and contempt: they attached no value whatsoever to His Majesty's remarks.

I was to learn that some of the sons of the Emperor inherited the belief that what they did was admirable. One of them, Prince August-Wilhelm, known to the family as Au-Wi (pronounced Oh-Vee), had mediocre artistic taste and a mania for making crude and feeble sketches and presenting them, doubtless with kind intentions, to any lady or gentleman whom he thought fit to honor.

It was a continual surprise how little sense of proportion the famly had in measuring the qualities of their own performances.

"What a pity," Fräulein von Gersdorff sighed, looking through her pince-nez at one of these masterpieces, which Au-Wi had just thrust into her hand. "What a pity that our young Princes think so much of everything they do. They never seem to compare it with what others do, but believe it to be admirable simply because they did it."

"Ah," one of the counts answered, "that is a well-known Hohenzollern trait, the belief that what they do is intrinsically superior to what others can do. They think they can accomplish without pain what others achieve by endless hard work."

Though independent and unconventional—I will not say original—in his mode of thought, the Emperor resented independence in others if it opposed his own cherished ideas and opinions. He imagined himself to be more liberal-minded than he was. He had a phenomenal memory for facts and a talent for seizing the most interesting—not necessarily the most important—points of any subject under discussion. Unfortunately, his reasoning was essentially superficial and his deductions often glaringly false.

"*Er ist doch der Kaiser*"—But he is the Emperor. This was the answer invariably heard at any attempt to criticize the actions of the imperial master of Germany.

*

I have a vivid recollection of an exhibition of flowers that I visited with Their Majesties and the Princess. In the part of the exhibition near the entrance, the wall was covered with an enormous canvas on which was painted what purported to be a portion of the gardens of the

Achilleion, the Emperor's palace at Corfu. There were marble steps in the foreground leading the spectator into a bed of real tulips arranged in front of this artistic atrocity that had been copied from a picture postcard. The display was the work of a young gardener, who, in frockcoat and white kid gloves, stood in front of his masterpiece, looking nervous, but obviously prepared for the congratulations of royalty.

The Princess admired the canvas and told the artist that it was *sehr nett*—very nice—although she whispered to me that the sea in the picture was not a bit like the real sea in Corfu.

When the Emperor and Empress arrived, they were conducted through the smiling, bowing crowd at the entrance and immediately halted in front of the dreadful canvas. The complacent woman who was the curator of the exhibition introduced the painting and its creator, who stood beside it in a radiance of glory. The Emperor stared across the tulips at the canvas, while the Empress murmured a dubious "sehr nett," and the ladies and gentlemen of the suite concentrated their pince-nez on the picture. The young gardener was, briefly, lifted to the highest pinnacle of bliss.

It was a crude and inartistic performance, but I was surprised at the anger shown by the Emperor. He was extraordinarily sensitive with regard to the palace in Corfu and the impression which it conveyed to the public. Yet one would think that he would have grown somewhat indifferent to the loyal attempts to illustrate himself, his family, and his dwelling places in well meant but ignorant ways. It was one of the penalties that attached itself to any public position.

But the Emperor stood before the canvas in a dead silence, his face growing stern and darker, and a shiver of apprehension fell on the smiling crowd. The young gardener wilted and his face grew white. The curator, smitten with dismay, was murmuring phrases which broke off suddenly in the middle, and the Emperor kept on staring at the picture. He was furious, and saw in the picture merely a caricature of his beloved Achilleion. At last, breaking the silence, he thrust his head forward: "*That*," and he nodded at the picture, quite ignoring the beautiful tulips that surrounded it, "*that* is supposed to be my garden in Corfu. It's not *a bit* like it—not the *least* like it." His voice rose in an angry crescendo. "It's horrible, horrible!" He hissed the word *grässlich* between his teeth and flung himself around so abruptly that it was difficult for us to get out of his way.

It never seemed to occur to him that this was the naive, well-meaning, and loyally intended work of an artistically uneducated man, or that in any case it was not meant to be looked at closely, but its effect judged from a distance, or that the crushed individual who was responsible for it would suffer miserably at the thought of the time and labor he had expended, only to achieve a ghastly public failure.

*

Even in those first early days at Homburg, it was noticeable what a difference the presence of the Emperor made in the atmosphere of the court. A certain vitality and a certain strain were visible. Everybody was to be ready to go anywhere and do anything at a moment's notice—to be in the appropriate costume necessary for walking, riding, or driving. From early morning till night there was hardly a moment of respite from duty, and my own day was a crowded one, with hardly time left for the necessary frequent changes of costume which were one of the chief burdens of existence at court.

Women's dress in 1902, when I began my *Dienst*—service—was very uncomfortable, and quite unsuited to the vigorous life we had to lead. Skirts were long—"just off" (the ground), dressmakers called it—which often meant that they were really "just on." Precariously perched hats were fastened by long pins to the bun of hair that we wore on the top of our heads, and in a wind the hats dragged painfully at their moorings. For luncheon and dinner we had to have dresses with long trains, the bodices of which were tight and boned severely along every seam. How hot and uncomfortable they were! No wonder the ladies of the court moved with slow "dignity" and were inclined to be stout.

For me, who had always to "be there"—who might never lose sight of an extremely lively ten year old (she turned ten in September, a few weeks after my arrival), yet must always be trim and tidy, always fit to appear before royalty—it was extraordinarily difficult to preserve an appearance of neatness. One who possessed no maid was further challenged by the evening frocks that hooked up behind; however many fastenings by a feat of superdexterity one managed to close by one's own contorted efforts, there were two or three in the middle of the back that remained entirely out of reach. There was also the harrowing possibility of finding that one had gone astray at the beginning, fastening the first hook into the second eye, a fatal proceeding.

All housemaids retired at six to their own homes, and, as my quarters were in a remote part of any Schloss where the court happened to be staying, the nightmare problem of who I could get to "do me up at the back" often became acute. Sometimes I heard footsteps outside my bedroom door and hastened out to the passage, only to see some elderly general or colonel of the suite pass by. He would make a grave military salute, and I would utter a stifled groan and escape backwards. More than once, I at last called upon a passing footman to lend me his aid.

Silk blouses, their high collars stiffened with whalebone, the ends of which soon worked through, bruising the neck, were the usual accompaniment of walking costume at the court. How torturing their tightness and weight! But His Majesty walked, and so did we. Often, we drove out some distance beyond Homburg among the mountains and forest, descended from our carriage, and tramped along at a brisk pace for several miles, when the carriages met us and we returned.

It was a strenuous existence for the entourage; the Emperor wished us to be always mobilized for active service.

*

When the afternoons were too hot to walk, His Majesty played lawn tennis. Grass courts are practically nonexistent in Germany and are used only by those people who do not take lawn tennis seriously. All good courts are made of a kind of concrete first used at Homburg, the composition of which is supposed to be a secret. It is an excellent preparation, possessing a certain elasticity approximating turf, and has the advantage of drying quickly. Even if turf lawns could be grown as they are in England—and I have never met with any that remotely resembled their close, fine texture—the heavy thunderstorms which prevail in Germany in hot weather would frequently make them unusable.

His Majesty played lawn tennis in rather crude-looking shirts and ties and usually wore a Panama hat. Unlike most men, he looked perhaps less well in such a getup. Young officers from the neighboring barracks were often sent for to join a set, and Fräulein von Thadden, who was an expert player, frequently had to upset her arrangements for the afternoon when requested to play with His Majesty. As the Princess grew older, she, too, became quite a respectable player, as did all the young Princes, especially the athletic Crown Prince and Adalbert.

In Berlin, during the wet weather, the Emperor had difficulty getting the exercise he needed, so he had a covered tennis court built on the grounds of Mon-Bijou Schloss, a short five minutes' walk from the palace on the *Lustgarten*. Here, when the weather was persistently rainy, His Majesty, in what was a frightfully overheated building, played with any young officers who were fairly expert. None of them enjoyed the honor very much. The oppressive temperature, combined with the nervous apprehension natural to the occasion—the fear lest an unlucky ball, with the hideous perversity of inanimate things, might perhaps rebound with force against the sacred person of His Majesty, or, as sometimes happened, fall into the midst of the tea table presided over by the Empress—paralyzed the hand of even the least imaginative lieutenant.

"I feel unstrung," confided one of them to me. "Suppose I give His Majesty a black eye?"

"Nobody gets a black eye at tennis."

"No, but still, it might happen, and you know von

Braun's ball went bang into the Empress's teacup and flung the tea all over her gown. His mother was in tears when she heard of it.''

*

Ausflüge und Landpartien—excursions and picnics—were an integral part of German life in the summer, and the *Hof*—court—lagged no whit behind. Though the Emperor detested cold, damp weather, he led an open-air existence and lost no opportunity of being *im Freien*—outdoors. He breakfasted, drank tea, and ate supper in the garden whenever the weather permitted. It was probably for this reason that the principal German meal, *Mittagessen*—lunch—whose elaborateness does not allow it to be served *al fresco*, still kept its place in the middle of the day, allowing the simple supper to be served out of doors in the cool of the evening. It was a healthy custom.

Near Homburg was an ancient Roman fortress which had been excavated and restored by the Emperor. He had rebuilt, at his own expense, portions of the old Roman settlement. The newness of the buildings, the freshly painted barracks of the Roman militia with Latin inscriptions over the doorways, the brightness of the glazed brick walls, gave a somewhat jarring sense of unreality to the whole *Burg*—fortress—and raised the question of whether it was advisable to attempt to reconstruct the past in quite such a conscientious manner—whether the actual ruins, scanty though they may have been, did not tell their tale better than these up-to-date buildings so curiously well equipped with modern appliances.

Excursions either on horseback or by carriage to *Saalburg* were a delightful feature of the stay in Homburg, and often the whole party was permitted to excavate for remains in likely spots. The Empress once disinterred a beautiful bowl, and it was not unusual to come across fine specimens of pottery or ironwork. Everybody was supplied with a short wooden implement for digging in the soft loam, and the royalties, including Prince Joachim and the Princess, and the ladies and gentlemen of the court labored industriously summer afternoons under the direction of Professor Jacobi, who carefully checked any undue exuberance in digging that might have led to disastrous results.

Those digging parties gave opportunity for the exercise of a characteristic form of German humor. Often a broken cup or vase or an ancient Roman dagger shaped in an excellent imitation from a chocolate paste was embedded in the soil the night before. The ardent excavator, glowing with the success of discovery, would find to his chagrin that, at the solemn washing of his find which took place with ceremony in the presence of the assembled company after supper, not only the encumbering soil but the whole fabric of the "precious antique" dissolved into a hopeless chocolate ruin.

*

The Hohenzollern egocentricity and militarism so evident in the Kaiser had deep roots. Not supporting this characteristic of heritage, I took particular exception to Carlyle's *History of Frederick the Great*, in which Carlyle, to the delight of German military officers, said many approving things about the virtues of Frederick's father, Frederick Wilhelm I, a man whom I had always maintained was a most disagreeable, brow-beating, merely brutal person who had tried to stifle rather than to develop the best qualities of his son, and with the greatest difficulty had even to be restrained from ordering his execution.

Regrettably, since Carlyle wrote his famous book, Frederick Wilhelm I had been held up to the German people as an example worthy to be followed, and his treatment of his children was not only condoned but commended as the only suitable method of dealing with the rising generation if one were to develop in them the strength of mind, the courage, and the iron determination that was desired in every son of the Fatherland. I preferred as a more accurate portrait the lesser-known *Memoirs* of Wilhelmina of Bayreuth, Frederick Wilhelm I's eldest daughter, who wrote in no dubious fashion of the severity and brutality of her royal father, not shrinking even from accusing him, doubtless with perfect truth and in spite of Carlyle's scepticism on the subject, of throwing the dinner plates at his wife and children when, as frequently happened, their conduct displeased him.

Every Prussian officer, every Prussian schoolmaster I ever met invariably maintained that the military capacity, strength of will, tenacity of purpose, and far-sighted sagacity and statesmanship of Frederick the Great were the direct fruits of his father's harsh treatment, and would never have ripened if those other less desirable traits of character—his taste for French literature, French dress, French music, French wigs and amusements—had not been stamped out in early youth by his heavy-footed parent. It was necessary, they asserted, that in childhood his spirit be crushed, indeed broken, by constant grinding military discipline, by the continual performance of demeaning tasks, and by separation from the society of those he loved.

I mention this history of Frederick the Great—the Emperor's grandfather—because the stern, relentless subordination to the grim purpose and reality of life of all childhood dreams, desires, and yearnings was exacted by the Prussian military governors who believed that in no other way could a boy be made into a satisfactory soldier.

Every Prussian prince and every German child was taught the same thing, taken away from feminine ministrations at the age of seven, given into the hands of young officers whose business it was to bring him up under strict military tutelage. His tender, plastic mind, at the most impressionable, most susceptible age, was henceforth chiefly surrounded by martial influences, was encouraged above all to believe that the most honorable, the most necessary career for him was that of a soldier.

I expressed my dismay at this philosophy of child-rearing once to Countess Keller. "Ah, but all that harshness and severity—see what it did for Frederick!" She closed her hand tightly, making it into a fist and shaking it. "It was that that made him great, that gave him . . ."

"Oh, how can you say that," I interposed, "when you can read in every line of Frederick's letters which he wrote when he grew older how he deplored that his childhood and youth had been so maimed and crushed by lack of sympathy and affection?"

"No, indeed, he would have grown up just a foolish, flute-playing, frivolous, good-for-nothing," the Countess continued, "if it had not been for his father's firmness and determination to make him a good soldier."

"Yes, I know, always drilling," I said. "Enough to make him detest the army. He did detest it, he says so himself—

anybody would when they had to grind at it from morning till night as he did—all the machine-made, all the soul-destroying part!''

Countess Keller laughed. She was a kind-hearted soul, but she was firmly convinced of the virtues of unmitigated harshness in developing the correct military spirit. After all, had it not led to the rise of Prussia among European states, to all the glory that was to follow?

*

It did not take long to learn that my small charge had inherited the temperament of her lineage. What Carlyle called ''Hohenzollern choler'' and a foot-stamping manner of expressing opinions exhibited themselves early. Victoria Louise was a high-strung, nervous child of generous, way-ward impulses, a child who needed a calm routine for the healthy development and cultivation of her mind and body, but who was, by the circumstances of her birth, kept in a restless vortex of activity.

She was nearly ten when I first knew her, a well-grown child with pale features and a lively, alert expression. She wore her hair cut in ''bangs'' across her forehead and hanging in long nursery ringlets over her shoulders. Those ringlets were produced, in what was naturally straight hair, by the art of her English nurse, whom I often watched with fascination, as she brushed the shining strands around her finger, forming without any extraneous aid, beautiful and regular curls.

There were but two people of whom the Princess stood in awe. Papa, of course, was one, and her English nurse, Miss Matcham, or Nana, was the other. Nana was a disciplinarian of the first water and brooked no interference with her own laws, which, in a court where many overlapping interests existed, bred many difficulties.

She had been thirteen years in the service of the Empress, had brought up the younger children from birth, watched by them many nights when they were ill, and had saved the life of Prince Joachim. The Prince had had a delicate infancy, and had grown into a brooding, super-sensitive child, the darling of his mother, and the one who was, ultimately, to break her heart.

One by one, Nana's nurslings were taken from her, but not without fierce opposition on her part. As was the German custom, Prussian princes were given early into military hands. However, the shrewd old nurse had a strong opinion—shared by the Empress—that an inexperienced young officer was no person to be entrusted with a child's physical and mental needs. The nurse battled, often successfully, for her charges, invading even the professorial departments, and, aided and abetted by Dr. Zunker, the court doctor, had entirely routed educational authorities, who withdrew baffled and disconcerted.

Her triumphs were short-lived. An elaborate education machine equipped with expert professors for every subject, with a carefully planned program in which every hour of the day was rigidly mapped out, could not be stayed for the whims of one obstructive woman obviously prejudiced against German institutions. The frequent skirmishes developed into the nature of a military campaign. It was not good for the children to be the center of warring elements, so at last the inevitable happened: with much reluctance, Nana's dismissal to England—with ample pension, of course—was decided on.

When I first made her acquaintance in Homburg, her influence was waning, her autocratic rule was loosening, and her departure was delayed only by the beneficent hand of Her Majesty, which shrank from the final severance of a faithful, if somewhat injudicious, servant. Nana subsequently asserted that I had been sent as an instrument of Providence to console her during her last few weeks; and though I was not conscious of any qualifications for the office of consoler, I may lay claim to having been an efficient safety valve for her emotions, which flooded over me.

She was uncompromisingly British, and it was at once her strength and her undoing. She refused to strike her flag to any mere lady-in-waiting, or to Fräulein von Thadden. "Do you think I was going to stand her putting the thermometer in the bath water to see how hot it was?" Nana asked me indignantly, referring to von Thadden; and, the Ober-Gouvernante still being in quarantine, I agreed that it was the kind of thing no one could be expected to bear.

If the German association modified nothing in her character, the same could not be said of her speech, which, while still British in outward form, became in the course of years warped from its original purity. "At Christmas," she told me, when showing the gifts the Empress had given her, "last year I became a set of teaspoons, and the year before I became a lovely silver teapot." She had confused the German word *bekommen*—to get—with the similar-sounding but different-meaning English word.

Of the more than seventy castles and estates owned by the Emperor, the New Palace in Potsdam, a cheerful-looking red Schloss built by Frederick the Great, was considered home.

CHAPTER THREE

AT THE NEW PALACE

At the beginning of September, we were warned to begin
our preparations for returning from Homburg to the *Neues
Palais*—the New Palace—at Potsdam, where the recovered
Obergouvernante was waiting to share my labors, and
where, I was assured, there was a regular routine.

The ladies of the court had maids and footmen, but I
had no one to help me, and as my day was well filled up
from early morning till late at night, I had to pack feverishly in the small intervals of time stolen from my other
responsibilities.

At half-past seven one evening, I went down to the
courtyard where the carriages were waiting. I was supposed
to accompany the Princess to the station, but at the last
moment something changed, and I was sent off with a young
adjutant whose English vocabulary was very limited. We
drove down the long street filled with people waiting to see

Their Majesties go by. They cheered and waved handkerchiefs. We assumed friendly expressions, but we had been warned by Countess Keller against responding to any demonstrations of loyalty or respect that might mistakenly be offered to me by misguided American or other tourists; we were to meet such enthusiasm with icy indifference and not usurp the royal. "Do not so much as raise a brow or lift the corner of a lip, even if you see someone you know in the crowd!" the Countess emphasized.

But the people lining the street to the railway station were a hilarious crowd, obviously out to enjoy themselves and resolved to cheer everyone in the royal carriages, regardless of who they might be. I responded with more than my eyelids, and the officer saluted blatantly.

At the station the royal waiting room was decorated with flags and evergreens, and we were joined there by Their Majesties, my Princess, and Prince Joachim. The royal train, painted in blue and cream with gold trimmings, was alongside the platform, the regulation carpet was laid down, maids and valets peeped furtively from the windows of distant compartments, footmen were hurrying to and fro, and ladies and gentlemen of the suite continued their normal occupation of waiting and chatting. Eventually, Their Majesties emerged from the waiting room and walked over the red carpet into the train. We all boarded after them, and our journey began among the frantic *"Hoch lebe der Kaiser!"*—Long live the Emperor!—of the crowd outside.

We in England may believe in our own loyalty, but we could never compete with a German crowd in giving it expression. We have never been able quite to abandon ourselves to unrestrained, wild enthusiasm, have always been a little too self-conscious, too afraid of being absurd. The German is untrammelled by considerations of that kind; he revels in his emotions, encourages his wife and family to revel in theirs, waves patriotic flags on the least provocation. In those years, he would put his small son of six into a complete miniature Hussar uniform and let him swagger about in the streets, sing *"Heil dir im Sieger-Kranz"*—"Hail You in the Victor's Crown," the German national anthem—and was rather proud than ashamed at being moved to tears of pride as his Kaiser passed by. No nation is more emotionally patriotic than the German.

As long as the daylight lasted, outside every wayside station and crossing was a palpitating crowd of little girls wearing wreaths of wilted flowers on their heads, of bare-legged boys waving Prussian flags, of perspiring officials of *Verein*—any kind of association for doing anything—in hot-looking dress suits and tall chimney-pot hats: there they stood as they had obviously been standing for some hours, wedged together in one solid, impenetrable mass, leaning heavily upon each other in rows against the station railings, while on the platform, where no one else was allowed to intrude, the stationmaster, in his militaristic blue uniform, remained saluting with his hand at his red cap as the train steamed slowly by. Always the same station and the same crowd, it seemed, with just a different name over the booking office door, the same *Eingang* and *Ausgang*—entrance and exit—the same brown, peasant faces gazing through the railings.

The Princess and Prince Joachim had their supper in the dining car with Count Blumenthal, Herr Porger, and I; they ate their soup and *kalte Schnitzel*—cold cuts—in full view of the shouting crowd.

We had to hurry our meal so the tables could be relaid for the supper of Their Majesties and the suite. We swallowed one course after another with headlong speed, curtailing conversation. When the last mouthful was dispatched and the children went to say goodnight to their parents, the rest of us retired to the sleeping cars provided for the night, although it was much too early to think of going to bed.

The royal train, in which I later made many journeys, was, as may be imagined, "replete with every modern convenience." This did not prevent it from banging and shaking to an appalling extent. One was hurled backwards and forwards and jolted and jerked with every form of movement known to science. Sometimes we seemed to be moving over rippled granite, and then a horizontal spasm mixed up with weird scrunchings seized the whole train, which appeared to be having some kind of hysterical fit. Occasionally, we pulled up with a jolt and a jar and remained stationary for a few minutes before resuming our shuddering, jerking journey, which stretched every mile into a nightmare length.

Time seems interminably long in such circumstances, and the hours dragged on slowly. An attempt at undressing forced into the foreground the question of how—in view of the difficulty of taking off clothes—one was ever likely to be able to put them on again. Brush and comb, hairpins, all went sliding away on the floor; after washing in a basin in which a miniature tempest of soap-tipped wavecrests was raging, I renounced the adventure of undressing and lay down uncomfortably in most of my clothes to wait for morning.

Through the ventilator came a choking, smoke-laden odor. The pillow, covered with beautifully fine linen, was hard as the nether millstone and produced a dislocated feeling in my neck; the sheets and blankets were of the finest, but no one wants to go to bed in one's garments of the day.

We were not due to arrive in Wildpark, the station of the New Palace, until eight o'clock in the morning—nine hours more of the terrible shaking. I lay down, turned out the electric light, and became for the rest of the night a mere oscillating body, whirled continually back and forth through space.

Fortunately, dawn comes early in the late summer, and at the first faint grayness I sat up giddily and watched the flat, dew-bathed landscape glide by, so different from the hilly region we had left the night before.

About five o'clock, there was a low tap at my door, and Nana, with her finger on her lip, handed me a cup of tea she had managed to produce from somewhere. "I knew you'd not sleep much," she whispered. "Did you ever know trains to shake like this one? You'd think they'd manage to take His Majesty along at a more comfortable pace, wouldn't you? A royal train, indeed! Enough to shake you to pieces."

I drank her tea, and she came and sat beside me and conversed—or I should say, talked, for it was more outpouring than conversation—in a hoarse whisper, so that she wouldn't disturb Count Blumenthal, who was supposed to have been sleeping in the next *coupé*, but who was probably lying awake yearning for the end of the trip.

The grayness of the fields departed, and they were threaded with gleams of color as the sun slowly penetrated the clouds. Great ragged eddies of mist began to rise, and cattle stood about half plunged in an ocean of vapor. The peasants were at work; the women with red handkerchiefs tied over their heads kneeled among the bright green of the potato crops. The dreary night was over.

The train rattled and jerked along, and Nana's voice continued to croon in my ear, words of warning, admonishment, advice. I listened without hearing or comprehension. About seven o'clock another soft tap, and the door slid back to reveal a footman with a tray of tea and Zwieback. "You'll have your proper breakfast when you arrive at the New Palace," said Nana, "but you won't get it much before nine. You'd better have some more."

I accepted the fresh tea with pleasure and listened as I drank it to the movement in the corridor. There was the sound of subdued voices—everybody was getting up. Soon, some of the ladies came and sat beside me, pointing out interesting objects in the landscape. Countess Keller was the first to spot a round, green dome visible over some trees.

"There, there!" she cried. "That is the roof of the New Palace; we shall be there soon." She squeezed my hand. "I hope you will be very happy there." She told me it was an important moment in my life, the moment when I was to enter the "real home" of the Emperor and Empress. "Like Windsor to your king and queen," she explained, fearing that the forty castles which the Emperor possessed might have created some confusion in my mind. "Here is their real home, you know."

The train, which had proceeded much more evenly

since we entered the Prussian district, glided smoothly into a station and came to a stop. A few officers were waiting at the door of the simple wooden *Wartesaal*—waiting room—which a few years later was to be replaced by a substantial stone building with lifts and luxuriously furnished waiting rooms.

There was a sudden opening of carriage doors and activity of footmen and *Jäger*—riflemen. The Emperor, enveloped in a long gray cavalry cloak, strode across the platform with the Empress and his children, saluted the waiting officers, paused for a word with each, and drove away. A long row of carriages was waiting. Everything was admirably organized; there was no confusion, no delay. My turn came, and I was whirled away out of the station yard across a road where people were standing, kept in order by a green-clad *Gendarm*, driven along a tree-shaded avenue, past some sentries who were guarding a small iron gate, over the *Mopke*, a big open gravelled space bordered by fine buildings on each side, and past the front of the huge palace, which reminded me of Versailles. I descended at a broad flight of stone steps and was ushered by a footman through what looked like a window but was really a door, into a corridor, up a wooden staircase painted white, and into the apartment which was to be my home for the next seven years. It was a lofty room, and in spite of its bare, uninhabited look, had an air of brightness and repose. The sunshine flooded it with welcome; outside birds were singing; a dachshund, one of twelve the Emperor doted on, looked up at me from the courtyard as I stood in the open French windows, and wagged his tail.

*

Although I was to make visits to thirty of the palaces and country houses belonging to the Emperor, I resided in only nine, and of these, the New Palace easily held the first place in my affections. For one thing, it bore the aspect of a permanent home, while other, perhaps more beautiful royal residences seemed more a hotel, in which one never quite settled down but remained with boxes only partially unpacked, waiting for the notice of departure.

The New Palace, situated about twenty miles from Berlin, was built by Frederick the Great in the rococo style of Louis XV on a very marshy piece of ground. Why he did not choose a better site—where good sites are so many—remains one of those mysteries which deepens with time.

"It was probably in a spirit of pure obstinacy," maintained Baron von Mirbach, an elderly gentleman-in-waiting to the Empress. "People said it was impossible to build a palace on such a spot, and so he set out to prove that it was not. He also wished to show that there was still money left in his coffers after the Silesian Wars. But he did not really want the palace, and never lived in it for any length of time."

It was a cheerful-looking red building, with queer dimpled monstrous cherub heads and wreaths of flowers in yellow sandstone engirdling the upper windows. On the edge of the roof and along the terrace below stood rows of pseudo-Greek sandstone statues in flowing draperies, with whose features the frost often took liberties, making necessary a yearly renovation and replacement of noses and fingers. Along the raised terraces and against the railing stood large orange trees in tubs, which every autumn were taken up to the "orangerie" and brought back to the terraces in the spring.

On one side lay the big *Sandhof*—a gravelled courtyard
—divided by high iron railings edged with grass and flowers
from the Mopke, where in former days Frederick drilled his
soldiers.

On the other side of the Mopke stood the royal stables,
the kitchens, the chapel, and, divided by a beautiful stone
arcade, two *Communs*—barracks—one of which housed the
palace guard and its commandant and his family.

The Sandhof faced the apartments of the Emperor and
Empress, which on the other side had a view onto the
spacious garden laid out in trim beds with fountains on each
side—a garden to look at rather than to walk in. Hidden
away in corners behind big beech hedges were other shady
gardens of trees, rose gardens with grassy lawns, the children's garden, and a garden with a tea house, where the
royal family breakfasted in the summertime.

Most of the old palaces were conspicuous for their
splendor and still more for their inconvenience—they were
structurally almost incapable of being adapted to modern
requirements. The New Palace was no exception, although
wonders had been done in the matter of adequate heating
apparatus and bathrooms.

But there was no way of overcoming the difficulty
caused by the lack of any passage in the wing where the
apartment of the Princess—the *Wohnung der Prinzessin*—
was located. Here, two magnificent salons had been transformed into bedrooms, one for the Princess and one for the
Obergouvernante. These were obviously originally intended
as reception rooms, having doors at each end and in the middle, and were the only means of communication between
the sitting room and the dining room, so that whoever

passed from one to the other was obliged to travel the whole length of one of these rooms, unless one went downstairs and passed through the courtyard to another staircase, which was what the servants had to do in all weather.

In a smaller but beautiful salon that formed the entrance to the Wohnung der Prinzessin, a cook stove had been placed in the massive marble fireplace for the purpose of keeping dishes warm—all of the food for the palace was prepared in a kitchen in the Communs on the far side of the Mopke and connected with the palace by a long underground passage through which the food was brought.

The sitting room I occupied on first coming to the New Palace had remained the same as when it was built around 1770. Its walls were covered with small irregular pieces of dark blue glass set in cement and carried up into the center of the ceiling, in which was inserted a circle of small mirrors, where at night, if once chanced to look up, the lamplight reflected. Over the marble chimneypiece bearing the cipher of Frederick the Great was another high mirror of the Louis XV period, with a golden-rayed sun fixed in its upper part.

Above the blue salon was an equally spacious bedroom at an angle of the palace wing with bull's-eye windows facing north and east. It was also furnished, like most German bedrooms, to serve as a sitting room, and contained a sofa, a large center table, and an *escritoire*, besides the necessary cupboards and wardrobes. It was heated in winter by a tall, chocolate-colored tiled stove—the *Kachelofen*. In cold weather, the Ofen was lit with wood at an early hour of the morning; though offensive to a sense of beauty, the Kachelofen could be trusted to keep a warm temperature at a minimum expenditure of fuel.

"I don't know why English people always want to *look* at a fire," said Fräulein von Gersdorff, defending the superiority and effectiveness of the national heating system. "It isn't the look of a fire that warms you. I never felt the cold so much anywhere as in England. All that beautiful coal warming the chimney, while I sat shivering two yards away from it!"

The New Palace had an alluring aspect. It was palatial, of course, looked at as a whole; but there was something home-like, gracious, and friendly in my particular corner of it, in the flowers which were growing on each balcony, in the canary whose notes could be heard trilling from the nearby dining room of the Princess, in the face of a white-capped elderly housemaid who entered with a bow, a *"Guten Tag,"* and an expression of delight at my arrival. She came and shook hands and said something congratulatory and welcoming. It was intensely pleasant and human, this obvious kindness and good-will. From that hour, Frau Pusch, the housemaid, was the cushion and buffer of my existence, intervening between me and the harsh world. She packed and unpacked and mended and ironed my clothes, fetched and carried with smiles and good cheer. And she taught me German.

*

There were permanent officials, constantly on duty at the Court of Prussia, who lived in Potsdam or Berlin, and had, during the period of their service, rooms allotted to them in whichever palaces were for the time occupied by the Emperor and Empress. These were the ladies and gentlemen of the court, the entourage, the people with whom I worked, ate, visited, walked, and shared the mutual challenges of the court life.

My own experience testifies to the truth of what I had read somewhere, that the chief function of a lady- or gentleman-in-waiting is to stand in a draft and smile. "Standing and waiting," said Countess Keller, "is the chief part of our lives; it makes one mentally and bodily weary till one gets used to it." Hand-shaking, too, was practiced to a considerable extent. It did not seem to matter how many times people had met before in the day and shaken hands, they liked to do it again while waiting for dinner. It helped to pass the time away, and gave an excuse for walking about from group to group.

My place at the oval table was at one end between Count Blumenthal and Herr Porger. The Emperor and Empress were seated at the sides opposite each other, and the guests, intermingled with court ladies and gentlemen, radiated right and left. Footmen wore the court livery, which included ill-fitting gaiters, and waited behind every chair. The Emperor's Jäger, in green uniform, attended exclusively to his master's wants.

Red and white wine and champagne were served to all the guests, but neither the Emperor nor the Empress drank anything but fruit juice. The Emperor had a horror of excessive indulgence in alcohol. "You English people," he said to me one day, "you drink those awful fiery spirits—whisky, brandy, what not. How can you imbibe such quantities of poisonous liquid—ruining your constitutions? Simply ruining them! Whisky and soda everywhere! I tasted it once—it's like liquid fire! Ugh! Your drinking habits are fearful!"

He admonished me for our national failings, as always, with an uplifted finger and a serious face, and despite my feeble assertions that although we still drank more than was good for us, published statistics had shown that year by year the percentage of drunkenness in the army had decreased as had crimes due to drunkenness. His Majesty had more faith in his own observations and continued to shake his finger at me as though I were personally responsible.

Dinner was finished in forty-five minutes. At a sign from the Empress everyone rose, and, the ladies preceding the gentlemen, we filed slowly into the salon, where coffee was served and everyone stood and drank it. This standing about after dinner was one of the most tedious of all court duties. It sometimes lasted for an hour. The Empress and Emperor never sat down, but moved from one group to another, talking to guests. The rest of us propped ourselves surreptitiously against projecting pieces of furniture and tried to look as happy as circumstances permitted.

If there were many important guests, the children dined alone with Count Blumenthal and myself and were expected to speak English. Twice a week after supper, I took Prince Joachim away and read English with him in his room while the governor sat listening in a chair, his long red-striped military gray legs stretched out before him, his hands clasped on his knee, and an absorbed look in his eyes.

The book chosen was Stevenson's *Treasure Island*. The Prince stipulated that whatever we read it should not be about *Musterkinder*—model children—the kind abounding in certain books but happily seldom met in real life. I considered the Prince's objection to Musterkinder a hopeful and healthy sign.

Before many pages of *Treasure Island* were turned, he pronounced it *prachtvoll*—magnificent. (There were few,

if any, original books in the German language written especially for boys; they had to content themselves with translations of James Fenimore Cooper's works, *Robinson
Crusoe, The Swiss Family Robinson*, and, only of late, *The
Adventures of Sherlock Holmes*.)

The governor, in spite of his thirty years and his military experience, also fell immediately under the spell of the
story. When the hour came to an end, the Prince begged for
an extension of his lesson, and Count Blumenthal pulled out
his watch and granted another ten minutes before bedtime.
"*Schnell, schnell*"—quick, quick—the Prince implored, and
I hurried on toward the fatal Black Spot and the fate of the
blind man, and it was determined I would come again as
quickly as possible because they both were anxious to know
what happened next.

After the children's bedtime, the winter evenings at the
New Palace were very quiet. The Empress and her ladies
would sit around the big table in one of the salons with their
needlework, while the Emperor looked at the English papers
spread about or, as often happened, read extracts from them
aloud. He usually wore glasses when reading and was very
fond of *Punch*, especially of the political cartoons, in which
he so frequently figured—as a sea-serpent, an organ-grinder,
or just his imperial self with exaggerated moustaches and
portentous frown. I always tried to hide *Punch* when I was
downstairs. His Majesty liked to thrust those embarrassing
pictures under my nose.

"What d'you think of that?" he would say. "Nice, isn't
it? Good likeness, eh?" It was difficult to find a suitable
answer on the spur of the moment.

About ten o'clock the Empress would rise and depart,

followed by the ladies, who all turned and made a curtsy to the Emperor as they went past. He regarded them with a rather mocking gaze. When the Emperor was away, the ladies dined upstairs in the apartment of the Empress and sat afterwards in her private salon, one of the loveliest rooms in the palace, all pale yellow satin and silver moldings.

Often, after everyone had retired for the night, I spent an hour or two developing and printing the photographs Sissy and I had taken during the day. At one time, Count Blumenthal wished Prince Joachim to learn the process of developing in a darkroom, so I agreed one evening to give him a demonstration in my bedroom of how it was done. But Joachim wanted to hurry things and would not allow the necessary time for developing; finally, he knocked over the big paraffin lamp.

Fortunately, I managed to catch the lamp as it fell sideways—otherwise, there would have been a horrible mess—but the hot globe made a nasty burn on my wrist. I decided that teaching the Prince the elements of photography was something better left alone. A vision of Prince Joachim in flames and me trying in vain to put him out with my dressing gown haunted my slumbers that night, broken by the pain of my burn.

My wrist had a large blister on the inner side, of which I took no notice after the first night, as it ceased to pain me any more, but in an unguarded moment Countess Keller saw it and demanded explanations. She made a terrible fuss and told Fräulein von Thadden to dress it for me. The wound, which had been healing in a normal fashion, was tied up in a bandage, which, of course, stuck. Fräulein von Thadden, who knew nothing about the simplest surgery, in spite of my protests proceeded the next day to pull the bandage, skin and all, with great firmness from the wound. "It hurts," I protested. "It should be soaked off."

"My dear miss, you must learn to suffer pain if necessary," she replied, and gave another pull, but this time I was holding the bandages. At that moment, Dr. Zunker, sent by Countess Keller, passed through the bedroom. Having seen von Thadden's attempt to pull off the bandage, he gave her a lecture—at which she was much annoyed—as to the proper removal of bandages.

It was curious how ignorant these German ladies were of the most elementary surgery. They seemed to depend entirely on Dr. Zunker and became agitated when the usual childish accidents happened. Once, in Bellevue Schloss in Berlin, I came across Countess Keller, very upset. "Oh, poor little Irma"—a child who had come to the *Kinderschaft* to spend the afternoon with the Princess—"has cut her head rather badly. Will you see if you can do anything?"

Countess Keller produced a sterilized bandage from somewhere, and we rushed to the sufferer, who was surrounded by an anxious and sympathetic crowd, including the Empress and Fräulein von Thadden. It was not really much of a cut, and after washing it with weak disinfectant, I applied one of those neat cross-over bandages which one learns how to make in first-aid courses. Then, it not being my afternoon for "service," I retired, catching a glimpse as I went up the staircase of a breathless gentleman, carrying a black case, getting hastily out of a royal carriage. Obviously, the doctor had been summoned.

The following day, Countess Keller told me with a smile of approval that my bandaging had been much commended by the doctor, who was told that it was the work of the English "miss." "These English are so *praktisch*—practical," he sighed.

I only relate this trivial incident because I found that the idea that I was *praktisch* in an emergency did more to give me a settled position and respect at the court than any amount of learning and accomplishments would have done. I had never dreamed, when bandaging the village boys for practice at home in England, that these slight shreds of surgical knowledge would prove so useful. Yet often in life does one find that a little knowledge is far from being a dangerous thing—so long as one realizes its littleness.

*

There were four ladies in the permanent entourage of the Empress, three of whom had been given the title of *Exzellenz* after long service, having been with the Empress from the time of her marriage, when she was only Princess Wilhelm. The Hof was the permanent home of these ladies, and they never left in all those years, except for the three-week summer holiday, when they went to take the *Kur*— a rest cure—in the mountains.

The lady who held the post of *Oberhofmeisterin*— equivalent to the English Mistress of the Robes—Countess Therese von Brockdorff, was a woman of remarkable independence of thought and character, humorous, broad-minded, full of insight and intuition, and gifted with great common sense and a blunt manner of speaking the truth— which was almost uncanny at court, where a system of keeping things under wrap, hiding facts, was an inevitable condition of existence. Countess von Brockdorff's downright manner did not make her beloved, but she had, to my mind, one of the finest natures I encountered in Germany.

Unfortunately, her influence was not felt as much as one might have expected in the court itself, which remained impenetrable to progressive thought. Such names as Darwin and Herbert Spencer were looked upon with mistrust and dislike. Nobody at court would think of reading their books, but they actively disliked their doctrines—whatever they were. The wonderful world of science and discovery, as applied to the amelioration of the conditions of human life, was, as far as the court was concerned, a closed book. Louis Pasteur's name, for example, was hardly known there—and considering the fears of the Emperor, this was a peculiar ignorance. The Emperor had a great horror of every possible kind of infection, especially of the ordinary cold. Whenever he caught the complaint, he retired to bed at once and cancelled all engagements until the worst was over. He gave everyone the same advice: "Go to bed and sweat."

Countess Keller, of the same age as Countess von Brockdorff—in her early fifties, perhaps—had control of the education of the Emperor's children, the boys until they were sent to *Kadettenschule*, and the Princess until she grew up and was confirmed. It was Countess Keller who had arranged for my employ, who had corresponded with me previous to my arrival, and who had greeted me with such warmth and understanding. She was kind-hearted and conscientious, possessed a sense of humor, and was devoted to the royal family.

The third of the four ladies residing in the palace was Countess Armgard Stolberg, of the noble family of Stolberg-Wernigerode. She was extraordinarily bright and pleasant, and, being the youngest, was the closest to me as a fellow colleague.

Then there was Fräulein von Gersdorff. She represented, so to say, the Arts, which she had cultivated all her life in an amateur fashion. She sang and played the piano and drew portraits in pencil, which were harsh and unbecoming likenesses without the slightest charm. The Fräulein was high-flown and idealistic, though neither of these qualities appeared in her artistic work, which expressed an implacable intention to get people down on paper exactly as they were without any of those softening illusions sought after in the best style of portraiture. She spoke with a queer drawling voice in a tone that carried far, and she had irritating habits, such as a propensity for always nibbling at things. Even at the dinner table, she would keep dabbing the tips of her fingers on the tablecloth to pick up breadcrumbs, at which she pecked like a bird as she talked. She was also fond of inveighing in public against marriage and extolling the virtues of a single life, which, in view of the many married people of which the court was composed, was tactless and misplaced. "Do stop talking nonsense, Clare," the Empress would say mildly.

Of the gentlemen, Count Robert von Zedlitz-Trutzschler, known simply as Count Zedlitz—the author of some interesting memoirs of his experiences at the court—had, at the time of my arrival, just been appointed Master of the Household. His period of service coincided with my own, and he quit the same year I did. Count Zedlitz was always ready to discuss political matters with me, beginning with a gentle air of raillery. I was eager to discuss anything but the Boer War.

Count Zedlitz only wanted to stir up a little patriotism on my part—just to see what it was like—to while away that tedious time before dinner. "Yes, the United States might still have been a British possession," I sighed, "if we had not had a foolish German king on the throne, who sent Hanoverian soldiers, poor things! to fight his battles for him."

"And the Americans beat you," he said, feigning sympathy.

"The American colonists, who were of British blood, beat the King's troops," I replied. "George Washington was an Englishman before he signed that Declaration of Independence and became an American. He and his little hatchet! I expect even that was imported from Sheffield."

"Well, I suppose that you in England cherish hopes of someday winning America back again—reconquering it, eh?"

I laughed at what I thought was the Count's little joke, but he was quite serious.

"Why not?" he said. "We Germans would. A country colonized chiefly by the British?"

"What a queer idea," I said. "I don't think it's ever occurred to us. Reconquering it? You mean with fire and sword, blood and iron?"

"Well, that's the only way, isn't it?" said the Count. And, just as the conversation threatened to become interesting, a *Kammerdiener*—a valet—threw open the double doors for the entrance of the Empress. (Ordinary people, of course, were allowed to use only half of the available doorspace.) That was the way with all conversations at court—cut off in their bloom—the result being that only trivialities were discussed. Those double doors often sprang open at the wrong moment, nipping delicious fragments of ideas in the bud.

Baron von Mirbach, a white-haired, white-bearded, rosy-complexioned old gentleman, was the *Kammerherr*— gentleman-in-waiting—to the Empress. He had a mania for building churches and collected enormous sums of money from the rich for this purpose. Some of the court ladies had served as models for the stained-glass saints in the windows of his churches; the profile of Countess von Brockdorff wearing the halo of St. Theresa looked placidly down on worshippers at the Emperor William Memorial Church.

The one I liked best of all the gentlemen in attendance on the Empress was Herr von Knesebeck, handsome and with a style about him. He was what everyone recognizes as a gentleman and had none of those petty views of life, none of the narrownesses, that flourish in a court atmosphere.

Some of the conscientious keepers of Her Majesty's purse objected here and there to small items of expenditure. A strict economy was, they decided, to be a salient characteristic of the Prussian Court. But Herr von Knesebeck's ideas were more munificent. When they gave five marks to an old workman on Her Majesty's behalf, Knesebeck gave twenty.

Herr von Knesebeck spoke excellent English and subscribed to an English newspaper, which he studied with diligence; his judgments on men and events were well considered and worthy of respect. He made excellent speeches, too, short and to the point, and was usually in attendance on visiting English royalties. He was the only gentleman of the court whose conduct I never heard any-one criticize.

He died before the war, and everyone who had known him grieved sorely. Herr von Knesebeck was the only person, other than the Emperor himself, whom the Empress had permitted to smoke in her presence.

The morning ride in Berlin. The Emperor and Empress in front; behind and center is Countess Stolberg. One can clearly see the phlegmatic piebald, Harlequin, the Emperor's preferred mount. The Emperor's withered arm prevented him from raising the horse's head for the photograph.

ROYAL ROUTINE

Life at the New Palace settled into a certain sameness. The Princess's day began with breakfast at seven-thirty, except on Sundays and on holidays, when she ate it at nine with her parents and her brother. Never was there a child who galloped through the first meal of the day with such reckless abandon. Finishing, she would fling down her knife and fork, the last mouthful still unconsumed, and depart to the Empress, who liked to see Sissy before lessons began.

At two minutes to eight, she returned breathless to the schoolroom—a dull, stately apartment with oil paintings of Prussian queens and electresses of Brandenburg decorating the walls. The Princess's footman had seen that everything needed was present—clean dusters, chalk, sponge, and water. The lady on duty was either myself or the thin, pale-faced Fräulein von Thadden. Sometimes a knock came at the door and, when opened, the smilingly apologetic face of the

Empress was revealed. She would slip in and take my place, pursuing her needlework while listening to the lesson.

The Princess was not a docile or an industrious child; her work was careless, owing chiefly to the usual rapidity with which she did everything. Her spelling was phonetic, and she was annoyed at English irregularities in this respect. Still, she was ambitious and fond of approval, especially from her favorite brother, Oskar.

Morning lessons ended at twelve o'clock, and then we took a short walk until it was time to dress for the one o'clock Mittagessen, which was eaten in the company of Their Majesties and the suite.

We dined in the Apollo *Saal*, a wonderful room decorated with painted panels that roused the indignation of Fräulein von Thadden, who objected to the scanty draperies and fleshiness of the simpering nymphs and cupids who eternally disported themselves among the never-fading garlands of flowers of the rococo period.

The *Speisekarte*—menu—of the royal table was written in German, and occasionally English dishes appeared on it, their names slightly disguised: "Apple-pei," "Brot-pudding." After lunch and the escape from the long, tedious waiting that followed, the children were allowed to go out together—pony cart rides, horseback riding, games in the courtyard.

On Sunday, the Princess and Prince Joachim entertained their friends to tea and supper. First, they would take them for a drive somewhere in the neighborhood, to the huge delight of the tourists, who shrieked and cheered, waved pocket handkerchiefs, and rushed apoplectically, with the greatest risk to their health, those fat mothers and fathers in their hot Sunday clothes, along the sandy walks, yelling, *"Die Prinzessin! Die Kleine Prinzessin. Ach! wie niedlich!"*

It was remarkable that however much the governor and I attempted to let the boys play by themselves and keep the girls to purely feminine amusements, it invariably ended in the amalgamation of the two parties; the running and jumping, the gymnastics over the parallel bars, the games of Verstecken were keener and swifter when the Princess took part. There were few boys who could beat her in running or jumping, and when Count Blumenthal jeered at a boy for behaving like a *Mädchen*, I found it easy to retort that one Mädchen could out-jump and out-run all his boys, and that he had better speak more respectfully in the future of our sex.

In the midst of this, Nana departed. Before going, she presented me with a quantity of numbers of a magazine called *Science for All*, which demonstrated how to make torpedoes, airships, and electric engines. She told me she had taken it "to improve herself," but most of the pages were uncut.

The Empress parted from Nana with the greatest reluctance and only under pressure from Fräulein von Thadden, who claimed to have suffered many things at her hands. With Nana's departure, the Princess became more and more difficult to manage, more unruly and rebellious, much worse than she had been in Homburg, and I could not but be aware of the unpleasant atmosphere that surrounded her. She grieved after her Nana but carefully hid her feelings. Fräulein von Thadden, still weak from her illness and occasionally unable to assume her duties, had obviously no former experience of children, and her ideas of their treatment were odd, old-fashioned, and difficult to understand.

Von Thadden was in a constant warfare, too, with old Dr. Zunker, who came over every morning in the train from Berlin to see the two children. He and the Empress were on one side, while Fräulein von Thadden, the ladies of the court, and Herr Gern, the Princess's tutor, stood shoulder to shoulder in opposition.

I tried in vain to preserve a neutral attitude, but I was not in sympathy with von Thadden's methods. The Empress disliked her intensely and called her a *Prinzipienreiter*—a stickler for rules. The Princess was of an affectionate disposition, however, and was for a time completely under von Thadden's influence. The Obergouvernante exercised that power over the child's conscience in harmful ways that made her nervous and wretched.

Often when I went to say goodnight to Sissy, I would find her crying bitterly into her pillow. This always happened when the Empress was away. I found out later that it was an axiom of Fräulein von Thadden's educational methods that at bedtime one worked upon a child's conscience; through some hypnotic power she possessed, she was able to do it very effectively. Day by day, the small disobediences and omissions of the child's life were made to appear enormous wickednesses, and von Thadden's strange travesty of piety was used to its full extent to give her power over the mind of the child.

We were saved, almost literally, by the cavalry. The Princess was permitted by the Empress to ride for half an hour twice a week, and, after a preliminary trial with Herr Kaspar, the *Sattelmeister*, I was pronounced sufficiently competent to accompany her.

"You will be very careful," said Fräulein von Thadden,

"and not ride very fast. I am going to take riding lessons soon and shall then be able to accompany Sissy. You must only ride for half an hour. She is so naughty she will try to ride longer."

That naughty Princess, learning she was allowed to ride, came leaping into my room, flung her arms around me, and screamed with delight.

Close to the New Palace was the lovely Wildpark, a game preserve with sandy paths under avenues of spreading beeches; here, under the supervision of Herr Kaspar, in splendid uniform, and a couple of grooms, we indulged in exhilarating gallops. The Princess soon developed into a practiced and fearless horsewoman with an excellent seat in the saddle and a light hand. Before long, she was learning to jump logs and hedges, to the horror and admiration of Her Majesty and the court.

Our gallops became *langgestreckt*—long and drawn-out. We rode a good way in a very short time. Soon we were promoted to rides on the *Bornstedter Feld*, the cavalry exercise ground about a half mile away, a sandy plain where we could let out the horses and settle down for a long, swinging gallop.

Nothing made the Princess so happy, so good-tempered, as those rides. They were exactly the outlet she needed for her exuberant vitality. She passionately adored animals, and their presence worked on her, as it does on all who understand and sympathize with them, a calming influence. When riding, all the irritabilities fell away from her, and as we galloped down the grassy stretches and smelled the pinewood of the forest, she would turn a radiant face to me and say, "Lovely, isn't it?"

In wet or frosty weather, we rode in the *Reitbahn*—riding school—that was attached to the Royal Mews. The *Bahn* had a layer of sawdust covering the floor and walls lined with mirrors so we could get glimpses of ourselves as we cantered past.

Herr Kaspar was delighted to have the opportunity to further our equestrian education. We took lessons in making *voltes* and circles at the word of command, in "passaging." We galloped and trotted and enjoyed ourselves immensely while the rain beat outside or the snow fell in thick flurries.

Suddenly, and for no reason that I could divine, Fräulein von Thadden stopped the rides. One day I went into Sissy's bedroom and there she sat, full of sulky resentment. "I hate-hate-hate von Thadden," she said, stamping her foot.

"Why? What's she done?"

"She won't let me ride—and Mamma said I could ride."

"But why not, if your mamma says you may?"

At that moment, the Obergouvernante came in, looking extremely annoyed. She had decided the Princess was to take a walk with me and would not alter her decision. "You must learn to bear disappointment, to give up the things you like," said the Spartan governess. Her eyes had dark circles around them, and it struck me that she was still extremely unwell.

"Mamma has already ordered the horses," Sissy pleaded.

"Then I will telephone to the stables and say they are not to come," pursued the inflexible von Thadden. "You are not riding today."

Now, Dr. Zunker, who, in spite of the fact that he spent

only half an hour a day in the palace, was a tremendous gossip. Having no disdain about pumping footmen and ladies' maids for the information he needed, he soon learned about the governess's arbitrary action, and he immediately issued an edict that the Princess must ride *three* times a week and for an *hour* instead of a half hour—not as a pleasure, but as a necessary measure of health.

*

From the Augustastift, an aristocratic ladies' school in Potsdam in which the Empress was much interested, three suitable young women of good family were chosen to provide the Princess with the necessary society of children of her own age. Every morning they were fetched at half-past seven by a royal carriage and brought to the New Palace, where they shared the lessons and the games of the Princess until twelve, when they were taken back to the Stift. When the court was staying in Berlin, the *Stiftskinder* were driven straight to Bellevue under a lady's escort.

The Augusta-Stift was one of the few boarding schools in Germany. Most of these establishments were founded on the sites of ancient convents and were converted to their secular use at the time of the Reformation. The head of the community retained the title of *Äbtissin*, or Abbess, and her robes of offices approximated closely a nun's habit, although, being Protestant, no one had to take any vows.

The families that had given lands or other endowments had the right to send their daughters to be educated free, and these girls, if they remained unmarried, were given a suite of rooms in the Stift, together with board and a small but sufficient yearly income.

As far as an outsider could gather of the life in the Stifts, it was old-fashioned and unprogressive. Some Stifts were so aristocratic that a candidate was not admitted if she could not show sixteen quarterings of nobility in her family tree.

Girls in high-class German schools led a very different life than those in similar institutions in England. Their whole existence was absorbed in the acquisition of knowledge. The exercise they took was not a matter of pleasure, but of health. If they did anything naughty or were untidy, they wore ribbon rosettes with colors that showed graduated degrees of infamy, and they were expected to weep bitterly when they didn't know their lessons.

As soon as the German schoolgirls were confirmed, they left school and blossomed into fashionably dressed, handsome young women, with hair done in the latest fashion and a decided penchant for young lieutenants. Their highest ambition was to be married as soon as possible, and they never again turned their thoughts in the direction of knowledge. They made excellent, self-sacrificing wives and mothers, and helped to preserve in their husbands that attitude of infallibility which was the prerogative of German men. They were as opposed to the self-possessed, slangy, sporting English schoolgirl with her multifarious ambitions as can be imagined. German schoolgirls never desired to go on the stage, never wanted a vote, and were perfectly content with the limited prospect which life offered to their sex.

There had been some heart-burning among the parents of the young ladies of the Stift, as each one considered that her child had the qualifications to be a companion to royalty; but the final decision was made by the headmistress and the Princess's tutor. The choice made was undoubtedly a wise one, although some of us ventured the opinion that the girls in question were too well brought up—we desired to see a little more natural, healthy naughtiness exhibited.

So, in their ill-fitting black frocks, in hard-round, black straw sailor hats, with their luxuriant hair strained brutally off their foreheads into the tightest, hardest of coils, every morning came three little girls to share the studies and recreations of the Princess. This quartette of young people worked and played together amicably until their confirmation.

The Princess had a vital curiosity, a trait she shared with her father. She liked, if possible, to merge herself into crowds to watch people going about their daily affairs, to see young people making love, old people cooking or reading the papers. She knew all about the brothers of the Stiftskinder. One particular friend among the boarders at the Stift—not one who came daily but one who was invited frequently to the palace—was a nice American girl called Yvette Borup. She had a brother who accompanied Peary on his expedition to the Arctic. After coming through all the dangers and hardships of such an expedition, a year or two later he drowned in America while boating—but at the time of which I write, he was absent with Peary, and there were few days when the Princess did not wonder "where Yvette's brother has got to now."

*

Shortly after we arrived at the New Palace, Princess May, a small niece of the Empress, the child of her sister, the Duchess of Schleswig-Holstein-Sonderburg-Glücksburg, came to spend a week or two with her cousin. Her visit marked the last effort on the part of the Princess to take an interest in her dolls. She was, however, an amused spectator of the unflinching realism with which Princess May—

an inventive child whose dolls suffered many and varied experiences—shaped the fragments of her dream of human life, the stormy channel crossings, the illnesses and cheerful funerals of her large family.

The passion of the Princess was animals, and during Princess May's visit, the Emperor, who was staying a few days at Cadinen, his country house in East Prussia, where he carried out farming operations on a large scale, sent the Princess a tiny, dimpled piglet.

From my bedroom window I suddenly caught sight of this infant swine, looking newly scrubbed and washed, with a bit of blue ribbon tied round the tender curve of his tail. He was sprinting across the great sandy Hof, pursued by several footmen and the two Princesses.

Victoria Louise was charmed with "Papa's *Scherkel*," and annoyed that she could not keep him in her own rooms. He was instead comfortably installed in the stable at Lindstedt, a villa belonging to the Emperor that was close to the gate of the New Palace, and where, being a pig of placid disposition, he put on flesh at a rapid rate, quickly losing the innocent gaiety of his early days, and developing a daily fatness, so that toward Christmas the usual tragic fate of pigs befell him.

His mistress suffered no sentimental regrets and ate without a qualm the savory sausages he provided. She did, however, retain a grateful memory of the nice sum he brought her, for, naturally, although she never paid for his keep, she demanded and received the sum for which the butcher had purchased his remains. "I wish Papa would give me another pig," she sighed when money was scarce. "He was so useful."

*

Soon after the Emperor's return from Cadinen, in early November, a severe frost set in, in what was to be the harshest German winter during my stay there. There was no snow at first, only a bitter east wind that came sweeping from the Russian steppes edged with ice and clasped the country in a grip of iron. It was gray weather with a leaden sky that promised snow if the cold should ever relax. Everywhere it froze hard, and the sentries outside—I heard them in the early hours of the morning when the cold was at its fiercest, walking up and down the Sandhof—were provided with fur-lined caps and coats and enormous fur-lined boots and gloves; otherwise, they would have been frozen at their posts.

The lakes and ponds, of which there were many in the neighborhood of Potsdam, were covered with ice. People were even skating on parts of the Havel River. The Princess begged to try her new skates, and at last, after elaborate precautions had been taken to test the ice—all the stoutest footmen and gardeners were made to stomp up and down on it in a collected mass—it was deemed safe for the sport of royalty.

Every day after lessons Sissy and Joachim, Count Blumenthal, and I drove to a large pond—nearly a lake— that lay by *Charlottenhof*, a strange little summer palace of one of the former Hohenzollern kings. We could easily have walked—it was only a short way through the gardens of *Sans Souci*—but the children preferred not to lose any time.

Neither of them knew anything about skating, nor did the governor, who shuffled about miserably on his skates, chiefly, as he explained, with the objective of keeping warm.

I was by no means an expert, but for a day or two I enjoyed the pre-eminence that belongs to those who know something when the rest know nothing. My pleasure was short-lived. Herr Gern, the Princess's tutor, appeared with his skates and crushed us all with his manifest superiority. He was a strong, sturdy young man, who skated with ease but without grace. The Princess and Prince Joachim quickly copied him, picking up a street-boy method of getting along by means of short, hurried strokes in the worst possible style.

One day the Duchess of Albany came with her young daughter Princess Alice, later Countess of Athlone. (The Empress had hoped to secure Princess Alice as a wife for one of her elder sons, but she preferred to marry an Englishman, much to the court's chagrin.) Princess Alice was an expert skater, and the English gentleman-in-waiting to the Duchess, Sir Robert Collins, was an artist on skates and illustrated in his own lean person the very poetry of motion. Not young, Sir Robert, with effortless ease, glided up and down, backwards and forwards, with an apparent absence of effort. Herr Gern, inclined to assume airs of superiority, humbly acknowledged the presence of a master. Count Blumenthal, in a series of convulsive waddling strokes, retired shamefacedly behind the pond's island, from whence Sir Robert fetched him out and gave him a few kindly hints.

Occasionally, the Empress would come on these jaunts and would skate leaning on Herr Gern's arm, for her ankle was still rather weak from the past summer's sprain. The most uncomfortable moments spent on the slippery surface, however, were those when the Emperor, in his warm gray cavalry cloak and surrounded by a party of adjutants and officers, wended his way in our direction. Inexpert performers realized the extreme risk of trying to bow to His Majesty on skates, and fled to the shelter of the island.

Misfortunes in the way of tumbles caused an unholy joy in the Emperor's heart. It pleased him to see people lose their dignity. One day when Princess Alice and I, skating with great dash and confidence hand in hand, came, after a convulsive flounder, to a sudden fall, the imperial laughter gloated wholeheartedly over our prostrate bodies.

Ladders and ropes were always laid ready on the bank in case of accident. One afternoon, Prince Oskar and the Princess—she delighting in the company of her favorite brother—decided to practice some lifesaving. I, on my skates, represented to the best of my ability the victim of an ice catastrophe, lying down and clutching at the rope, which, after many failed efforts, they managed to throw in my direction. When it came to pulling me "out," although I was not *in* but already *on* the surface of the ice, their well-meant endeavors only resulted in themselves being dragged backwards, while I remained exactly where I was.

The next day, the Emperor wanted to know how I liked being "rescued." "They didn't rescue me one inch, Your Majesty," I replied. "I should have been drowned ten times over." He chuckled over this and said he would like to see the experiment repeated in his presence, one royal desire that was to remain forever unfulfilled.

*

November was a busy month, and it was a distinct advantage to the court—although not to the Emperor, who received much criticism in the newspapers for his actions—

that, in November 1902, he decided to pay a visit to England. The Empress grasped the opportunity of his absence to visit Prince Au-Wi and Prince Oskar at Plön.

In these early years of my stay, the Crown Prince and Prince Eitel-Frederick (Fritz) were in Bonn studying at the university, Prince Adalbert was with the navy at Kiel or roaming about the world on a warship, and Princes Au-Wi and Oskar lived together in Plön in a pleasant country house with their governor and various teachers and enjoyed the companionship of the young cadets of the aristocratic Kadettenschule which was nearby. (Au-Wi and Oskar had always been inseparable companions; as children they had slept in the same bed and had even contracted measles at the same time.)

With the absence of Their Majesties, our life reverted to an absence of ceremony, the blessedness of which I was again reminded recently when I found a copy of a letter I had written during that time:

> Last night I went to Prince Joachim's room to give him his English lesson, but *Treasure Island* was sorely interrupted by Princess May of Glücksburg playing on the accordion in the room next to us. Prince Joachim and Graf Blumenthal both rushed in to her, threatening all sorts of things if she didn't stop! Yesterday afternoon, the Prince and Princesses went to Berlin; one of them had to go to the dentist and have a tooth out, so we had a special saloon and red carpet down at the private waiting-room and a comfortable journey to Berlin.

We had two footmen with us and two carriages met us in Berlin, where there was more red carpet. We drove first to the dentist and then to the zoo. So that people might not know us we each assumed different names. Sissy was "Marie" and Joachim, "Stephen," and they called me, who had no need of disguise, "Tante Mimi." But I think a good many people knew the Princess. She is too often seen in Berlin to hope to remain unrecognized.

The man who looked after the monkeys gave us a private performance of two chimpanzees, who drank tea, played the harp, put on neckties and hats, and danced, sending the children into fits of laughter. We saw the lions, bears, and seals, but had no time for the elephants, as we had to return by the five o'clock train.

Such simple pleasures had to be snatched during the absence of Their Majesties. The rest of the time we led a rather dawdling existence, tedious, tiring, and futile, that ate into one's strength and energies without any equivalent satisfaction of achievement.

*

November also held the birthday of the Empress, a celebration at the New Palace. The most striking among her presents were the dozen hats given by His Majesty, chosen by himself. They were arranged on stands on the billiard table of the room where the birthday table was erected—a table beautifully enwreathed and garlanded by autumn leaves mixed with fruits, bunches of tiny red crabapples, clusters of green and black grapes, small melons, and gourds. It is a perilous business for any man to set out to buy a dozen hats for his wife without consulting her tastes and wishes on the subject, but the Emperor was not a man to recoil from such an enterprise. Though the hats were beautiful and obviously the most expensive of their kind, they raised, I found, certain doubts and queries in the mind of the woman observer.

Does any woman in the world, be she ever so much an Empress, really desire to have hats thrust on her by the dozen without any trying on or any of that delicious hovering between two decisions which makes hat-buying so thrillingly charming—above all, without reference to the costume with which the headgear must be worn? The ordinary masculine mind is not sufficiently subtle to number among its greatest achievements the purchase of successful feminine millinery; even an emperor ought to realize his limits. But Wilhelm never did.

On the evening of Her Majesty's birthday, a performance was usually given in the rococo theatre built by Frederick the Great. One year, the newly crowned King and Queen of Norway were present. They stayed at the New Palace with their small son Olaf, an amusing, quaint, old-fashioned child who charmed everybody, especially the Emperor, with whom he chatted in a confidential fearless manner, treating His Majesty as a friend and companion and inviting him to help in building his house of bricks.

Sissy, thirteen, and the only child still living at home, with her mother in an official photograph taken on the Empress's birthday in 1905.

CHAPTER FIVE

THE SEASON IN BERLIN

Berlin was a city that grew on one. It had no hidden beauties, no unexpected nooks of quiet, old-world buildings. It was all aggravatingly new and prosperous. Yet it was not without certain pleasing aspects—its tree-planted streets, for instance, and the *Tiergarten*, a big park in the very heart of the city, full of trees and sheets of water that froze for skaters in the winter and hosted perspiring rowers in the summer. In the wide shaded paths and roads of the Tiergarten, the Emperor, when in residence at the capital, rode and walked every day.

Indeed, one of the features of Berlin was its excellent riding roads, and one of the Emperor's favorite routes was the road between the royal Schloss and the *Grunewald*. Although riding through Berlin was a tedious process, owing to numerous intersecting side streets of asphalt, the Emperor went on horseback all the way from his own door and back again, refusing to travel part of the way by automobile as the Empress did; her horses were sent on ahead with the grooms to a certain spot in the forest where she joined her husband.

Once, as Their Majesties rode together in the early morning, the horse of the Empress stumbled and fell, turning a complete somersault and throwing its rider on her head—fortunately, without serious injury, thanks to the hard straw hat she was wearing.

It is a dreadful business for an empress to fall from her horse, even when she receives no particular harm. It usually happens before a crowd of people, some of whom are necessarily held responsible for the accident. On this occasion, one or two officials became hysterical and shed tears, while the Emperor, under the stress, used some rather sharp words of censure. The adjutants scattered themselves wildly over the surface of the earth in search of a doctor, while Princes Oskar and Joachim, who were riding with their parents, did the same.

Prince Oskar discovered no doctor, but he did manage to find a Droschke with a miserable-looking horse and a dirty, unkempt driver, who was sitting, dreaming on his box, in front of a house, waiting for his fare. Prince Oskar ordered him to come and drive Her Majesty home, but the Droschke driver demurred, saying he was already engaged and could not leave his farc in the lurch. The Prince insisted, but the faithful cabman still refused the proffered honor of driving the Empress home. Finally, the Prince drew his sword and bade the driver in the name of military authority—paramount in Germany—to proceed with him at once to the indicated spot. Grumbling loudly, the driver did as he was told.

Her Majesty, who was protesting at being treated as an injured person, would have preferred to remount her horse and ride home quietly, but she had to get into the evil-smelling, dirty vehicle with Countess Stolberg and, escorted by her two sons and two crestfallen officials, go home, where a frightened young military doctor thought, after a short examination, that it was advisable for the Empress to keep to her bed.

Wilhelm always appeared in his Hussar's uniform when riding in Berlin, as did the twelve officers of his escort. They made a vivid break of color against the dingy walls of the palace. Whenever the Emperor and his retinue emerged into the big square—the Lustgarten—outside the Schloss, a crowd gathered. At these times, the police did not allow anyone to cross the square. If we had been out shopping on foot, we were not permitted to re-enter the Schloss unless we could produce our *Einlasskarte*, with which every member of the royal household was furnished—orange for *Herrschaften*, persons of rank, and blue for *Dienerschaft*, servants. I always carried mine in my purse, for it was not the least use to reply to the burly *Dienstmann's* question, "Why do you want to go into the Schloss?" "Because I live there."

These rides of the Emperor, two or three times a week, through the streets of his capital, mounted on a splendid horse, surrounded by glittering officers, helped to impose his personality upon the people and added materially to his popularity. His saddle horses were tall, big-boned animals, trained with special care to accommodate the lack of power in his left hand. But he had a good seat on horseback, and on those winter afternoons it was one of the sights of Berlin to watch his progress through the streets, along the broad alleys of the Tiergarten, under the center arch of the *Brandenburger-Tor*, on each side of which sentries were posted, and up Linden Avenue, where the windows of the big hotels were packed with tourists anxious to see the Emperor, while on the pavement, people stood patiently waiting in the cold to see him pass by.

The Master of the Horse confided to me his agonies of apprehension on these actions and said he had implored the Emperor to give up these rides over the slippery asphalt of the square, but it was in vain. The Emperor knew the impression he made on people and believed it well worth the risk. It was a triumphant ride: the enthusiastic greetings of the people, the shrill cries of Berlin's schoolchildren, who saw in the figure on the white horse the personification of the glory and might of the German Empire.

Even democratic Americans who saw the sight confessed to feeling strangely stirred. "You know, I felt like cheerin', too, when I saw William comin' along like that," said one of them to me. "He does understand how to keep the center of the stage, that man, and the sun flashin' on all those swords as they rode, and the blues and reds of the uniforms! I tell you, he's some Kaiser, he is. He knows how to dress the part. He's got an instinct for the spectacular. He's clever, I tell you, if he has done some foolish things. He plays to the gallery, and it's what you've got to do, I guess, nowadays if you want to be a power in politics."

Berlin was a city that developed under the Emperor's hand; it was everywhere stamped by his tastes. One feature of the new streets was the frequency of small, open, tree-shaded spaces furnished with benches, where the poor women and children of the neighborhood enjoyed fresh air. Unfortunately, the Emperor's taste was second rate. He was attracted in art, whether in painting, sculpture, or music, to the mediocre, so that the statues of Berlin were somewhat of a blot on the town—all the statues of the kings and electors of the Hohenzollern line which the Emperor presented to the town. During the first few winters of their introduction, when morning dawned, some were occasionally discovered to be minus a nose or other necessary feature which had been broken off during the night. These outrages were always attributed by the Emperor to the Socialists, but a young artist of the modern school once told me that he believed the perpetrators were art students, furious at what they considered to be a crime against German taste.

The cathedral, erected on the site of the old one on the banks of the Spree opposite the castle, was built on a plan approved by the Emperor and was much criticized. The interior was bare and inartistic in the extreme, unworthy of a town of the size and wealth of Berlin. The cathedral seemed to embody the spirit of Lutheranism—plain, unadorned, and with no uplifting of the spirit to the worship of an ideal.

The social life in Berlin was not what one would expect in the center of a great empire. There were neither smartly nor poorly dressed people, no congregating of the aristocratic class who take the lead in social life. There was no fashionable time or place for people to walk or drive, and fine equipages, excepting those belonging to the court, were absent. From time to time, the Emperor tried in vain to create a fashionable atmosphere. One season he instituted a *Korso*, which was to emulate the afternoon procession of carriages in Hyde Park. He himself daily drove in the Tiergarten with his coach-and-four; his Master of the Horse appeared with another, and all frequenters of court functions were invited to come with their carriages, but the result was a dismal failure.

Countess Stolberg remarked, "What is the use of the Emperor trying to imitate London? Your season is in May and June, ours is in January and February—no time for driving slowly up and down and chatting. If we drive at all, we drive in closed carriages wrapped up in furs, and we are thankful to get to our journey's end as soon as possible."

When the Emperor would hold a levee—a *Cercle*, as it was called in Berlin—it took place at 9:30 P.M., and I would watch the carriages as they came into the courtyard and arranged themselves row on row to wait for the return of the officers. Never had I beheld such a collection of wretched vehicles. Every last equipage that would hold together, every poor, trembling, worn-out horse—the horses of Berlin were a crying scandal and shame to any decent community before the advent of the automobile mercifully drove them off the street—was pressed into service, and it was strange to see tall, handsome men in brilliant uniforms descending from shabby carriages with drivers who appeared to have made no effort to their own toilette or that of the horses.

Conspicuous among the crowd of officers in full-dress uniform were the Cuirassiers of the guard in their white tunics and high-topped boots. There was an incessant clanking of swords. Once, after watching the stream of courtiers pass, I stepped to the windows on the opposite side of the corridor and looked out through the night into the dimly lit courtyard (the excellent electric illuminating of the Berlin streets had not yet penetrated to the Schloss, which was appallingly ill-lit). I was struck by the contrast of row upon row of broken-down animals and men with their wretched vehicles waiting in the sleet.

In Berlin, more than in any other German town, there was a lack of the polish and courtesy which is supposed to be acquired where people congregate in large numbers. The shop assistants were distinctly rude, and it amused me to note the rapid change from boorishness to humility of the young man or woman behind the counter upon becoming aware that a court carriage was waiting outside for me.

*

The Berlin palace was an ugly gray pile of buildings skirted on one side by the River Spree. Inside was a gloomy, sunless courtyard, paved with cobblestones. In the center of the Hof was a statue of St. George and the Dragon, the latter curling uncomfortably around the hoofs of St. George's horse, an estimable steed which, instead of shying, as our experience of horses would lead us to expect, gallantly aided its master's spear-thrust by dancing a kind of tango on the dragon's vitals.

Along one side of the courtyard, in the basement of the Schloss, were the barracks of the Schloss Guard. When the court was in residence, the guard spent its time in perpetual rushes and drummings. No princely personage could arrive or depart without a line of soldiers presenting arms to the throbbing drumbeat. One could hear, intermittently from early morning till late at night, the rapid beat of feet on the cobblestones as the soldiers snatched their arms and fell into line, then the silence, the military command, and the long continuous rumble while the royal or princely personage of whatever size or age descended from his or her carriage, saluted, and disappeared into the Schloss.

Poor Princess May of Glücksburg was, on the occasion of a visit, more than a bit intimidated by this practice. She was, at first, running about the courtyard, giving Jacky, the Princess's dog, rides in the handcart. Having hitherto led a quiet life in the ancestral Schloss in the country, she did not connect the guards' constant movements—in and out of the guardhouse every five minutes or less, hardly having time to eat their soup, constantly seizing their weapons and lining up to present arms—with her presence. When the Princess realized that these honors were being lavished on her own small person, and that she was expected to wave her finger backwards and forwards at the soldiers in a sign of dismissal, she was abashed, and, as she was far too shy to shake her finger at anyone, she chose to play in a more secluded spot.

*

In January, two festivals broke into lessons. One was the *Krönungstag*—the anniversary of the accession of the Emperor—which was celebrated by a series of tedious ceremonies at which the whole family was present. The day began with a service in the chapel at ten o'clock in the morning, at which, in the first few years I lived there, women were obliged to appear in court dress—later done away with by order of the Emperor—with long trains. Those of royal birth had their trains carried by pages in red. For these functions, tickets were issued to the gallery high up in the dome of the chapel and given to anyone connected with the court. It was no light task, first to climb up the interminable steps of the winding stair that led to this vantage point, where no seats were allowed, and once there, to endure the suffocating crush. The only amusement was to observe the behavior of the crowd—to watch, for example, the lady who had received a ticket through an ambassador and thought that, however late she appeared, she had a right to a place in the front row, and the footman's wife, who was already there, refusing to recognize social superiority—except in her own case, which allowed her precedence over a mere waiting-maid.

A few days after this festival was the anniversary of His Majesty's birthday, and the day was kept with zeal and earnestness from early morning until night. At half-past nine in the morning, the Emperor received congratulations from members of the household. On tables arranged in one of the smaller salons were spread out the gifts received from family and friends. The Princess's present was a source of anxiety. Sometimes it took the form of a blotting-book, the cover worked or painted by herself, or a photograph frame, or perhaps a sketch of her own, something costing little, excepting the expenditure of time and patience. The Emperor was always pleased with his daughter's gifts, and he valued them more than the silver statuettes, the oil paintings, and the jewelled cigarette cases lavished on him by the other members of his family.

On the evening of the Emperor's birthday, there was the usual performance of the opera, but no tickets were sold and the seats were occupied entirely by guests of His Majesty. The whole house was decorated with wreaths of flowers, and the *Parkett*—stalls—were filled with the gentlemen of the diplomatic corps, ambassadors and envoys from the remotest parts of the world: Chinese mandarins in yellow silk robes, wearing peacock feathers in their caps, Turks and Egyptians in red fezzes, mingled with the uniforms of every existing army in the world. The ladies were seated in a dress circle, in a line with the royal box.

I received a ticket for a loge—a stage box—the best possible place for an uninterrupted view of the house. From this vantage point, I could see many notable royal personalities, as well as some unusual events.

Before the entrance of the Emperor and the Empress, the Intendant of the Theatre, in full uniform, came to the front of the box and rapped loudly three times on the floor with his wand of office. At once that queer gaggling jamble of incoherent sound which rises from a crowd of people was hushed. Their Majesties and their guests slowly advanced, bowed to the audience, and took their places.

On one birthday, for some reason, the evening concerts took place, instead of at the opera, in the beautiful *Weissersaal*. Several soloists sang, and there was a large band of string and wind instruments. Suddenly, during the playing of a piece, a door opened in the empty musicians' gallery which ran across the Saal at right angles to the box where I was sitting, and I was startled to see a man enter on hands and knees and creep slowly across the floor to the opposite side. Following him a few paces behind, in the same stealthy manner, came a fat, unwieldly woman. They were distinctly visible through the white marble balustrades as they moved slowly along, the woman getting into constant difficulties with her skirt, which much impeded her progress. The first thought that crossed my mind was could this perhaps be the preliminary to an anarchist bomb? The rotundity of the woman was reassuring. She did not look to be of the stuff of which conspirators are made; nevertheless, her movements were suspicious.

I touched the hand of Countess Stolberg and nodded in the direction of the two grovellers on the gallery floor. She started, and then an angry flush of indignation spread over her face. She whispered to me that they were the wife and son of a *Kastellan*, one of the officials in charge of the Schloss. They had chosen this extraordinary manner of seeing and hearing something of the festivities. Foolishly, as it turned out, for the Emperor saw them, with the result that the unfortunate husband and father of the guilty pair nearly lost his comfortable position, while the son was punished and the wife fell into disgrace.

At the same concert one of the chorus singers went out of his mind. At all state concerts there was a long intermission, when the Emperor and Empress would move around among the invited. Not until His Majesty commanded was the signal given by a gentle drumroll for the concert to begin again. On this night, after a very short interval, indeed, the drum was heard, and everybody hurried back in some surprise to the red velvet chairs from which they had just risen to wander about and talk.

The Emperor knew that someone had blundered, as he had given no order to continue, but he let the mistake pass and returned to his place beside the Empress. The person who had given the signal, however, a singer in the chorus who for some time had been giving his friends cause for uneasiness, continued to drum energetically for several minutes. Finally, he jumped up and ran from the Schloss, pursued by a pink-stockinged footman as far as the courtyard gates, where he then escaped into the darkness of the crowded streets.

On another birthday, the guests included King Edward VII of England and Queen Alexandra, who were visiting Berlin in the year before the King's death. The performance on this birthday was *Sardanapalus*, which strictly speaking, is hardly to be classed with opera at all, consisting as it does of a series of pictures interspersed with songs. The last scene is a realistic representation of the funeral pyre of Sardanapalus, to which slaves bring all the treasures of the house to be consumed by the fire. Beginning with little licking tongues of flame, the fire soon spreads to a wide and vivid blaze in which Sardanapalus's entire household perishes. At the moment before the curtain finally descends, the whole stage has the appearance of a glowing furnace threaded with leaping flames and rolling billows of smoke.

King Edward, tired from his hard day's work in Berlin, had indulged in a short nap during the performance and woke to consciousness at the moment of most intense conflagration, when he was, for a few moments, much excited and alarmed, believing that the fire was real and wondering why the firemen were still inactively stationed in the wings. With some difficulty, the Empress managed to convince him that there was no danger.

*

After the Emperor's birthday, the season was in full swing. There were four state balls and various *Cours*—receptions—and levees, but the balls were the chief events of the season. With his customary thoroughness, the Emperor did not permit any dancing at court that failed to measure up to a certain standard of excellence. Every young debutante, every young officer eager to dance before royalty had to first satisfy the fastidious judgment of the court dancing mistress, Frau Wolden, who held several *Tanzproben*, or trial dances, in the *Weissersaal*. Frau Wolden was only slightly less a personality than His Majesty; it was whispered that once in a forgetful moment she had, indeed, sunk onto the throne itself.

Frau Wolden upheld with a stern hand the dignity of the court, and her scathing remarks on the attitudes and steps of certain young provincials of both sexes who thought to introduce fashionable irregularities into the dances, made them realize their error at once. Her real age was unknown. She owned with pride to seventy, and would lift her silk skirts and show her wonderfully fine ankles in graceful tiptoe turns as if in derision of awkward flat-footed youth. To the day of her death, she retained all her marvelous grace of movement.

Twice a week, Frau Wolden came to the castle to give dancing lessons to Prince Joachim and the Princess. Other boys and girls of the same age were invited to complete the class and were drilled by the old lady in the intricacies of the minuet and gavotte, old-world dances that were mainstays of the Berlin court balls.

*

When Beerbohm Tree came with his company to Berlin for a week or ten days to show the Germans something about stage management, the Empress wished the Princess to see the English actor but feared there was nothing suitable in his repertoire. However, after carefully rereading *Richard II*, she decided that it was appropriate for stimulating historical interest, and the Princess, to her joy, accompanied Their Majesties.

Tree's stay in Berlin must have been fraught for him

with peculiar anxiety, for on the Sunday when he gave two performances, all his German scene-shifters deserted him to go to the funeral of a notable Socialist. Tree was left to grapple as he could with the situation. There were terribly long waits between the scenes of *Antony and Cleopatra*, at which Their Majesties were present, and once the curtain went up prematurely, revealing British stage carpenters among the splendors of ancient Egypt.

The Berlin Opera House, which stood only a few yards from the royal Schloss, was built by Frederick the Great and, though a fine building, was not up to date in its accommodations for performers or audience. After the terrible fire in Chicago, where, for want of adequate exits, many lives were lost, hideous iron staircases were constructed outside the Opera House by order of the Emperor. These, while giving some additional sense of security to the audience, altogether spoiled the appearance of the building.

A Berlin opera audience was not known for smartness; a morning blouse and tweed skirt, with a pair of rather weary-looking kid gloves, were considered by the ladies as quite sufficient for the Parkett. However, when the Emperor's presence was announced beforehand, no one was admitted who was not in evening dress.

Life in the Berlin Schloss was very different from that in the New Palace. When lessons were being held, the Princess had to drive every morning with the lady on duty to the Bellevue Schloss, at the other side of the Tiergarten, where her tutor gave lessons from eight to twelve. In the mornings, the Obergouvernante took *Dienst*—duty—in Bellevue, returning at one o'clock for luncheon in the tiny dining room of the Princess's apartments, whose walls were made entirely of mirrors bordered by wreaths of painted flowers.

Bellevue was one of those plain, unpretentious palaces which were built in the middle of the eighteenth century and had the advantage of a large garden full of grass and trees. It was sometimes the scene of great Easter egg hunts, in which the Emperor took an active part. About twenty children were invited, and preparations in the way of gifts were only a little less than those at Christmas. The Empress gave every person in her service a piece of Berlin porcelain—hand-painted coffee- or teacups, dessert plates, vases, candlesticks. Flowers were arranged to look like eggs and sent to the suite from Her Majesty. Each of the children invited to the *Eiersuchen* received a huge cardboard egg filled with toys, postcards, trinkets, and bonbons, besides a variety of chocolate eggs wrapped in bright-colored papers.

The eggs had to be looked for in various hiding places, and each child was given a basket to hold what was found. If the weather promised to keep fine, the eggs were hidden in the garden, but if it appeared likely to be wet, the hunt took place in the Schloss. Sometimes the Emperor insisted on hiding all the eggs himself, as he considered that he knew the best places for them; but once he made an unfortunate choice of the porcelain stoves as appropriate nesting places. The chocolate eggs melted away under the influence of the heat and betrayed their presence by long, brown stalactites dripping to the floor below.

The egg parties were apt to be a bit stiff—the children were overawed and probably over-admonished before coming as to their behavior. But one of them was saved by the Prince of Saxe-Altenburg. He arrived at Bellevue clad in an immaculate white sailor suit and a white linen cap, but in his earnest pursuit of eggs, he thrust himself into the heart of the sootiest bushes, conscientiously penetrated the most tangled thorny shrubs, and explored the coke-cellar of the greenhouse—emerging at last with his face covered with black smears and the dazzling whiteness of his garments seriously diminished.

When the children reassembled with their eggs, this small Prince, regardless of the smuts on his hands and nose, smiled at Their Majesties and produced from his pocket a pair of motor-goggles, which he put on with great joy. He then swept a sunshiny glance at the girls and boys and turned to the Emperor and grinned confidently. This effectively broke the ice. The children giggled, lapsed into naturalness, and forgot that they were wearing their best frocks, while they followed the motor-goggled Prince in a wild chase around bushes and flowerbeds. All went home smudgy; it was an unusually good time.

*

Once I was admiring the blue satin curtains in one room of Bellevue—they were quite new, which was unusual—and the Princess said, "Yes, of course; that is because of the Shah of Persia."

"Why?" I asked, wondering what the Shah had to do with new curtains at Bellevue.

"Oh, don't you know? He and his suite stayed here once, and they used to kill sheep in this room and wipe their hands on the curtains. They had to be replaced, of course!"

She further added that the "old Shah"—the one who threw chicken bones and asparagus ends over his shoulder to the servants standing behind—tried to imitate European manners and eat with a fork instead of his fingers, but being unaccustomed to the implement, compromised by picking up the meat with his fingers, sticking it on the fork, and conveying it to his mouth.

"When Great-Grandmamma Augusta once offered him a dish of strawberries, instead of taking a few on his plate, he just ate them from the dish—while she held it! Fancy! Great-Grandmamma Augusta, who was so particular! Everyone had a fit!"

May 24, 1913, the wedding banquet of Victoria Louise and the Duke of Brunswick, held in the Weisser Saal of the Berlin Schloss. From bottom, beginning with the butler pouring: Crown Princess Cecilia, the Duke of Cumberland, Queen Mary, the Emperor, Duchess Thrya of Cumberland (hidden), Crown Prince Wilhelm, and the Grand Duchess of Hesse. Across the table, from right to left, Princess Fritz, King George V, the Empress, Pol and Sissy, Czar Nicholas II, the Grand Duchess Louise, and Prince Waldemar of Denmark.

HOLIDAYS

About the middle of November there were great charity bazaars in Berlin. The ladies of the court attended and made large purchases of clothing on behalf of Her Majesty. I often accompanied one of them to the various shops in Berlin and gasped at the wholesale manner of her orders—fifteen cushions and twenty-five photograph frames selected in as many seconds.

Enormous bales of goods began to arrive and were placed in the *Marmorsaal*, a splendid apartment which was used for the entertainment of royal guests, but which, in the weeks before Christmas, took on a more homely, human aspect, piled up with warm garments, heaps of toys, books, almanacs, cakes of soap, boots, and shoes. I can still feel in my nose the disagreeable tingle, similar to a mild form of hay fever, caused by the fluffiness of those piles of flannelette garments, thick woolly stockings and socks which I helped to sort and count.

Every man, woman, and child having any connection
with the royal estates in Cadinen, Hubertus-Stock, Rominten,
Berlin, or at the New Palace was remembered, and the Empress always chose their various gifts personally.

The *Inspektor*, or clergyman, of every district furnished
a list of every family with the name and age of each member.
Everybody received one garment at least and a toy, if a child,
a book, and one or two packages of *Pfefferkuchen*—
gingerbread. Often there were families of nine or ten children,
and nearly every year one more infant was added to their list.
The Empress, distributing the little cakes of soap, told us how
the peasants preferred to keep them as souvenirs rather than
use them, and would bring them out with pride, still in careful wrappings, to show Her Majesty a year or more later.

One person, whose idea of the German Empress was
that she spent her life in a series of domestic duties, sent her
a small parcel with the following letter:

> Most Excellent Majesty, Berlin
> Most Gracious Empress:
> May it please your Majesty, I crave your
> Majesty's patronage, hailing from the Emerald Isle:
> the enclose [sic] cover for painting arranging china
> is procurable in any shade of linen. I have the
> honor to remain with the profoundest veneration,
> Your Majesty's most dutiful servant,
> James Barker (Belfast)

The "enclose cover" was a green apron with a large
pocket. As such gifts were never accepted without payment,
it was put on one side with the idea of being returned.

Her Majesty, however, happened to need something as a protection for her dress when handling the fluffy garments and found the green apron to supply that want. It was worn every day by the Empress for the next few weeks. Obviously, James Barker, even if his literary style was not of the highest order, had an instinct for supplying the right thing at the right time. The "Irish apron" was the subject of constant praise, and during "the wearin' o' the green," Her Majesty frequently expressed appreciation of its practical utility. It was, I believe, the only apron Her Majesty ever wore.

To the Princess, the approach of Christmas was a serious time for many reasons, chiefly financial. Until she was seventeen, she received only a personal allowance of five marks a month, out of which she was expected to buy her own stamps and to spare a Sunday contribution toward the collection. It may be a breach of confidence of the highest order to reveal that this contribution never exceeded ten *Pfennige*—one penny in English coin—and I can never forget the look of sorrowful indignation when one day I put the smallest silver coin of German currency, a fifty-Pfennig piece worth less than a sixpence, in the collection plate. "How am I going to buy my stamps when you are so reckless?" she demanded outside the chapel door.

The balancing of her accounts was always fraught with many sighs and groans. "Thirty-five Pfennigs too little," she would announce, drawing the bottom line. So as soon as Christmas began to loom in the distance there were many anxious consultations as to how to obtain the necessary presents for her relatives. Of course, Papa and Mamma had to have something special and made by her—something bought ready-made in a shop was not to be thought of. "Cushions and lampshades seem to be the only things," said the Princess, "and Mamma has twenty-four lampshades and dozens and dozens of cushions. We must think of something cheap. I'm so awfully poor."

Fortunately, the powers that controlled the purse-strings decreed that all materials for presents should be bought out of the Princess's own money, but that in the matter of "making up" the exchequer would provide the needed funds. So the harassed child was forced into the manufacture of those articles which are cheap in the initial outlay but expensive to complete: slippers, worked picture frames, cushions.

One Christmas, at an acute crisis when for some reason the list of presents expanded to twenty-eight, the advent into fashion of ribbonwork saved her from despair. She begged some odd pieces of silk and brocade from Her Majesty's workroom for the purpose of making glove and handkerchief sachets.

Ribbonwork, as everyone knows who has done it, is capable of achieving the maximum effect with the minimum of effort. While I hastily sketched simple designs of apple-blossoms or violets on the corners of everything, the Princess sat and worked feverishly. She was an indefatigable and rapid needlewoman—too rapid, perhaps, to be accurate—and got through a tremendous amount of work if someone would read to her. To this day, certain portions of *Kidnapped* are inextricably interwoven in my mind with the sound of the long-drawn ribbons and an intensely absorbed face surrounded by tumbled golden hair, bending in the lamplight over her self-imposed task.

Sometimes the Princess and Prince Joachim would sit in the evening with the Empress, working on the very presents destined for her, and she was required to ignore what they were doing and to turn her eyes conscientiously in another direction. They erected newspaper screens around themselves and if the screens fell down, as frequently happened, Mamma had to shut her eyes or turn away until the camouflage was rebuilt.

For six weeks before Christmas, those who happened near a railway line would have noticed the passing of luggage trains bearing nothing but "small" pine trees, ten to twelve feet high. They were the thinnings of the pine forests of the *Thuringer Wald* and came down daily to Berlin and other large towns to supply the dealers. Every public square became a miniature pine wood. Even stringent police regulations were relaxed. In the broad streets were dealers in trees and sellers of toys, Pfefferkuchen, filigree ornaments, airships, toy flying machines, and other Christmas luxuries.

Hardly any house in Germany, whether the inhabitants were young or old, rich or poor, was without a tree at Christmas. One saw them in lonely signal boxes on the railway, in poverty-stricken cottage windows, in workshops, in barracks, in churches and chapels.

At the New Palace, the glory and brightness were concentrated in the big *Muschelsaal*. Here, in that wonderful hall of shells, a row of big Christmas trees was arranged, one for every child of the Emperor, one for His Majesty and the Empress, and another for the ladies-in-waiting—nine trees in all, and two for the servants' distribution. In addition, everyone had to have a private tree. It would be a terrible thing to find a single sitting room without a pine tree and tinsel ornaments.

The Muschelsaal occupied the center of the palace. On its walls were every variety of shell, arranged in fantastic patterns: roses, stars, and spirals of every kind, while the middle pillars were decorated with beautiful stone or marble in an irregular rockwork. Here were also found large lumps of amber from the shores of the Baltic Sea (one with a fly clearly visible below the surface), pieces of blue lapis lazuli, green malachite, red jasper, and ringed onyx, alabaster, porphyry, quartz of every shape and color, highly polished and set in cement on the square pillars that upheld the roof. They sparkled in a thousand colors under the wax lights of the candelabra and the twinkling tapers of the trees.

The trees were decorated almost entirely by the Princes and their sister. Besides the candles, they were hung with *Konfekt*—chocolate rings. Then they added plenty of silver lametta and angels' hair, filmy silvery threads that gave an impression of hoar frost, and a *Christbaumengel* with wide-open wings or a large silver star was put at the top of each tree.

A further inroad on our time was made by the practice of carol-singing, which took place—on account of the piano—in the salon of the Princess, leading out from that of the Obergouvernante. Every one of the ladies and gentlemen of the palace who possessed the faintest pretension to vocal ability was pressed into service, and the unfortunate *Hofprediger*, or court chaplain, was given the herculean task of training this group to sing together in some kind of time and tune.

We were a very scratch choir. Fräulein von Gersdorff, the arts expert, who posed as a musical critic, was our leading soprano, but she had a trick of suddenly changing without warning to the alto, taking the rest of the feeble and uncertain upper voices with her and leaving those who had been singing alto in horrid doubt as to whether they should fly to the rescue of the demoralized sopranos or go on singing their own parts. "I thought the altos were weak," she would explain afterwards in that queer, deep voice of hers. "I thought I would help them a little."

We begged her not to desert her own part without warning, as her booming, powerful voice drowned any efforts of her colleagues to stay the impending decline, and they were dragged down against their will, with frightful results. I don't know why it was that Fräulein von Gersdorff, who should have been our chief support with her sweet voice, should almost invariably have been the cause of our downfall. What she really seemed to want was to sing both parts simultaneously.

All the sons of the Emperor stayed in the New Palace during Christmas, and they, too, were invited to come and help swell the chorus, although they often grew restive, being summoned from their rooms for "one more practice." Prince Adalbert put in an appearance occasionally and brought his equerry, who had the only trained man's voice in the party. We had built great hopes upon him, as he had declared himself capable of singing bass, but his idea was to boom out the air an octave below the treble, which was, of course, unsatisfactory.

By means of ceaseless drilling, the Princess and Prince Joachim were taught to sing alto; the Hofprediger himself sang tenor; and the ladies managed the treble well. We had great hopes of being able to perform a capella. But, however well we sang beforehand, at the critical moment this design was always abandoned. Someone had a cold, another was not sure of C sharp, and most of us were nervous. After much discussion, we fell back on the support of the piano.

All over Germany, the *Bescherung*, or presentation of Christmas gifts, took place on *Weihnachtsabend*—Christmas Eve. The real business of Bescherung, however, began on the day before Christmas Eve. The Empress rushed from one *Kinderheim*—children's home—to another, to hospitals and schools, with the same ready smile, the same fresh look of interest in the oft-repeated ceremony, the oft-sung carol. She never tired of giving pleasure to others, and when, in later years, I would hear criticism of her being less than clever, I would rise quickly to her defense. No other woman in the world would have been so suited to the Emperor's varying moods, his suddenness, his volcanic outbursts of energy. In the presence of her husband, she was self-sacrificing and self-effacing; when apart from him, she showed plenty of initiative and self-confidence.

Christmas Eve was a busy day, too, for the Princess. In the morning, she decorated a small tree for two needy children, girls who were chosen by the Hofprediger with the help of a deaconess who visited the poorer quarters of town. These two children with their mother or an elder sister were invited to come to the palace, where they were given coffee and cake in the little kitchen of the Wohnung der Prinzessin.

While they consumed their coffee and cake, the Princess directed her footman to draw down all the blinds of the big salon, shutting out the winter daylight to create a proper background for the twinkling lights on the tree, which were reflected from the mirrors of the room. On a table was spread a complete suit of clothing for each child, including boots and stockings, a large basket of food, containing among other things *Leberwurst*, *Blutwurst*, and coffee, sugar, Pfefferkuchen, and other Christmas delicacies. There was a large doll on each side of the table, staring into the middle distance with the usual doll-look of vacuity.

The Bescherung for the servants of the Princess, including the grooms and stablemen, took place at eleven o'clock on the morning of Christmas Eve. The men from the stables came across the Mopke in their neat livery and followed the housemaids and the footmen, who entered the Muschel-Saal and stood around a decorated tree to receive the little plates, eggcups, and *Biergläser*, bought with the Princess's pocket money, and packages of Pfefferkuchen. The blinds were again drawn; no Christmas tree can do itself justice in the daylight.

Elsewhere on the palace grounds, the Emperor walked, his pockets full of gold and silver coins that he distributed to whomever he chanced to meet: gardener, sentry, schoolgirl, officer. The sentry, of course, was prevented from taking the coin (usually a twenty-mark piece) when on duty, and it was placed in the sentry-box until the guard was relieved. It was always notable how many gardeners were out on the paths on Christmas Eve, sweeping away invisible leaves, but the Emperor's selection of a route was random and there was little to be gained by guessing the course of his wanderings.

One Christmas, the Princess was walking with four of her brothers down the wide drive of the *Neuergarten*, when in the distance, they saw the Emperor approaching. Prince Fritz laughingly suggested that there might be a chance of receiving some Christmas money, so under his orders they stood in military formation beside the road, saluting (at least the Princes did—the Princess merely kept "eyes front"), as the Emperor drew near. He returned the salute, and said, in English, in a gruff voice as he passed, "No, you won't get anything—all labor in vain," and gave an emphatic nod. The would-be recipients giggled at each other. "He might have given us a mark each," Sissy complained.

At two o'clock, the Bescherung to the servants took place in the *Schildersaal*. Long tables were laid down the center of the room, on which were arranged everyone's presents. Two or three large trees were lighted, and in the corner stood the piano to reinforce the carol-singing efforts of our choir. In poured a crowd of white-capped house-maids, green-clad Jägers, footmen, and Kammerdiener. All the ladies were assembled in décolleté evening dress, and those who had undertaken to sing carols were trembling, especially when the leading soprano whispered that she had a sore throat and couldn't sing a note.

Then the Empress, also in evening dress, arrived with the Princess and the Princes in full uniform. The choir timidly sang the first carol, which sounded thin and chirpy in the large room. It was listened to with the greatest respect, however, if not pleasure, and then another was sung at the request of the Empress, while everybody waited patiently.

Her Majesty then walked round and showed everybody their presents—dress-pieces, counterpanes, curtains, clocks. She began with the housekeeper, and, as year after year the tables were arranged in the same order, the whole ceremony was soon at an end, and they all trooped away with their cutlery, silver, pictures, and photographs, leaving nothing behind but the bare tables with their white cloths and the Christmas trees.

After a short pause, the party moved to the apartment of the Empress, where carols were sung for the pleasure of His Majesty. There was the last acrimonious dispute as to whether they should be sung with or without accompaniment, ending, as was confidently expected, in favor of the moral support of the piano. One lady was warned about her E, which was inclined to be a little flat, and the question hurriedly discussed as to whether somebody who had been singing seconds had now better join the trebles weakened by incipient colds. Nothing was settled when the door from the next room opened and His Majesty stepped in, bowed, and stood in an attitude of attention not unmixed with boredom, which made everybody's blood run cold.

The Hofprediger's face wore a look of concentrated anxiety and apprehension as he counted the first bar and plunged into the accompaniment. The top E was safely passed, and the adjutants were booming their tenor and bass with praiseworthy conscientiousness if little skill. We settled down to verses two and three with renewed confidence.

The second high E was on the downgrade and the third one almost as painful, but as soon as the last note died away, the Princess and Prince Joachim began to recite the *Weihnachtsgeschichte*, which is customary for every Prussian prince and princess to repeat yearly from the age of six until confirmation. When they were halfway through, we sang *Stille Nacht*. They finished the Christmas story to the end, and a third carol was performed. Sometimes His Majesty would take hold of a hymn book and sing along with the rest of us; everyone felt his attempted harmony was sehr nett—very nice—if not particularly brilliant.

At the impossible hour of four o'clock, we filed in to dinner. It was given early so that the guests could still be in time for their private festivities at home. All the Emperor's old adjutants and court officials were invited, and we assembled in the big salons near the Jasper Gallery. Dinner was served at small oval tables. Monster carp were brought, boiled in ale and looking plethoric and porpoise-like, and the meal wound up with English plum-pudding and mince pies served with flaming brandy sauce. The German gentlemen were not fond of plum-pudding—they thought it horrible stuff—but they liked the mince pies, especially the brandy sauce part.

As soon as dinner was finished, the Emperor gave a signal and the doors to the Muschelsaal were thrown open. The whole row of lighted trees ranged the length of the immense hall and shed the clear, soft, subdued light of multitudinous wax tapers. (Before I left the service of the court, electricity was installed in the Muschelsaal, and much of the old glamour of the Christmas scene departed—the candles seemed to burn faintly, and the green of the foliage was faded.)

Round the Saal, tables were arranged as at a bazaar, and each lady had one to herself, loaded with presents. The Emperor would sometimes walk round and show his own gift, usually a beautiful fur, where it lay on each person's table; but one of the charms of His Majesty was that he had no stereotyped line of conduct: if he didn't feel like walking round and making himself agreeable, he didn't do it. He was no slave to precedent.

The Empress gave one principal present and scattered with liberal hand small trifles such as workbags, pincushions, books, small articles of jewelry. All the adjutants and generals received something handsome and substantial: one had a Turkish rug; another, a bronze bust of the Emperor; a third, a pair of silver candelabra. But whatever else they got, a large plate of nuts, cakes, and chocolates accompanied each table, and those gentlemen who had to return to Berlin early were soon seen, aided by footmen, pouring their nuts and gingerbread into large brown paper bags and carrying them away under one arm, looking for all the world like children with a Sunday school treat.

The tables of the Empress and the Emperor were covered with offerings from their relatives in England and elsewhere, but the chief interest was in the presents to the Princess. When she was twelve, on her Christmas table appeared the plans of a tiny *Bauernhaus*—a peasant house—the gift of her father. It was built the following spring in the children's garden at the New Palace.

Another Christmas she received from the Emperor a pony cart to replace the blue-lined Turkish victoria of the Sultan, which was now deemed too childish and theatrical. The ponies were promoted to a workmanlike vehicle of light-colored ash, capable of holding six persons.

Perhaps, however, the most charming of all the Christmas presents the Emperor gave his daughter was a beautiful Arab mare called Irene. She was brought from the stables at the time of the Bescherung and led up the terrace steps into the big hall in front of the Muschelsaal, where she stood gazing round in her well-bred gentle manner at all the ladies in their evening finery. She looked at them out of her beautiful eyes with a fearless, disdainful air, and the lights of the candles shone on the stain of her bright strawberry coat.

By six o'clock on Christmas Eve, the household, one by one, slipped away and left the imperial family to spend the rest of the evening in each other's society. The Muschelsaal was the family rendezvous. As soon as it was dark, the Christmas trees were lighted and tea and supper were taken in the shadow of their branches. The Emperor sat at a table writing his New Year cards or reading, sometimes aloud, sometimes to himself; everybody was busy examining and comparing presents or writing letters of thanks.

Christmas Day itself passed quietly, the luncheon strictly *en famille*—none of the suite was even present, and as many as could be spared of the married servants were sent home to be at least part of the day with their families.

*

The Prussian Court was awakened on New Year's Day by the sound of trumpets blaring forth old German chorales as the band of the regiment in garrison slowly marched around the palace playing solemn and stately music. The previous evening, in the society of a few intimate friends, everybody had partaken of *Pfannkuchen*— in Berlin, a sort of doughnut—and a punch that was not to be drunk inadvisedly if one were to avoid a morning headache.

It was the custom to send postcards with New Year greetings to acquaintances in the palace, and footmen were constantly arriving from the Princes with these small offerings. One New Year's Eve, having retired earlier than the occasion warranted, I was awakened from my first pleasant dreams by an urgent rapping on the outside of my double door. A masculine voice responded to my inquiry, saying he had something to deliver to me from the Emperor, so I hastily rose and huddled on a dressing gown. At my door, a Jäger handed me an envelope bearing the imperial cipher which contained a picture postcard of His Majesty's yacht, the *Hohenzollern*, and the New Year's wishes of the Emperor inscribed in his own handwriting.

Breakfast on the first day of the year was a hasty event. At eight o'clock the royal special train, containing the whole of the imperial family and the suite, footmen and maids in attendance, was off to Berlin for the *Gratulationscour*, when all foreign ambassadors, in their state carriages driven by bewigged coachmen and footmen in bright red, blue, or yellow uniforms, drove from their embassies to wish the Emperor the compliments of the season. Joyous crowds lined *Unter den Linden* to watch the pageant progress toward the Schloss.

One quaint ceremony on New Year's Day was the presentation to the Emperor, as he sat at table, of sausages and hard-boiled eggs by the *Halloren*, a guild of salt-workers who lived in Saxony. It was the Princess who introduced the Halloren sausage to my notice. On the second or third day of the year, she burst into my room with a small sandwich—German sandwiches have bread on one side of them only—made of an extremely thin and delicate piece of pink sausage. I was expected to eat it with great solemnity, and I conscientiously tried to praise it, declaring that there was a "nameless something" about the flavor which distinguished it from all other sausages. I later discovered that it was a rare and not-to-be-repeated favor to share even the smallest piece of this wonderful delicacy. Every day this sausage appeared at the eleven o'clock lunch, but no one was allowed to partake of it but the Princess herself.

The Emperor with his dachshunds aboard his yacht, the *Hohenzollern*, which was built in the design of military battleships at a cost of four-and-a-half million marks.

IN THE COUNTRY

The estate of Cadinen was in East Prussia, ten miles from
Elbing, near the Russian border. Only a year or two before
my arrival, the Emperor had purchased a large property
there for the purpose of conducting some experiments in
farming. Cadinen and its glories were such a frequent topic
of Sissy's conversation that I had a lively interest in my first
journey there—where the children were to spend two
months of their summer holiday—in June 1903.

We travelled all night from Berlin, a long, slow trip. The
train passed through flat, uninteresting country, especially
during the last few miles where the railways approached the
Frischeshaff, that curious muddy lagoon formed by the
waters of the sluggish Vistula and separated from the Gulf of
Danzig by a thin strip of sand that stretched for two hundred
miles along the coast. Tile-factories—*Ziegeleien*—were numerous along that strip of land, one owned by the Emperor.

Our special train carried the usual portentous amount of luggage, three tutors, one doctor, Countess Keller, Count Blumenthal, several footmen, and many maids. In addition to Sissy and Prince Joachim, we took, to my delight, the Princes Max and Freddy of Hesse. And this was just the children's train. Her Majesty was to join us later, when the *Kielerwoche*—the Kiel boat show and regatta—was over, and bring Prince Oskar and the newly moustached Prince Au-Wi with her from Plön.

His Majesty almost never went to Cadinen at the same time as his family—there was not sufficient room for their suites, however reduced, and the Emperor didn't like to reduce his following. As it was, some of the servants and all of the stable-people—riding master, royal grooms, and stable boys—were lodged in the various inns and cottages that dotted the village.

Once, with a sudden determination to see how the Empress was getting on, the Emperor arrived for three or four days, announcing his plans only a few hours before-hand. An instant general shuffle of apartments was made, everybody packing up their things and squeezing themselves into out-of-the-way holes and corners. Every house in the village that had a decent room to spare was requisitioned, but only two were available; somebody suggested a tent on the lawn, but there were no tents. Most of His Majesty's adjutants had to use the train, shunted onto a siding, as a hotel, sleeping and dressing there in much discomfort. "We only have accommodation for a toothbrush and a cake of soap," complained one Kammerherr, "yet we must change into four different costumes every day."

In 1903, there was not a train platform at Cadinen. We

descended from the blue-and-gold royal train right into the meadow. Great purple columbines, yellow and blue lupines were growing over the line itself. No road was visible except a sandy cart track full of ruts. There, looking entirely out of place, four royal carriages waited to take us up to the Schloss. A farm cart drawn by a yoke of oxen would have been more appropriate. We bumped toward the Schloss, the coachman wisely avoiding the track and driving over the meadow, past the Emperor's Ziegelei.

The Schloss, a yellow-painted villa, stood in a small garden with an orchard of cherry trees around it. It was opposite the village green and a duck pond, around which other houses were clustered. The chief beauty of its garden was a lovely avenue of chestnut trees, but they grew too close to the house and made some of the bedrooms so dark that on a dull day one could not read or write without a lamp on the writing table.

We were greeted by an unruly flock of geese who gabbled and cackled their way over from the duck pond, only to be driven off at the last moment by a goose-girl, who, with her knitting and tight plait of hair, looked as if she had stepped straight out of a fairy-tale book.

To the right, in the view of the Schloss windows, was a large farmyard surrounded by cowsheds; to the left was a smithy, from whence a constant busy clinking floated in the windows.

The servants at Cadinen were the peasant women of the neighborhood—clean, strong, healthy-looking people who usually worked barefoot in the fields for a wage of three-pence a day, but with the arrival of the court were thrust into print dresses and boots and little flat caps. These women spoke with an East Prussian accent, and only came for an hour or two in the mornings and again in the afternoons. In the meantime, they shed their hats and gowns and returned to the fields; the Inspektor did not approve of their absence at harvest time. Cadinen was an area unpenetrated by the Reformation; the population was mostly of Polish blood, and all were Catholics. Occasionally, we had a glimpse of the old Polish customs now dying out. Once an old woman servant of the *Landrat*—a district administrator —was sent to the Schloss on some errand. When the Empress appeared in the garden, the servant fell on her knees at Her Majesty's feet and kissed the skirt of her dress with fervor. But there was nothing abject in her manner when she rose up and talked to the Empress.

In the Schloss garden was an untidy pond from which arose every moment of the day and night a ceaseless moaning. This relentless cry quickly got on everyone's nerves, and the grownups were all snappy and cross during the first few days of the stay. It was the cry of the *Unken*, a loathsome black frog which inhabited the pond—not to be confused with the large green frogs whose cheerful croak was welcome. Indeed, the term *Unkenruf*—Unken cry— was used in Germany to express any persistently ominous prediction, and it was a very expressive term. There were few things more depressing than the call of those tiny creatures.

Motivated by our sufferings, Prince Max found a butterfly net and managed to catch a good many of the Unken, which floated on the top of the pond and were invisible except for a tiny green spot over each eye. Max became expert at locating them and enjoyed the sport every day after dinner, catching over a hundred Unken in two or three days. The horrid, slimy, glutinous things—which Sissy handled without any qualms—were a bright flame color underneath and deep black above. Max would carefully transfer them in a water can to the *Haff*, and everyone was much relieved by their change in quarters.

The charm of Cadinen was its simplicity. There were no tourists, no "respectable" people, just workers in the fields and crowds of barefoot, sunburnt children. Pigs, sheep, and chickens pervaded the place, all of them belonging to His Majesty.

In those early years, there was no sentry, and only a few private detectives hovered around, trying to look like summer tourists. And they succeeded. It was a long time before I discovered that those gentlemen who seemed to be staying at the inn rather a long time were there for our protection. I had thought they were travelling salesmen and wondered what on earth they sold at a place where people had no money to spend and so few wants.

To the children, who had seen little of the farming process, the estate was a constant delight, and they made themselves a nuisance to the smithy, a delightful man who had been at sea and travelled afar, and was still young and handsome.

"So useful," the Princess said as she watched him work. "Much better than learning the date of the Silesian Wars, isn't it?" Sometimes she helped to blow the bellows. The smith enjoyed, or perhaps just endured, their presence in his shop and gave them each a tiny model anvil as a present.

In the afternoons, we drove into the forest, and the children lit a fire and cooked potatoes in it. Max, Freddy,

Joachim, and Sissy devoured quantities of the potatoes with butter and salt. I was presented with two small ash-covered specimens, which I ate with gratitude.

All summer, the children ran in and out of the cottages, fed the chickens, stroked the cats, patted the dogs, and hung over the calves and pigs with constant worship. At last, the Empress grew afraid of infection, and the children were kept out of the cottages, which were old, unsanitary, and picturesque, with heaps of potatoes in one corner and a sitting hen in another.

A chapel, capable of holding twenty people, was built on the top of a steep hill in the orchard. Every Sunday morning we trudged, panting, up to the *Gottesdienst*. A stalwart clergyman came over from Elbing to hold the service. He stood at the door of the church, a man so tall and thick-boned he overwhelmed the tiny chapel, and shook hands with each of the worshippers, saying *"Grüss Gott"*— God greet you.

From the doorway of the chapel, we had a wide overview of the Haff, which was muddy except at sunrise, when it was blue, and at sunset, when it turned yellow, pink, and then blood red. Beyond the Haff was the clear stripe of deep blue, the waters of the Baltic, or the *Ostsee*, as it was called in Germany.

We grew to know the Haff very well, for most afternoons the children were taken across it in a steamer to bathe at a place called Kahlberg on the farther shore. Their steamer, the *Raduane*, was hired from someone in Danzig for a few weeks every summer. It was manned by three mariners whom the children considered—with good reason—to be the cleverest people they had ever met.

Vigand was the captain; another man attended to the machinery; and a third hovered around fetching campstools and answering questions. Prince Joachim, under Vigand's strict tutoring, took lessons in steering.

The doctor and both the tutors, two maids, two footmen, Countess Keller and myself, and two dogs accompanied the children. We took tea onto the shore as well as bath towels and changes of dry garments. The Princess had a knack of falling into a wave fully dressed, so we had to be prepared for emergencies.

The Haff was a greasy, oily, smelly stretch of water in the hot weather, so stagnant that small weeds grew on its surface. It suffered occasional violent storms which dispelled the oil, but tossed the tiny steamer up and down in a manner most disagreeable to indifferent sailors. Fortunately, it only took half an hour to get to the opposite side, but even that was too long for some people—Count Blumenthal among them—and they succumbed to the horrors of seasickness almost in sight of port.

On the other side we had to get into a boat and row to shore, walk over a stretch of sand, and there, on the other side, lay the sand dunes with the beautiful clean Baltic dimpling in a burst of white foam. In the distance to the left could be seen the houses and pensions of the fishing village of Kahlberg, to which visitors came in the season. The far end of the shore was reserved for the use of the royal children, so they were able to enjoy themselves without restrictions.

It was perhaps the least interesting bit of coast to be found anywhere. The Baltic was practically tideless, and the shore had no rocks to break the long monotony of sand. The sun blazed fiercely, and nowhere was there the least shelter from the intense heat. But Sissy and Joachim and Max and Freddy thought it was the loveliest spot on earth; it was the only seaside place they knew. They dug sand castles and paddled in the waves, being allowed to bathe after discussions and consultations with Dr. Zunker.

Five minutes was the limit of time allowed for us to play in the water, and Countess Keller stood, watch in hand, on the shore and called "Time's up—come out," at the end of what seemed a mere flash of seconds. "We haven't even had time to get our bathing dresses wet," the Princess would argue, and a heated discussion would begin, to the effect that the Countess must have misread the time. The lady would stand on the shore, commanding, waving her arms, imploring with increasing vehemence, and the Princess, secure in the water, would duck under the waves, emerge, and sputter, "One minute more, dear Countess, one minute more: I know your watch is fast, you said so this morning," and she would plunge under again, while the outraged Countess, angered by the illogical reasoning, would threaten to stop the bathing altogether. Finally, the dripping Princess would obey.

This scene was enacted daily, even when the doctor conceded ten minutes in the ocean instead of five. Often, the Princess would plunge under as soon as the Countess opened her mouth to speak, and once she shrieked, "*Unsere Zukunft liegt auf dem Wasser*"—Our future lies on the water—as a wave swallowed her up and nothing but a row of pink toes remained visible.

After bathing we had tea, which was brought to the shore in stone screw-topped bottles and drunk out of silver tumblers. After tea, everyone looked for *Bernstein*—amber—for the coast of the Baltic was the only place in Europe where it was found.

When it was time to return to the steamer, a long row of spectators, many with cameras, was waiting to see us embark. The joy with which the children met Vigand after their short separation was touching. When the Empress and the two older Princes arrived at Cadinen, they accompanied us to Kahlberg and were introduced to Vigand and his crew; these heroes had been described in detail to Her Majesty long before she saw them.

Prince Joachim's steering, in the meanwhile, was occasionally somewhat erratic, but improved day by day until he was able to take us into haven and bring up alongside the pier in a most masterly manner.

*

One of those inexplicable tales which, though totally devoid of foundation are firmly accepted and tenaciously held, was a curious rumor among the German people to the effect that the Princess was deaf and dumb. How this extraordinary idea arose can never be known, for at every stage of her existence the Princess lagged no way behind other children in volubility of expression and quickness of hearing.

Once, while at the shore, a forester, a loyal German subject, approached Dr. Zunker while he was watching Joachim and Sissy paddling in the brine a short distance away. The forester expressed his unmitigated sorrow at the misfortune suffered by the imperial family in that their only daughter should be so afflicted. At that moment, one of those spells of *zanken* broke out between the Princess and her brother.

" Do you hear that?" Dr. Zunker asked. "Can you hear your deaf-and-dumb Princess talking?" Indeed, her voice carried quite a distance. "Go a little nearer and listen."

The man stopped and drank in the sounds as though they were heavenly music. He turned with his face radiating joy. "*Gott sei Dank!*"—God be thanked—he exclaimed, and he departed to spread the glad tidings.

Many people were harder to convince. One dear old lady in Berlin was always making doubtful inquiries of me on this subject, and, like the Apostle Thomas, she refused to believe. "Ach, yes!" she would say, "Of course, you dare not tell me the truth. You have to say that she is all right."

"Of course," I mocked, "it is essential for a deaf-and-dumb person to have an English teacher, isn't it?—and another one for French? She is deaf and dumb in three languages." The lady was still doubtful.

*

My days in Cadinen were lengthened by my decision to subtract from my sleeping hours for the purpose of having a few private moments. Every morning at five o'clock the *Lampier*—the old man who trimmed the lamps and cleaned the shoes—would knock softly at my door. I would rouse hastily, dress, and creep warily past the rooms where everyone slept, down the back staircase and into the yard. There in the morning sunshine, the wrinkled *Hühnerfrau* was feeding her flock of ducks and chickens. Slipping like a conspirator through the wet bushes into the stable yard round the corner, I would come upon the smiling Sattelmeister, Herr Kaspar, standing beside two horses held by stable boys. We bowed to each other in the German fashion, mounted, and rode away into the glory of the dewy morning. The rides in the lovely woods on those very early summer mornings were the only hours I could call my own. Every minute of the day from half-past eight had its appointed task.

Our rides were over roads not as good as those to which we were accustomed; they were full of slippery beds of clay and were quite dangerous after a rain, as were the fourteen wooden bridges which crossed the wimpling stream meandering aimlessly among the trees. When it was impossible to ride in the forest, we rode in the cornfields and the stubblefields from which the oats had been cleared and which were magnificent for a good stretching gallop.

The fields were filled with Canterbury bells, blue cornflowers, and scarlet poppies, masses of campanulas, yellow foxgloves, deep heliotrope, shimmery yellow bearded rye, and the darker, reddish brown of the wheat. Sometimes, galloping through the riotous color of the fields, we would come unexpectedly upon one of the peasant women, kneeling before a tiny wooden shrine hidden in the standing corn.

I can close my eyes and see it all again, feel the flap of the black stork's wing that once sailed close above my head, frightened from his morning drink, and see the dew-gummed branches in the green depths of the forest and the ferns in the crevices of the rocks that trembled at our passing.

*

Under the Emperor's auspices, his Ziegelei became a factory for the manufacture of objects of art. Della Robbia plaques, busts of the Emperor and Empress, ornamental vases and dishes were made there, instead of the bricks and tiles that it formerly produced. This pottery went to be sold in the Berlin shops, much to the indignation of the German earthenware merchants. They were unable to compete with the Emperor, who sold cheaply regardless of the cost of production.

The clay at Cadinen was not at all suitable for making fine earthenware, as was demonstrated to the Emperor, who had a vision of inaugurating a new era in pottery. On my last visit, he confided to me that a bed of wonderful clay had been discovered in the neighborhood that might easily prove epoch-making in the history of ceramics. I knew those beds of clay. They were the ones in the forest that made the paths slippery and dangerous for the horses.

One could not help but be sorry for the officials of the factory, many of whom had been brought from the pleasures of Berlin to what they considered the dreary miseries of Cadinen. They were to be pitied because they were competent men, struggling to satisfy an employer who understood nothing of the difficulties of their job, who did not realize the various properties of the clay with which they had to work, and how impossible it was to create fine porcelain from an earth containing only the coarser ingredients and impregnated with iron.

Many of these potters were artists who had been taken from factories where they worked under the best conditions, with the right materials, and who could produce masterpieces of the ceramic art. Here in the *Cadiner Fabrik*, they struggled. They were baffled by want of the right material. It could be procured elsewhere, so they sent for clay from Dresden and with it expressed their sense of beauty, but the Emperor was not satisfied. He wanted beautiful pottery made from clay of a nature fit only for tiles and brick—*his* clay.

As tiles and bricks, the clay was beautiful, with its dark red cinnamon tones blotched with iron pyrites. The cathedral of Frauenburg was built of those bricks and tiles and glowed in the sun with tints of rose and cinnamon dappled with gray and black.

The factory had been experimenting for seven years when I last saw it. The shelves were filled with terra cotta, the highly glazed pieces that must be fired at an extreme temperature. Every one had a flaw. The clay would not stand the heat.

The master potter was irritated and disappointed. Yet the Emperor was pleased and told the man to keep on trying. On this visit, in the presence of the whole of his suite (the Emperor liked them to be as interested as himself in his endeavors), His Majesty heaped—there is no other word— from the crowded shelves of the warehouse, terra cotta busts of himself and large vases and other pottery on our assemblage. My share of the spoils was a bust of himself and two flower vases.

The Ziegelei was not the only experiment that occupied the Emperor's imagination at Cadinen. He talked a good deal about crossing the ordinary domestic cow with the Indian buffalo or some analogous male, and had visions of creating an entirely new type of domestic kine. He ignored all the difficulties that may arise in the way of those who try to persuade nature into new paths, and he spoke of this new breed of cattle as if it were already grazing in his meadow. After a time, the project disappeared into the limbo of the many other things that the Emperor was going to do, and his herds remained East Prussian, black and white in aspect, and of the usual placid type.

*

The last Sunday of our stay in Cadinen was devoted to the *Kinderfest*—a treat for the schoolchildren of the village —given by the Empress. The peasants scrubbed and washed and starched and ironed their children to a pitch of painful perfection, but none of them wore anything in the shape of finery nor curled or waved their abundant locks for the occasion. The girls' tight pigtails were tied a trifle tighter and the boys' heads were shaved almost to the bone. The most conspicuous change in their attire was the presence of shoes and stockings, which handicapped their activities. All the light-footed boys and girls who usually skipped down the grassy lanes became slow-footed, slouching, awkward louts, moving with stiff propriety.

The festivities began with coffee and cake at three o'clock—tea was unknown in that district. The cake was a kind with currants stuck in it randomly, and the coffee, which we can hope was not as strong as it looked, was imbibed by infants of the tenderest age, babes in arms, who sipped it eagerly from their mothers' cups apparently without any evil effects.

After cake and coffee, games were played. "The very stupidest games I ever saw," said the Princess, who preferred something more exciting than the German equivalent of Here We Go 'Round the Mulberry Bush. So she organized sack races among the boys, tucking the small urchins into their sacks and instructing them how to hop along, cheering on the son of the blacksmith, whom she obviously desired to see the winner.

At half-past six, the Fest was finished, but at the Schloss, the children continued it on their own. Prince Joachim had discovered that one of the footmen and one of the cooks were harmonica players and proposed that they should be sent for and an impromptu dance held on the lawn.

The cook arrived first in his white cap and apron, looking embarrassed at being called upon to perform before royalty. He made a deep bow to Her Majesty and was conducted by the young Princes to the garden seat and requested to begin at once. He flung himself into a waltz with the ardor of a true musician, and they all slipped merrily upon the grass. Presently, a fat, red-faced footman arrived with a second harmonica, bowed, and took his place beside the cook.

The two went hard at it. Infrequent discords arose, whereupon they regarded one another sternly, each tacitly accusing the other, but it never disturbed the rhythm, and the dancers hopped energetically in spite of the heat and their hard day's work. The cook, an artistic soul, wagged his head in time to the music and gazed upwards toward the heavens, but the fat footman, a man of another temperament altogether, sat stolidly and moved nothing but his fingers. Bedtime for the children was long passed before the musicians were reluctantly dismissed.

On the last day at Cadinen, the luggage was packed and carried downstairs and loaded into carts by a quarter-section of soldiers sent over from Elbing. The brown-faced young men penetrated every room, grinning and shouldering everything they could find, while harassed footmen rushed about with lists in their hands which they consulted hurriedly.

*

His Majesty had purchased the whole estate of Cadinen "as is," and he proceeded to improve it. Gradually, he changed the prevailing simplicity of everything and built new stables as well as an enormous German gothic arch leading to a large automobile garage, which contained ample accommodation for grooms and chauffeurs. He pulled down the old cottages and erected some pseudo-English gabled cottages, the plans for which he boasted had been sent to him from England, from Lord Esher. The peasant women never looked very much at home in them and were always sighing after the old cottages—much to the anger of the Emperor, who considered the women ingrates. Personally, I thought the whole business a desecration.

Even the duck pond, the enchanted spot where the Princess from her window watched every evening as the farm horses waded in, where the herd of cows came and stood in the water switching their tails and taking long deliberate drafts after milking time, was done away with, filled up, and the green levelled and kept smoothly rolled. No children or dogs played on it any more, the horses and cattle went another way home, and sentries, those adjutants of royalty, were posted where the geese had waddled across the grass.

Year by year as we paid our visit, some of the glamour faded, and it became by degrees a royal residence instead of a jolly country house. Excursion trains from Danzig and Königsberg were run to it. Crowds of perspiring tourists gaped round the gateway. The last time I saw Cadinen, on a flying visit of a few hours while travelling with Their Majesties from Rominten, there were forbidding sentry boxes starkly painted in black and white standing at the gates of the little yellow Schloss, and from the yard one could clearly hear the Unkenruf.

The Emperor, seated in front, and his ministers. From left: Bulow, Mackensen, Prince Rupprecht, Bayern, Crown Prince Wilhelm, Pieussen, Wüttemberg, Ludendorff, Kluck, Emmich, Faldenhayn, Einem, Hasseler, Beseler, Hindenburg, Bethmann-Hollweg, Heeringen, Tirpitz.

THE MILITARY INFLUENCE

Those calm days in my first year with the royal family fore-shadowed but vaguely the years that were to follow, but even then one was dimly conscious of an uneasy, restless spirit which seemed to conceal potentialities of trouble; there were faint mutterings, a distant thunder, of the approaching storm, if one had only understood the signs of the times.

Potsdam, near the New Palace, was known to most people as a great military center, the home of the Life Guards and the infantry regiments in which the sons of the Emperor received their early initiation into military duties. Huge square barracks were built everywhere, often on ill-chosen sites where they blocked out much of the scenery.

All through the day, rolling through the town were military forage-wagons, piled up with hay or straw, and other carts, loaded with *Kommisbrot*, the loaves of soldier's bread, indigestible to ordinary capacities, but decidedly satisfying in quality. Bread and cheese and soup, with a little coffee, were the German soldier's standby. He was not pampered in times of peace.

When I first came to the court, I suffered from the usual British ignorances and prejudices, and I sympathized with a teacher who mentioned the tax she paid out of her salary. The taxes all over the Empire had risen frightfully. The sums voted for the enormous increases in the navy had to come, as the Emperor did not seem to realize, out of the pockets of his people. Also, the Herero War in *Südwestafrika* was not going any too well and had already cost twice the original estimate.

"We don't have to pay taxes in England," I told the teacher, "until our income gets a good deal higher than that."

"Oh," she replied, "we pay this willingly. It is an *Ehren-Tax*, and we are glad to pay it. It is for the defense of the Fatherland. No one thinks of grumbling."

"It is all very well for you English to talk about disarmament," said a young officer in our company, "but where should we be if we disarmed, with the French on one side, eager to seize Elsass-Lothringen and the Russians on the other side of us none too friendly? We don't want to depend on friendliness, we want to depend on our good right arm." Here he shook his fist. "We Germans fear God and nobody else."

"You don't fear God," I said. "Most of you don't believe in Him, or if you do, you create one to your own liking—seven-tenths Bismarck and Clausewitz, and the rest made up of recollections of the old bloodthirsty heathen deities of Valhalla, or Thor and Siegfried. And as for Alsace-Lorraine, it never has been anything but a worry and plague since you've had it. It's your own bad consciences, not the French, that make you so apprehensive. You know in your own hearts that you would never rest while part of Germany was in the hands of an enemy.''

"But Elsass-Lothringen used to be part of Germany. It was taken away by Louis XIV.''

"Well, the people don't feel German—they feel French.''

"The people!'' the officer exclaimed. "Who cares what they feel? What do they know about such matters? It is their own fault if they are treated with severity. Do you know what they do? When we conquered them, they were a German-speaking race, and ever since then they've all learnt French—pretend they can't speak German!''

"Doesn't that show that they feel they are French?'' I persisted.

The officer took refuge in Ireland. Any German officer driven into a corner in an argument with the English invariably lands in Ireland. It is his chief refuge, and his misconceptions as to the cause of Irish political discontent are almost as bad as those of the average English person. If we don't understand the Irish question ourselves, unfortunate Germans, wanderingly helplessly among the turgid verbiage of our party newspapers, must remain hopelessly mystified.

*

One day a woman, the wife of a workman, who often did small dressmaking jobs for me, came to my rooms to fit a blouse. She looked upset, and when I asked the reason, she restrained her tears with difficulty.

"*Ach! gnädiges Fräulein!*" she said. "The Gendarm has been to my house, saying my son has been trying to evade his military service, and asking why he did not report himself at the proper time—my son whose *heissester Wunsch*—greatest desire—is to serve! He can hardly wait till the time comes, and *so ein Kerl*—such a fellow—to come to me and say things like that—my son who is so patriotic!" Here she broke down and sobbed, after an interval explaining that the mistake arose because her eldest son had died, and it was his name that had not been removed from the military register. "But to accuse us—honorable people...."

"But he is your only son now, isn't he?" I asked.

"Yes, now since der Johann died, of course he is our only one and not obliged to serve, but *gnädiges Fräulein*, it would break his heart not to go; and besides, you see, they get on much better afterwards. He hopes for a post on the *Eisenbahn*—railroad—so he must do his service, or he can't get it."

What she said was true; his chances in life would be immeasurably improved after his year's service. I never met a single German youth who did not look upon his military training as a matter of course.

Still, I noticed that the enthusiasm with which the recruits joined the army was completey overshadowed by the delirious delight with which they left it. After the big autumn maneuvers were over in September, the culminating point and test of the year's work, at which the Emperor was invariably present, trains loaded with home-going soldiers, sun-browned young men from twenty to twenty-two, looking fit and healthy, would pass along the line which ran through a field behind the New Palace, one of the few grass gallops in the neighborhood. Those trains were filled with cheering, yelling youths whose shouting almost drowned out the shrieks of the engine; they hung out of every window in perilous positions, quite disregarding the command inscribed on every carriage, *Nicht hinauslehnen*— Do not lean out. They waved their caps and hands out of the window at everybody they saw, at every cow, at every dog. At intervals, the cheers rose in a crescendo of sound, and one had glimpses in the thickly packed carriages of men performing gymnastics upside down. Sometimes a pair of legs would gyrate wildly at the windows.

"Why are they all so jolly?" I asked the Princess the first time we saw them, as we were galloping down the *Gruner Allee*.

"I suppose because they're so glad they've finished their service," she replied a bit ruefully. It was never admitted at the Prussian Court that a soldier ever gets tired of his service and longs for a normal, non-military existence. It was, instead, an accepted article of faith that every soldier of the Emperor's army became at once, through his training, an honorable, upright man, imbued with a penetrating love of his Fatherland and ready to sacrifice his life with joy for his Kaiser.

This creed was accepted so naturally as a self-evident fact that I wished the ladies of the court who had such an implicit faith in the noble spirit and angelic qualities of the individuals in their army could have read some of the anonymous letters that were almost daily to be found in the letterbag of the Princess, written by soldiers to the daughter of their Emperor.

In the absence of the Obergouvernante, it had been

my unpleasant duty to go through these epistles. Some were harmless enough, chiefly picture postcards smelling of bad tobacco and inscribed with "Greetings to Her Royal Highness Princess Victoria Louise of Prussia from her *allerunterthänigst*—most humble—so and so, now serving in the 15th Regiment of Infantry at Colmar." Monday mornings brought a large crop of such messages, evidently written during the Sunday evening leisure at some *Garten-restaurant*. They were usually at once consigned to the wastepaper basket or given to the footman to be burnt, for they were obviously unsanitary and bore a good many thumbmarks.

There were always among the correspondence a few letters which were ultimately handed over to the police. These letters often ran into several sheets and were of such a foul nature that a mere reading left one with a sense of being besmirched with unutterable filthiness. They were always from soldiers serving in the army, degenerates. I remember sending some of them over to one of the gentlemen of the Empress, whose duty it was to see that they were forwarded to the proper quarter. He acted as an extra-gentleman-in-waiting and only came on duty a few weeks of each year in the summertime when the Emperor was on one of his all-male cruises in the fjords of Norway, and the Empress was travelling or staying at Rominten. With what a face that elderly veteran of the Franco-Prussian War regarded those soldiers' letters. "How could one have imagined human nature to be so vile?" he asked sadly.

Every soldier in the Fatherland is trained not only to be an excellent soldier but also to be an excellent patriot. He is taught—if he does not already know them—the songs which breathe a passionate love of his Emperor and country; his barrack walls are hung with pictures showing, in greatly exaggerated colors and with an obvious lack of correct military knowledge on the part of the artist, famous incidents in the history of his regiment, melodramatic moments in which a triumphant German, in a spic-and-span uniform on a highly groomed horse and with a complete absence of bloodshed or any of the messy incidents which characterize real warfare, is killing, single-handedly, a dozen Frenchmen who lie in neat rows in front of him.

However ignorant and muddle-headed a German recruit might have been—and some of those who came from East and West Prussia were incredibly primitive and bucolic —he was painstakingly inspired with a feeling of national pride, a kindling in his heart of the belief that the German Empire was superior to every other country in the world, that the German people were the wisest and the best, and that to the Emperor all these superior qualities were due.

A great deal of overt brutality existed among the non-commissioned officers, which, when discovered, was severely punished, but for the most part it evaded detection. Finally, in 1904, a former German officer, an admirer of the Emperor and the army, wrote a book pointing out some of the military's gravest defects and the terrible lack of moral tone among its officers. He laid great stress on the ill-treatment of soldiers, not only by the non-commissioned officers, but also by the ill-tempered, drunken lieutenants who cruelly abused their position of authority and the private soldiers' helplessness. The former officer wrote of the low level of mental and moral culture of many officers and their failure to respect civilians. He unflinchingly highlighted the German officer's weakest spot: a false and exaggerated sense of his own importance.

He also drew attention to the well-known fact that many of the officers, owing to the smallness of their pay and the increasing luxury of living, were hopelessly in debt, giving rise to conditions which were morally debasing and often ended in deplorable scandals.

None of the military abuses which he cited and desired to see reformed were ever denied by the Germans. The book was, of course, suppressed by the government—yet everybody in Germany read it. It was quite easy to obtain copies of suppressed books, and, as a rule, the suppression greatly stimulated the sale. In Berlin, I saw notices in booksellers' windows that all forbidden books might be obtained on inquiry. If copies had been exhibited in the window, however, they would have been confiscated by the police.

One trait among German officers was the intense and enduring hatred toward France and Frenchmen. This dislike, instead of being extinguished with time, developed and increased, and the abuse that was constantly showered upon the French hardly seemed worthy of a great nation toward a gallant but unfortunate foe which, in 1870–71, had paid the bitter price of defeat and, one would have thought, might have been conciliated with immense advantage to Germany. But conciliation found no foothold in German schemes of statesmanship; the Germans considered it synonymous with weakness.

Sometime near the end of 1903, a French lady, Mademoiselle Lauru—the first Frenchwoman to be at the Prussian Court since the Franco-Prussian War—was appointed a governess to the Princess. Sissy awakened to the privilege of being fair in one's dealing with the hereditary enemy and received Mademoiselle with interest and friend-liness. From that time onward it was amusing to hear her talking with other children. When once she had been Prussian and patriotic, urging upon them the necessity of admitting that French people were hateful and despicable, now she was admitting that they were often charming and beautiful. The unanimity with which they all agreed that Mademoiselle was delightful gratified the Princess.

The hearts of the young officers were not softened; they believed in the decadence of France as an accomplished fact. One of them frequently rode with me. He was attached to the imperial stables and was a great talker, very satisfied with himself and his opinions. "France," he declared one wet and windy day when we were trotting around the riding school together, "France as a nation is finished— done with—going downhill every day—that is a well-known fact."

I was rather surprised, for I had recently been in France and had seen a good many evidences of prosperity and industry. I knew this officer was a man who had never been outside Germany. I disputed what he said.

"Ah," he replied, "France may appear right on the surface, but she will crumble into dust before long," and he rubbed his fingers together as though he could feel France breaking up in his hand. "Her population grows smaller every year. How can any nation progress if its people are dying out? Here in Germany the population increases every year—every large city has enormous increases. In a short time, the Germans will be spreading everywhere, and French influence will be shrinking." He went on for a long time demonstrating that nothing could prevent the absolute wiping out of France from the map of Europe, her complete extinction as a nation.

"I would like," I said, when he had finished, "to ask you your opinion of the future of England?"

"Oh, England!" he said, and turned in his saddle, looking back at me with something mocking and exultant in his tone. "There is a good deal to be said about England, but I think we have talked enough politics for this afternoon." So we began cantering, and his thoughts about England remained unspoken, though I had no doubt in my mind that they were not favorable to the British Empire.

*

By 1904 the six sons of the Emperor and Empress were growing into manhood: Crown Prince Wilhelm and Prince Eitel-Frederick, having completed the university at Bonn and passed their *Abiturien Examen* with credit to themselves and their teachers, were settled in Potsdam to perform their year of military service. They were living in their own quarters, known as the *Kabinettshaus*, but they came home to the New Palace nearly every day to visit their mother.

Prince Adalbert, after a two-year voyage with the German fleet (two years which coincided with my early tenure at court and therefore rendered Adalbert the least known to me of the royal children), lived at Kiel, and the two inseparable Princes, Oskar and Au-Wi, were leaving Plön to go to Bonn. Oskar and Au-Wi were charming boys, simple and pleasant, with highly developed senses of humor.

Au-Wi, the eldest of the two and an aspiring artist, loved to arrange color schemes for the ladies' dresses. He lso reduced Dr. Zunker to despair by dressing up in a variety of fancy costumes, including that of Hamlet and other Shakespearean characters and having himself photographed. The doctor literally wrung his hands at the sight of the pictures, which were circulated among the suite and gave rise to much criticism. Once the Prince came to dinner with the Empress in *Biedermeier* costume—what we should call "early Victorian"—with side-whiskers, stock, and coat and trousers of an old-fashioned cut. In this getup, he exactly resembled the photographs of England's Albert, the Prince Consort, his great-grandfather.

Oskar was a totally different temperament, fond of sport, hating the ceremonial side of court life, straight-forward, bluff, and kind. He early took to pipe-smoking, much to the horror of the Empress, and later on cleared his domestic life of unnecessary complications by marrying Countess Bassewitz, a young lady-in-waiting of the Empress, with whom he lived in Potsdam.

The youngest son, Prince Joachim, had been installed at Plön, where the Empress descended upon him frequently, much to the dismay of General von Gontard, his governor there, who was hard put to provide accommodations for the necessary suite.

The sons of the Emperor were unusually fortunate in their governor, who with his military training possessed the broad-minded, more tolerant liberal spirit of the age, and knew when to sink the martinet in the man. He realized that the formation of character is first of all a development from within, chiefly molded by the cast of the minds that surround it and not produced by outward circumstances.

The Crown Prince and Prince Fritz remained only a short time under von Gontard's charge before going to the university, but the younger Princes were in his care for some years at Plön, where I was once invited to stay for a few weeks to give Prince Joachim lessons in English.

Plön was a small, primitive town with just one long straggling street, a few shops, and at the end, close to the lake, the Kadettenschule, which had been the residence—and the burial place—of the old Danish kings. (Plön was a part of the disputed Holstein territory that Prussia seized from Denmark in 1865.) One afternoon, General von Gontard conducted me into the vault, where, side by side in their massive coffins, lay all that was left of some of the former majesties of Denmark. It was a gruesome place, old and neglected. The coffins were moldering to pieces: on the floor lay dust dropped from the ruined sides of kings.

As the boys were occupied all morning with their other studies, I, who was lodged in the *Prinzenvilla* under the fostering care of the wife of a private detective, had nothing to do until one o'clock. Thankfully, the governor allowed me to ride one of his two horses every morning—big, fine, cavalry chargers which fled away with me over the tree-shaded roads and fields. I had been allowed to bring my side-saddle from the New Palace. "The very first time," Herr Kaspar assured me, "that such a privilege has ever been granted to any lady at court."

Those morning excursions gave me the opportunity to explore the neighborhood, which I otherwise would not have seen. All this district of Holstein was rather flat but handsomely wooded, with many lakes adding a wistful, calm beauty to the sleepy landscape. There was something reminiscent of England in the farmhouses and the hedgerows—

which were never seen in Brandenburg, where the fields were unfenced.

At one o'clock I was at the Schloss for luncheon, where I had to speak English with the Prince and his cadets. After luncheon, the boys, including the Prince, all went with me down to the "island" which lay in the lake, where farming operations on a small scale were carried on.

A long, narrow road led to the island, which was really a peninsula, and there everybody, including the Prince and myself, engaged in the occupation—it being the season of harvest—of digging potatoes out of the ground and gathering them into heaps. The coachman and footman and a young officer all assisted. Some geese came along and gobbled up the stray small potatoes we threw in their direction, and the sun, reflected from the lake in front, shone brightly on us as we toiled, girt round with potato sacks to keep our clothes clean.

This participation in agricultural pursuits was part of the training devised by the governor, but, as he himself was not an agriculturist, I doubt whether it was really as beneficial as it might have been. Surely the propagation and development of seeds and the rearing of young animals would have been less monotonous than this incessant potato gathering.

At five, when the afternoon train to Kiel was seen in the distance, we took off our sack-aprons and went home to tea. I was free for an hour or so, until I gave an English lesson to the whole class of boys, which nearly always included the governor.

They had been reading Dickens's *A Christmas Carol*— everybody in Germany read Dickens and got quite a wrong

idea of modern English life from his books—but I produced
Conan Doyle's *Adventures of Brigadier Gerard* as being, in
my opinion, more suitable for boys. I never had a class that
hung so much on my words. As they all spoke with a very
bad accent, I read to them myself, so that they could hear
English, and then we discussed the story and the meaning
of obscure words and phrases.

One morning, I was invited to an English class taught
by an officer using self-teaching reading books. It amused
me to hear some of the pupils reciting "Rule Britannia" out
of their reading books. It sounded like a derisive challenge,
as they declaimed the poem with that clear, distinct utter-
ance specially cultivated in all German schools. I could with
difficulty keep from smiling to hear a young German piping
its bombastic lines, with Kiel and its rapidly increasing war-
fleet only an hour's journey away:

> All thine shall be the subject main
> And every shore it circles thine.
> Rule Britannia.

My general impression gained from the military ideal as
applied to education in Germany is that, while thorough and
practical, it ignores too much those other world influences
due to science, invention, and discovery, which day by day
are changing the conditions of life among the nations.
German military education seems to breed a class of men
who are earnest, loyal, and self-sacrificing, but who possess
extremely narrow views, who see and judge everything
from a purely military, autocratic standpoint and are quite
unable to sympathize with or understand the aspirations of

the normal human being toward personal initiative and liberty of action.

*

It is difficult for English people to realize with what passionate enthusiasm and full consciousness of its value as an inspiration for the present and future times the teaching of history was carried out in Germany. Textbooks were written with the view of convincing German youth that without the God-given blessing of the Hohenzollern race on the Prussian throne none of the past glories of the German people would have been possible.

"Oh, yes, you are right in England to be democratic. With you it is the people who have done everything; with us in Germany it is our rulers who have done all. That is why we look to the Kaiser for a lead. In England, your king has no power, you are practically a republic. Here the Kaiser is the supreme power. Our people have no capacity for rule. It would be nothing but confusion and jangling if the power were not in one hand. We do not understand what you call party government and calling each other disagreeable names at elections. We should not like it. The Socialists? Oh, of course, the Socialists are all right, too. They voice the wrongs of the people and give an impression that they are of importance. The Socialist vote? Well, it may be increasing, but, after all, the power—the real power—it all lies in the throne—in the Kaiser's hands...."

The speaker was a rather cynical schoolmaster with whom I frequently found myself falling into interesting political discussions in which we disagreed as to ultimate issues. He only echoed what everyone else said when he remarked that in Germany the people had, historically, done nothing, the rulers everything. I learned to recognize it as one of the stereotyped phrases which one encountered with irritating persistence.

"But," I objected one day, "I don't think that this is true. The German people have always shown as much initiative as those of other nations, but the rulers have gotten the credit. There was the War of Liberation, for example, when Prussia was crushed under Napoleon. It was the people, not the Prussian King, who made the first effort at independence. There were splendid patriots and leaders among the people. What about Scharnhorst and Stein and the *Tugendbund*? The King did nothing then—the people everything—it was only later on that the King was roused by the efforts of the people."

My companion was nonplussed. He was clearly unused to any point of view other than that which was commonly held.

"Of course," I continued, "Queen Louise made up a good deal for her husband's shortcomings, but her efforts would have been in vain without the help of the people."

"Oh, yes," he said, his face brightening. "You see, it was Queen Louise who saved Prussia." He was relieved to be able to find that after all it was a royal who had come to the rescue, even if it had been a woman.

"But Scharnhorst," I urged. "He was the son of a farmer, wasn't he? Not even of Prussian birth, but a Hanoverian. He reformed the army which afterwards beat Napoleon. And Stein? It was because he saw that the peasants were too much ground down, that the Prussian people had no liberty under their rules, that they were driven to fight without any enthusiasm for their cause—"

The schoolmaster was unhappy. He had not realized I had been reading up on Stein.

"That was the reason," I continued implacably, "for Napoleon's success, but as soon as Stein was given a free hand, he liberated the people from serfdom and things went better. It was he who laid the foundations of the future greatness of Prussia."

The schoolmaster laughed and abandoned further argument, remarking that he saw I was *höchst demokratisch* —highly democratic—and he found that amusing in anyone living at the Prussian Court.

*

One cold day of my first winter still haunts my memories. It was a day when the Princess was wandering through the state apartment of the Berlin Schloss with her brother and young cousins. She stopped on the white marble staircase to point out with pride one of the large military pictures hanging there, painted by Anton von Werner, in which a charging squadron of Ulanen, in brand-new blue and red uniforms with highly polished buttons and accoutrements, mounted on specklessly well-groomed, prancing horses whose shimmering coats reflected the blue sky above, occupied the forefront of the picture. Around them bombs were exploding picturesquely and harmlessly, and at a discreet distance in the rear there was a suggestion of fallen men and horses. In a further concession to the supposed realities of war, a thin trickle of blood flowed from beneath the helmet of the leading Ulan.

It was one of those pictures obviously painted by artists who judge of war by peace conditions and dare not, even if they would, reveal its tragic features, its bloodshed and horror of mangled limbs and torn flesh. The painting had a bright varnished appearance and was calculated to inspire unsophisticated youth with the idea of the splendor and magnificence of war.

The children stood in a row, looking at the painting, which nearly covered the entire wall of the landing. The little girls were hand in hand, and the boys in their sailor suits hung over the marble balustrade and criticized the picture. "Look at that man in front with his sword flashing. Isn't he splendid?" cried the Prussian Princess. "Papa had this picture painted; he told the artist how it was to be done. Isn't it fine?"

"My father says war isn't like that at all," objected little Max of Hesse, a bright sunny fellow, full of good common sense. "He says it's not so clean and bright and that shells tear the men and horses to pieces and it's horrible. He says no one dares paint war pictures as they really are—it would be discouraging for the soldiers."

"How silly you are, Max!" said the Princess. "Of course, Papa must know how it ought to be painted. And the soldiers do look like that—I've seen them galloping just as they do here." Prince Joachim agreed that the soldiers at reviews and on maneuvers were exactly like those in the picture. Prince Max looked unconvinced but said no more. He would learn soon enough of the truth of his convictions.

There were a good many of those sprawling canvases, of little artistic merit, but portraying triumphant moments in Prussian history. In one of the galleries was a picture of a well-known general on horseback with Fame allegorically attired as an angel floating in the sky above him with a laurel wreath in her hand, with which she obviously was about to enwreath his brow. In the background, the smoke and flames of burning villages were to be seen ascending heavenward. Crowds of peasants lay heaped about in attitudes of death or acute misery, but the smiling, about-to-be-crowned conqueror had his back turned to all those unpleasant incidents, for which, though plainly responsible, he repudiated all liability.

*

The Sattelmeister was a handsome old man who dyed his hair. Many German officers, both commissioned and non-commissioned, resorted to such help—not so much from personal vanity as because an appearance of age was detrimental to an officer's prospects of advancement. Baldness was not of so much consequence because the majority of officers of the regular army were bald before they were thirty—a result, it was supposed, of the constant wearing of the ill-ventilated *Pickelhaube*.

The Sattelmeister and I had many canters together in the Wildpark or over the *Exerzierplatz*. He was an enthusiastic conversationalist, which was of great benefit to the somewhat elementary German with which I began my career at court. He was also very intelligent and had a great respect for the English. We discussed many interesting matters; among other things, he, to my surprise, spoke bitterly against a proposed increase in the German Army which was being discussed in the *Reichstag*.

"We already have too many soldiers," he said, with his face darkening. "What do we want with more? It will only make trouble with other countries. It is an unnecessary burden on the people. And those who have to pay the piper may not call the tune. Too many soldiers is worse than too few—they become our master." This was from a man who had fought in the Franco-Prussian War and had been all his life a soldier.

"But," I laughed, "I thought that here in Germany everyone was so devoted to the army, so proud of it, so ready to pay the piper—all, of course, except the Socialists."

"The Socialists?" he demanded. "The Socialists are quite right—the people are getting tired of paying for the army. It is dangerous in many ways. Military service is all right, it is good to give a year to one's country—but we are going too far—too far. . . ."

We were passing those funny targets in the shape of men at which the soldiers of the garrison had been practicing shooting, and, commenting on the appearance of the wooden figures, I, in a bantering mood, suggested to him that in the minds of the soldiers they represented Englishmen. The Sattelmeister resented the idea. "*Gott bewahre!*" he exclaimed piously. "What have Germans and Englishmen to fight over?"

"Why, nothing at all," I answered.

"*Natürlich*—nothing!" he repeated. "But then there are politicians, there is *Weltpolitik* and *Wasserpolitik*." He was referring to the German Navy and the "future on the water." "And some politicians are like the Almighty, they can create something out of nothing. The German people don't want to fight, and I don't suppose English people do either, but if the politicians happen to be the *dumme Kerle* they often are, then there will be trouble, and the people will pay."

We were quiet a minute, and our horses jogged on down the lane beneath the acacia trees. "Elsass-Lothringen!"

he said. "We took it from the people, we drove many of them from their homes, and what good is it to us now? A constant danger. Are the people there happy and contented? No. When I go to Urville with the Empress, there is a tea for the children round the Schloss, and they put it in the *Tägliche Rundschau*—a paragraph describing it and the happiness and contentment of the people under German rule. It is all *Quatsch*. They are not happy. And when the children grow up, they are more bitter than their parents. Tea at the Schloss. You can't make a conquered people content by giving them Pfefferkuchen and coffee."

The Crown Prince and Duchess Cecilia of Mecklenburg, both enthusiastic members of the fashionable young set in Berlin, at the time of their engagement in 1904. The Crown Princess became a swift favorite with the German people, and no less so after she gave birth to four sons and two daughters.

VISITS AND CEREMONIES

With only Sissy left in the family nest, the Empress fought desperately against all attempts to separate her from her daughter. She would have liked to take the Princess with her on those weary interminable train journeys, with their cheering crowds and constant ceremonies, and the Emperor was equally willing to snatch the Princess off—the missed lessons interested him not a bit, as he was not a believer in education for women. Nevertheless, with Fräulein von Thadden being "firm," the Princess was rarely separated from her lessons, and mother and child would weep in each other's arms over a parting of a week.

In the spring of 1904, however, Fräulein von Thadden, still not well, went away for a long cure, and the Empress, profiting by her absence, decided to take the Princess with her on a visit to her sister, the Duchess of Schleswig-Holstein-Sonderburg-Glücksburg. After a few days, I went

to fetch my pupil back, while the Empress continued elsewhere with her ladies.

Schloss Glücksburg lay far north, and I had to travel
through Hamburg, changing at Flensburg in a queer little
narrow-gauge railway. The railway ran alongside the one
street of the tiny town of Glücksburg—a town of dreams
that looked at itself in the water of the lake all day and
seemed to have fallen into a doze. The Schloss arose
seemingly straight out of the lake, the walls washed by the
water on every side. Access to it was by a rough-looking
causeway. It had been built in 1508, and little—including
the water and sanitation systems—had been altered since
that time.

I was lodged in a nearby hotel but was required to leave
the hotel at 8:30 to dine with the Empress and the ducal
family at the Schloss in a dining room that was rather like
a crypt. We had cutlets and spinach, then kalte Schnitzel, all
served from the same enormous dish. This was followed by
a stodgy rice pudding with treacle sauce, which we ate from
silver plates.

The Empress departed the next day with Fräulein von
Gersdorff, who took me aside and told me that this was one
of the occasions when I had to be firm with the Empress,
fight valiantly in the armor of the absent von Thadden, and
say a lot of nasty things about the Princess missing her
lessons. I felt myself incapable of provoking one of those
dramatic scenes Fräulein von Thadden knew so well how
to engineer, and I contented myself with a gentle remon-
strance, which fell flat.

"Fräulein von Gersdorff told you to say that to me,"
said the Empress pleasantly. "Now, didn't she?" I laughed

—I ought to have frowned—and confessed that it was so. "Well, now you've said it," said the Empress triumphantly, "and you needn't think any more about it." We both broke into unrestrained laughter.

The Empress left, and I was given her vacated room, a funny place, where an oil lamp provided illumination. It was full of eerie shadows; the ghosts of dead kings and queens seemed to come forth from the ragged tapestry.

The following day, Sunday, the Duke and Duchess and their family of five girls and one boy, Sissy, and I, went to chapel. We went through an upstairs corridor of the Schloss, where a footman opened a door, and we found ourselves in the ducal pew, which was really a room, looking something like a library, as several bookcases of dilapidated ancient books stood against the walls. Two rows of chairs were placed facing a wall which was full of windows and through which could be seen the church and the heads of the tallest of the congregation whenever they stood up. Mostly, they remained invisible. The chairs upon which we sat had once been covered with red velvet; the nap was now gone, and they had a mangy look and were full of holes. To keep out the draft, a most hideous curtain of woolwork roses, no doubt the handicraft of some ancestress, hung over the door.

In the middle of the last hymn—of nine eight-lined verses!—the door of our gallery rattled violently, and a boy appeared with a bag slung at the end of a long rod. This he dexterously passed between the shoulders of the back row of worshippers, avoiding their hats, and collected our contributions. I don't think the ducal offerings amounted to much, as before the service there had been many inquiries after the smallest pieces of change.

The Duke Ferdinand of Glücksburg was the most silent man I ever met. I gathered from the Princess that *Onkel* Ferdinand was one person who did not get on well with Papa, that he had Danish rather than German leanings and never came, no matter how often invited by Papa, to the various gatherings of princes of Germany, who from time to time assembled in Berlin as a sign of cohesion and unity of the German Empire.

Onkel Ferdinand indeed remained implacably Danish. He wore Danish uniform at dinner and required his suite to do the same. Alas, even the settlement of the Great War did not fulfill the Duke's hopes of his estates reverting to Denmark—the borderline of the new frontier ran a few miles north of Glücksburg.

Of Onkel Ferdinand's five daughters, two married German princes, the eldest becoming the wife of Prince Charles Edward, Duke of Saxe-Coburg and Gotha, and mother of Princess Alice; and the second marrying, unhappily, as it transpired, her cousin, the artistic Prince Au-Wi.

The only interesting thing to do in Glücksburg was to visit the *Iduna*, the Empress's yacht, which lay in the harbor. Sissy loved to go there, for the captain fed us on delectable English foods—sandwiches made from Crosse & Blackwell's pastes, porridge of Quaker Oats.

On leaving Glücksburg, the Baron von Mirbach was sent by Her Majesty to escort the Princess home. The Duchess had provided us with a basket of food, upon which the Princess fell somewhere about ten o'clock. Perhaps it was our early breakfast and the hour's drive afterwards, but that chicken was one of the most delicious I have ever tasted, full of nutty flavor. Baron von Mirbach refused any share; he was unwilling to spoil his luncheon, ordered for twelve o'clock, the hour when we would arrive at Hamburg.

He kept warning us not to eat so much, as the celebrated *Hamburgerkücken* were to appear on the menu, but the Princess did not heed his warning. Consternation was written large on the face of Herr von Mirbach, who saw his twelve o'clock luncheon doomed, he thought, to failure. He was an apprehensive man, forever anticipating trouble.

Often Baron von Mirbach was, as far as I could discover, the only German of the court who appeared to have misgivings about the absolute excellence of German methods of government. On the contrary, he was gifted with a Cassandra-like facility of prophetic foreboding and denunciation, and he had a blunt, rather ferocious manner of stating things to the Empress, who valued him highly, while ridiculing all he said.

Once, at Cadinen, I was strolling along the straight, tree-bordered road leading from Elbing to Frauenburg. The road ran past the farmyard which nestled under the nose of the royal Schloss. In Germany it was considered a sign of super sensitiveness and deficiency in common sense to object to farmyard odors. In Hesse, does not every manure pile occupy a position in the main street directly underneath the windows of the best parlor? As I wandered past the cowsheds, I came upon Baron von Mirbach, his gaze fixed upon the telegraph poles, which could be followed for some distance in diminishing perspective. "*Dumm!*" he exclaimed, catching sight of me.

I stopped and looked at him inquiringly. "You allude, I suppose, to the telegraph poles?" I suggested. They had been erected since our last visit the year before and were one of the necessities of the Emperor's occupation of the newly acquired Cadinen estate.

He shook his head in a manner suggestive of feelings too deep for expression, and then, in a flood of abuse of government methods, pointed out in a series of arguments too rapid and involved for me to follow, that if the authorities had only had the sense to erect the posts on the other side of the road, the extension of the East Prussian telegraph system which was planned for the following year could have been carried out without the expense of the erection of a second line of posts. He said it was only a further example of the *kolossal* stupidity with which everything in Germany was managed.

I was gratified by what he said. "How comforting it is," I said, "to hear that English do not possess the only government in the world capable of making mistakes." He made a large gesture to the heavens as if invoking the aid of higher powers to give me understanding, and shaking his head, walked on up the road toward Elbing.

I often wondered if the prophetic, pessimistic Baron von Mirbach anticipated his own end in Russia? I am convinced that he did, but bravely went nevertheless to meet his fate.

In Hamburg, where there was a forty-minute stop, our saloon was invaded by two nervous, white-gloved waiters, preceded by a *maître d'hôtel*, carrying the luncheon. They made the regulation bows, and our table was spread with beautiful linen and decorated with flowers. We had thick soup, fillet of beef with several kinds of vegetables, and then the celebrated Hamburg chickens—young birds fattened on milk and oatmeal, of a peculiar deliciousness. Following the chickens, we were served cucumber salad and preserved strawberries and two puddings, one hot, one cold. There were only three of us to partake of this ample luncheon, but the Princess ate everything with the greatest appetite and told the hotelkeeper how delicious everything was. The look of doubt that had haunted the face of Baron von Mirbach gave place as one dish succeeded another to an expression of awe-stricken admiration. "I would never have believed that the Princess had such a good appetite," he murmured to me. "Absolutely splendid."

For the rest of the trip, I read *St. Winifred's* to the Princess, and von Mirbach indulged in the nap that his age and exertions demanded. I heard sometime later that he told Countess Keller that it was the pleasantest official journey he had ever experienced.

Von Mirbach was of the opinion that I had an ameliorating influence on the conduct and disposition of the Princess. However much I might have wished to lay claim to such a desirable result, in this case all the credit for her happy frame of mind must be given to the chickens—the one from Glücksburg and the plump babies of Hamburg. Good food has a wonderfully soothing effect, and we rarely got any in the palaces of the Emperor.

We arrived in Berlin at four o'clock, and a short three days later we started for Donau-Eschingen, where the Emperor was to shoot capercailzie for three days in the forest of Prince Max Egon von Fürstenburg, after which we were to visit Strausburg, and then return to the New Palace.

Prince von Fürstenburg was one of the wealthiest landowners in Germany, and he also possessed large estates in Austria. His country place had a spring rising in its garden, which, if rumor was to be believed, was the source of the Danube. The Prince kept a pack of foxhounds, had a large stable of the finest horses in the country, and was a patron of the arts, a sportsman, and a good all-around man of business. Also, he was young and handsome and lived with a stately and beautiful wife and a family of five lively children.

A German country house capable of accommodating an Emperor and Empress, as well as their daughter and the attendant suite for three days, must, I knew, be built on an extensive scale and possess, unlike Glücksburg, all the modern conveniences. So in one week, I visited the extreme north and south of Germany: I led a life of strict simplicity in the north, and in the south found every contemporary luxury.

The Emperor had given me an exhaustive lecture on the nature of this magnificent bird, the capercailzie—of its habit of drumming weirdly at dawn and sunset in a kind of intoxicated love-frenzy. I recognized it as kin to the blackcock of the Scottish pine woods. "Yes, blackcock—that's what they call it in England," he confirmed.

On the evening of our arrival, the Emperor went out to shoot, but I never heard if he was successful or not on either that or the other two nights of our stay. We heard no *Ha-la-li* that was performed on the hunter's horn whenever the Emperor had brought down his game.

The last day of the journey to Donau-Eschingen was spent at Metz, where the Emperor reviewed an army corps. Their entry into this town must have seemed strange indeed to Their Majesties. Here there was no welcome, no smile, not a single flag. The people who stood in the streets looked on idly, like spectators of a curious show, as the long procession of carriages with their outriders moved on. Countess

Stolberg remarked resentfully on the absence of enthusiasm. The names over the doors were French, the faces were French, and there was an atmosphere of French hostility.

Under an awning, in the burning sunshine, the Empress stood for two hours, smiling and bowing while the troops marched past. The Emperor was on his horse, a distance away, with his officers. On the roof of a neighboring building were gathered the only Germans in the town. Here was a flutter of white and a shouted *"Hochs!"*—a lonely outpost of patriotism. The rest of the beautiful town went on with its own affairs while the German soldiers marched and rode past.

One day, about five years after the end of the Boer War, a German lady who was dining at court drew me aside after dinner. "Today I have been talking to a German gentleman who has been living in your Orange River Free State, or whatever you call it, and he tells me that the Boers are quite content now to be under your government."

"They are?" I asked. "Is he quite sure?"

"Oh, quite certain. He knows. He is a German. They know he is a German. They tell him the truth. Now tell me: how do you manage it? And with so few soldiers, I am told—hardly any at all. How do you do it? And in five years! Look at us in Elsass-Lothringen. They will never be satisfied. We are always in fear of war. Tell us your secret." She laid her hand on my arm and looked at me intently as if she could surprise the secret out of me.

"Oh, I don't know," I replied lamely. "We've had a lot of practice at governing, and made an awful lot of mistakes, and we've learned a little by our past mistakes. I suppose that is one reason. And then we let them alone a good deal afterwards, and play cricket and football with them and things of that kind. We let them vote the same as the rest of us, and well, we don't treat them any differently from the rest, as far as I can make out—just let them alone to conspire or do as they like, and then if they know they can, they don't want to. See? And then our Tommies—our soldiers—are not brought up to be so patriotic as yours—so, of course, it's less galling: they'd just as soon chum up with the enemy afterward as not. . . . ''

"Cricket and football," the lady murmured, "and not too patriotic, and a vote, and let them conspire if they want to, and the soldiers are chummy. *Ach*—we cannot do that. It is a matter of national temperament, I suppose, but it is sad, very sad." She sighed and walked away looking troubled.

*

In view of the avowed love of nature and outdoor life among the German people, I often wondered at the conspicuous lack of beautiful private gardens to be found in nearly all parts of the Fatherland. (An exception were the gardens at Prince von Fürstenburg's Schloss: they were large and well kept; there were a rose garden, an ornamental pool with wildfowl swimming on it, and also the alleged source of the Danube, surrounded by a marble balustrade and presided over by a lady in marble on a pedestal, symbolizing the ancient river.)

All German gardeners seemed to walk about a good deal in wooden shoes wearing a blue apron. They were continually raking the sandy paths, they cleared up the dead leaves in the autumn, they mowed the grass with a scythe when they considered it sufficiently long—perhaps two or three

times a year!—and they could not imagine that people
wanted anything more. Some wildly enterprising garden-
lovers, however, would purchase one or two of those
grotesque china gnomes, and deposit them, one sitting,
the other standing, in the center of their garden, surrounded by painfully arranged rock work and a few smoky-
looking shrubs.

Once when the Empress was travelling with the
Princess from East Prussia to Berlin, she broke her journey
to take luncheon with a wealthy nobleman whose house and
estates lay not far from Danzig. The suite travelling with her
were included, and I was struck, as we drove up to the
house along a country lane bordered by plowed fields, by
the fact that here, in this big country place, where one might
have thought that the visit of the Empress would have stimulated everybody to do their best to improve the appearance
of the grounds, the grass on the lawn had not been cut. It
was, it is true, full of wildflowers—buttercups and cuckoo-
flowers and white marguerites—but I suspected there was
no aesthetic reason for leaving them there. They would be
made into hay later.

There were winding walks through the woodland
toward the *Aussichtspunkt*—the "view" so cherished and
noted by all good Germans. (As soon as a beauty spot was
discovered in Germany, it was "improved" by cutting down
trees if necessary: convenient paths were constructed converging on it, dangerous corners were fenced off, fence
posts were erected telling the traveller of the view to be seen
a little higher up, seats were carefully arranged where one
could sit and soak into one's soul whatever it was capable
of assimilating, and as one turned away, satiated, perhaps,

with the wonders of atmosphere and scenes, unobtrusively, tactfully, but nonetheless inevitably, nailed to the stem of an upstanding pine tree appeared the wooden tablet bearing the word *Erfrischung*—refreshments—with a rudely painted hand indicating the direction in which cake and coffee might be found. Nature and restaurants are closely associated in the German mind; a passionate enthusiasm for food is entwined with an intense admiration of the scenery.)

But here at the estate of the Count, the winding walk was a tangled wilderness; it could have been, with the exercise of a little of that love and care to which gardens respond so readily, a beautiful setting to the old house and to the troop of lovely children belonging to our host and hostess, who were people who had travelled widely and accumulated many art treasures.

These treasures did not, however, prevent their house from being in its interior arrangements ugly and uncomfortable. They had not been able to forego the chocolate walls so beloved in Germany. The big hall, with a curving staircase at one side, which, if it had been in an English house, would have been converted into a charming lounge with Persian rugs, tables and cozy chairs, plants and newspapers, was a bare place, the boards painted chocolate and no furniture in it except an iron stove and the usual coat rack. There was no sense of home. Yet the luncheon was served on costly china, our bouillon was drunk from bowls of eggshell porcelain, each unique, brought by our host from Japan, and our dessert knives were works of art in jade and mother-of-pearl. In the children's room hung original paintings by Richter, the children's artist *par excellence* of Germany.

"I like them to grow up with such things," said their father to the Empress. "It forms their taste unconsciously." The Empress agreed, although she afterwards said that she thought good reproductions would have been just as effective.

It was a bewildering visit. The courteous, cultured host and hostess—the latter in a wonderful gown from Vienna— the rosy children with their suite of schoolrooms and nurseries, the evidence of wealth and desire for beauty and artistic surroundings, and the lack of knowledge of how to attain it fully. The setting of all the beautiful things the Count had collected was hopeless—nobody and nothing looks good against a painted chocolate wall, even when green plush curtains are added.

*

Whitsuntide, or *Pfingsten*, was celebrated in German villages by the people placing big boughs of young larch on each side of their doorways to welcome the returning spring. Every street broke out in sudden growth of unaccustomed greenery, and in the churches young larch trees cut from the hillside were placed on each side of the altar.

In the New Palace, the day was feted with the *Schrippenfest*, a dinner instituted by Frederick the Great in honor of the garrison. All the previous week, the soldiers made long green garlands of pine and fir twigs. The garlands were wound around the arcade of the Communs and entwined on the posts that supported the wooden roof. Early on the morning of Whit Monday, big copper cauldrons with beef, prunes, and rice were set boiling out of doors. The feast had begun in a small way, with the distribution to the soldiers of *Schrippen*—small white loaves of bread—but over the years it had developed into a substantial meal.

The whole diplomatic corps and many officers and ladies were invited to the Schrippenfest, so there was a large assemblage at the military service that preceded the meals. After the service, the Emperor and Empress, their family and guests, ate with the soldiers. No one sat down; everyone ate the meat and prunes while standing—the ladies in their trained silk dresses, the ambassadors, generals, and adjutants all balancing a plateful of boiled beef and eating it wherever elbow room could be found.

When Their Majesties had finished, they walked down between the tables, inspecting the soldiers and asking them questions: Where have you come from? How long have you served? Have you had a good dinner?

The Emperor and his family possessed to an unusual degree what Kipling called the "common touch." They knew how to talk to poor men, working people, without any shadow of that patronizing affability often mistakenly employed by one class when trying to be nice to another. An absolutely frank and unreserved interest in other people's affairs was implied in Their Majesties' conversation, an obvious desire to know something of the conditions of other people's lives. It never became perfunctory, although it easily could have, especially in view of the thousands of soldiers and other people to whom the Emperor talked in the course of a year.

The Princess herself from childhood always had the knack of choosing the right thing to say to the poorest children she met. She wanted to know their names, how many brothers and sisters they had, what class they were in at school, and what they were going to be when they grew up. Once, one small boy answered, "a chimney sweep"—then a profession that one never assumed was chosen with deliberate forethought—but the Princess was never at a loss for something appropriate to say. She never appeared shy; she was at ease with herself and made everyone else feel the same. Sissy was not a devoted student, but she had initiative and judgment.

For this, I maintained she owed no small debt to her Tante Feo. About a mile from the New Palace lived the only unmarried sister of the Empress, the Princess Feodora of Schleswig-Holstein, a woman of many intellectual gifts and a striking and interesting personality. She had much influence over her nieces and nephews, and they spent a lot of time in her company.

Princess Feo's ideas were democratic. She detested the atmosphere of courts and the restrictions and ceremonies required of a court existence. She was also a clever artist and the author of several insightful books on the life of the peasantry. Her home was in a large farmhouse belonging to the Crown, known as *Bornstedter Gut*. The ground floor was inhabited by the bailiff and his family. The rest of the house belonged to Princess Feo, to whom it had been lent by her brother-in-law, the Emperor, with whom she was a great favorite, although their views clashed uncompromisingly on nearly all subjects.

Princess Feo refurbished Bornstedter Gut herself, shopping in Berlin like any ordinary *Bürgerfrau*. The Bornstedtergut was one of those solidly built, large yellow houses that abounded in the neighborhood of Potsdam. It had been the early home of the Emperor and Empress Frederick. Princess Feo changed it out of recognition.

German drawing rooms in private houses—known as

die kalte Pracht—cold splendor—were nightmares of ugliness. Had I not been in the splendid and hideous salons of Herr von Mirbach and Herr von Scholl, wealthiest of the *Landadel*, who still clung to the drab walls of their ancestors? Had I not imagined the paint ivory-white, in my mind re-hung the walls and banished the plush ornaments into the attics, planning how the spacious rooms might, with a little taste, be made charming?

In the big *Warenhaus Wertheim*, the first of those great stores built on the American principle that had begun to open in Berlin, there were grouped wonderful suites of furniture placed in rooms with modern wallpapers designed by artists. I begged the ladies of the court to go and look for themselves at these things, so they might use their influence to spread a cult of beauty. They were shocked at the idea. The Empress herself threw cold water on Wertheim's. Was the proprietor not a Jew? Had he not two stone bears (modelled by a famous animal sculptor) peeping down into the basin of the splashing fountain that he had erected under the portico in front of his palace of industry? It would never have done for a royal carriage to be seen drawing up there.

It was therefore a blow to the ladies and an annoyance to the Empress that her sister bought everything from Warenhaus Wertheim. It was spoken of in whispers—tacitly ignored—but everybody knew of the awful fact. Princess Feo only laughed at the ladies, laughed at the prejudices of her sister, and went on buying pretty, comfortable furniture, delightful curtains of the brightest design, cups and saucers, gaily painted tables and chairs, vibrant carpets for the floors, and ultra modern pictures for the plain blue flock paper of the walls—all from Wertheim.

Princess Feo loved the realities of life and refused to have things made easier for her because she was the sister of the Empress. She was only seven years older than her eldest nephew, the Crown Prince.

I first saw her at Bornstedt, where I had come to get Sissy, who had been spending the afternoon with her aunt. The carriage I was in drove past a big farmyard, where wagon horses were being harnessed, up to the door of a big stone house, pleasantly shaded by chestnut trees. As I got out of the carriage, a sudden eruption of screaming children, boys and girls of all ages in a state of heat and untidiness, among whom I recognized my Princess, burst from the dark doorway of a cow-house, trampled and stumbled over heaps of farmyard litter, and fled with shrieks up a ladder into a hayloft. They were pursued by a lady clad in a tweed skirt, a striped blouse, and a Panama hat, who likewise flew up the ladder with agility and disappeared. Uproarious screams issued from the loft. They were playing Verstecken, and the lady of the ladder was Princess Feodora.

Princess Feo loved to surround herself with clever, unconventional people, whatever their rank in life. With her it was an obsession that all her royal nephews and nieces should know life as it really was, not as seen blurred and transformed through a court atmosphere. She taught them many perhaps disagreeable truths about themselves, which they would have heard from no one else. The trend of modern thought and contemporary politics found in her an earnest and intelligent student. With poverty, with humble folks, she had an intense sympathy, a passionate tenderness for a simple struggling existence.

Although she possessed a sense of humor, in her books

she wrote only of the somber side of life, the bare sand-
dunes of her native Holstein, the resinous breath of its pine
woods, the chill sand bar on the shore of the seawaves. She
depicted the strenuous toil, unrelieved labor, and sordid
existences of the peasantry. "The only truths in life," she
had one of her characters say, "are founded upon work.
Everything else is false."

She was, unlike the Emperor, a staunch believer in
women's education. In this attitude, the Emperor was
decidedly behind the practices of his people. In Germany,
girls without money had a slim chance of marrying, so
the modern German girl, conscious of being greatly in
excess of the male population, sought to extend her sphere
of activities, and was no longer content to be merely a
good *Hausfrau* and to learn seventeen different ways of
making sausages.

Daughters were no longer being brought up on the
same lines as their mothers. Everywhere I was told that
household management was a thing of the past, that restaurants and a love of leisure had undermined the good old
ways, that girls preferred to train as doctors or dentists or
chemists, that they wanted to be factory inspectors rather
than cooks and domestic purveyors of home comforts.

The outlook of the ordinary middle-class woman—she
who kept perhaps one or, at most, two servants—was
bounded by the interests of her husband and family. She
scarcely kept in touch with the outside world, and if she
indulged in sport or any form of pleasure other than the
theatre—which was patronized by middle-class and comparatively poor people to an extent much greater than in
England—she would have been considered rather modern.

When one German said of another that she was *sehr modern*—they put the accent on the last syllable—then all the rest of her sex knew what to think of her.

The German woman was not well informed about the necessity of fresh air; she had hardly begun to master the secrets of domestic hygiene. She was extraordinarily subject to nerves, and the only holiday she took was a Kur of a few weeks every summer in some remote *Badeort*.

The energies of the middle-class woman were concentrated in the effort to save up enough money to take herself, her husband, and her family to the seaside or to the mountains during the *Ferien*—the children's summer holiday in July—when every hotel was packed to bursting point, prices were at their highest, and fitting accommodations were almost impossible to come by.

Probably the absence of housekeeping worries and the pleasure of eating meals which she herself had had no share in preparing were the major assets of her holiday. Her walks—she hated walks as a rule—were initiated by a desire to get rid of that superfluous flesh which pursued the German woman after her fortieth year, and her enjoyment of the scenery was perfunctory. She would stop at the *Aussichtspunkt*—observation point—carefully indicated by a signboard lest the traveller should not notice it—and let off the usual exclamations, "*Herrlich! Wunderschön! Prachtvoll!*" but her inner consciousness was liable to be absorbed by the narrowness of her own domestic life. The snatches of conversation that one overheard in the pine forests sounded singularly inappropriate to the environment of the speakers. One wondered why they should choose lovely glades of shimmering light and shade for the purpose of bemoaning the high price of meat, the delinquencies of Anna, and the fearful rapidity with which Hans wore out his shoes.

The German woman who appeared to me the most broad-minded and cultivated of her sex—cultivated, I mean in the wider sense, not merely having acquired a knowledge of several languages and certain historical and literary facts, but who possessed a wide and tolerant mental outlook— was the educated Jewish woman. She was invariably alert and up to date. She had artistic sense, her house was furnished in an original and tasteful manner, and she dressed herself beautifully. She was liberal in her charities, lavish in her hospitality, and had distinct social gifts. The Jewish woman was only just beginning to fight her way into German society, but she did it very efficiently and was well equipped for the struggle.

*

In the summer of 1904, the first automobile arrived at the New Palace, an innovation long resisted by the Empress and her ladies, who considered these vehicles lacking in royal dignity. The Emperor, however, cut short the eternal *zanken* by arriving one day from Berlin in a new Mercedes. Fräulein von Gersdorff moaned at seeing what she called "this hated machine" defiling the gravel where Frederick the Great had once set foot, but in spite of her protest, the Empress and the Princess got into the car and went for a trial trip.

In a very short time, six automobiles appeared in the stables. What relief they must have brought to the railway officials—what a savings in red carpet! We were always going on excursions in the automobiles. It was such a blessing to royalty to be able to fly past their loyal subjects and escape recognition until they were fifty yards farther on. The chauffeurs, of whom there were always two to each car, wore the royal Prussian eagle on their coats, but it was a subdued eagle that merged into the pattern, not at all easy to recognize when the cars were going fast.

*

In September 1904, twenty-three-year-old Crown Prince Wilhelm became engaged to the Duchess Cecilia of Mecklenburg-Schwerin. All my impressions of the Crown Prince had been pleasant ones, although, from a certain independence of manner and what was considered a modern outlook, he was not regarded with much favor by the ladies and gentlemen of the court, who considered Prince Fritz to have greater promise.

German royalties were peculiarly fortunate in having a wide range of choices for marriage partners—the Fatherland was rich in numerous, prolific princely families. These families were unremarkable for wealth or extent of territory—some were conspicuously poverty-stricken—but all of them were classed as *ebenbürtig*—equal in birth—to royalty. The German Empire was long the happy hunting ground for would-be bridegrooms from powerful thrones around the world.

The Crown Prince announced his engagement in a series of laconic telegrams. "We are engaged—Wilhelm and Cecile," was the message sent by the *Brautpaar*.

As soon as the announcement of this engagement became public, the postcard shops of Berlin—whose name is legion—became mere picture galleries for the illustration of every possible moment of the life and movements of the young couple. An army of photographers were employed to lie in wait and capture them under almost every conceivable life circumstance.

First there was the official photograph of the Brautpaar sitting hand in hand, the orthodox photographic pose for all newly engaged couples. Then there was one called "The First Congratulations": rows and rows of schoolchildren of Schwerin, each with a bouquet of wilted flowers, presenting in turn to the smiling Duchess while the Crown Prince stood by. "The First Drive" pictured them both in a sort of dog-cart, duly chaperoned, taking the air; and there were dozens more: playing tennis, drinking tea, nursing the dogs.

Although they were engaged in September, their marriage did not take place until the beginning of the following June, when Cecile turned eighteen. If ordinary weddings usually mean a time of considerable stress to everyone concerned, they are epochs of honeyed leisure compared with the ceremonies attendant on royal functions of the same kind. For weeks beforehand, none of us dared to let our thoughts wander from the impending event.

A few days before the state entry of the bride into the town, we all had to leave the New Palace and migrate to Berlin. A state entry means, for the bride, not only an entry in state carriage but in state attire, wearing a semi-evening dress and a long train. The day before it took place, the bride arrived with her mother and took up residence for the night in Bellevue. The next day was too hot to be agreeable, but all Berlin was astir early. The streets were decorated with wreaths and flags. Along the route, wooden stands had been erected: the entry was the only part of the state ceremony that the public could enjoy; the wedding occurred privately in the chapel of the Schloss.

The people of Berlin gathered at a very early hour, although the procession would not start before three, taking their places along the Tiergarten as near as they could to the Brandenburgertor. There, they stood from hour to hour waiting patiently in the heat.

In the stables, there was great activity. The eight fine black horses which drew the state carriage had been exercised daily together wearing the heavy red brass-studded harness. The coach was made almost entirely of glass in the upper panels, and was beautifully painted and decorated. Three handsomely clad footmen clung behind it, and two equally handsome pages held a precarious and uncomfortable footing behind the coachman's box, crowded up between it and the curvature of the coach in a complicated and mysterious manner. The ponderous vehicle swung heavily from side to side and had a peculiar cross-channel motion.

Its progress toward Bellevue—the sight of the eight slowly pacing horses, each wearing plumes of ostrich feathers, led at a foot's pace by grooms in red coats encrusted with gold lace—delighted the waiting crowd.

The guild of the master butchers of Berlin, in a long-established privilege, rode, in top hats and frockcoats, at the head of the bride's procession. They had been practicing their equestrian exercises for weeks. Many had never made acquaintance with a saddle before—except for a saddle of mutton. Quiet, staid horses of mature years suddenly rose in price and horse-dealers reaped a rich harvest from ancient but attractive nags that knew how to walk with an air of magnificence.

From the Schloss there was an excellent view of the long procession as it came at last slowly up the Linden. It stopped at the Brandenburgertor where the *Burgermeister* —the Lord Mayor of Berlin—had the pleasurable duty of making a speech of welcome to the bride, who was expected to make a short speech in reply. A bouquet was also presented by a galaxy of white-clad maidens. Then, headed by the black-coated butchers, among the fluttering pennants of the Uhläns, the coach swung slowly on its way.

The future Crown Princess was joyously responsive. She possessed to a high degree that capacity for appearing pleased and amused which is invaluable to royalties. The world to her was an intensely interesting place, and on that day Cecile drove triumphantly into the hearts of the people, where she remained enthroned throughout her life, a stimulating, charming presence.

Besides the bride, the coach contained the Empress and the Countess von Brockdorff. When it turned at last from the shouting, waving populace into the courtyard of the Schloss—the butchers having ridden in one gate and out the other—it met the Emperor, who was standing at the entrance to welcome Cecile, while the bridegroom waited at the head of his regiment, which formed the guard of honor for the occasion.

The wedding was held three days later, at five o'clock in the afternoon. Those people who were not invited to be present at the wedding ceremony in the chapel received invitations to the *Bildergalerie*—picture gallery—through which the wedding procession passed.

The guests were a mixed assembly; anyone having any connection with the bride or bridegroom—professors, school friends, teachers, footmen and their families, fellow students—all received tickets. They wore evening dress, and some very strange costumes were seen among the ladies. One I remember, an obviously homemade and inartistic affair, was trimmed with real waterlilies, which in the heat had turned a dismal brown and long before the procession drew near were depressingly dying on the ample bosom of the wearer.

The procession was headed by two heralds in tabards and twelve pages in red. The bride followed in a dress of silver tissue, led by the bridegroom in uniform. She had on her head the small jewelled crown which every Prussian bride wears on her wedding day, and her train was carried by four young ladies.

The Empress followed with the bride's brother, the Grand Duke of Mecklenburg-Schwerin, and the Emperor with the bride's mother, the Grand Duchess Anastasia. They were followed by a crowd of other royalties walking, as is the custom, hand in hand; they all looked very pleased with themselves, and those who happened to know me grinned delightedly and nodded as they passed. Some made odd pairings: the very tall Duchess of Aosta, for example, who walked with a tiny little Japanese gentleman. The Princess, who walked with Prince Joachim, made friendly demonstrations as she went by and shrieked with laughter when I responded with a very deep curtsy.

When the procession had vanished, an army of housemaids with brooms entered and began to sweep up the dirt and litter. It was typical on ceremonial occasions, when people were waiting around on red carpets to welcome royal guests or ambassadors weighted down with state secrets, that a print-gowned housemaid with a broom would appear, wielding her implement coolly in the midst of state events, as though sweeping were the most important business of life.

In the chapel, everybody stood the whole time—no chairs were admitted, except for one or two specially exalted guests—so the long address of the Lutheran clergyman, admonishing the bridal couple as to their duties to each other, seemed longer than perhaps it was.

Every lady was in court dress, wearing the regulation veil and long, heavy train which we had to hold on our arms during the service, as it was not to be displayed until the *Defilircour*—the reception line—which followed the ceremony.

From the chapel, the newly married pair walked into the adjacent Weissersaal, where, with the Emperor and Empress, they stood to receive the guests who passed quickly before them, bowing, we ladies now with our trains spread out.

When the Cour ended, we adjourned to dinner, which was laid in several different rooms at small round tables, except the one where the royalties sat, which was large. Here, more quaint ceremonies took place. The Prince von Furstenburg, the Marshal of the Court, served the Emperor with soup, and the other royal guests were also waited on by pages and gentlemen of birth who took the dishes from the footmen. The Truchess—the Lord High Steward—poured the wine, and in the middle of the dinner the Emperor toasted the Brautpaar.

The dinner was not too prolonged, however, for the climax of these stately formalities remained to be performed—the most beautiful, and perhaps for the hard-worked bridal pair, the most tiring ceremony of all—the Torch Dance, seen nowhere but at the Prussian Court, and once seen, never to be forgotten. I was last to experience this dramatic ceremony several years hence, and the memory of its grandeur remains with me forever as a symbol of a lost, past era.

The Emperor with his first grandson and heir to the Hohenzollern throne, Prince Wilhelm. The Prince was a withdrawn, sullen child until it was discovered that he was being mistreated at the hands of his nurse. Her immediate dismissal was one of the few times His Majesty interferred in the lives of his married children.

COOKING LESSONS

The Bauernhaus—peasant cottage—which the Emperor gave to his daughter the Christmas of 1904 was built in a side garden a little distance from the New Palace and was ready for occupation by the spring. It was solemnly dedicated, unlocked by the Emperor, and presented to the Princess, who was overjoyed at having a place where she could cook and wash clothes to her heart's content. Like most royal people, she was attracted chiefly toward occupations in which she was least likely to ever be engaged.

As I was the only lady in the palace who had the faintest theoretical or practical idea of the art of cooking, I was chosen to guide the children. Before we had the Bauernhaus we made toffee on a doll-stove in a doll-saucepan, but the brocaded chairs and sofas of the Wohnung der Prinzessin were an unsuitable environment for beginning cooks. Furthermore, the Princess didn't want to prepare food for dolls' appetites, she wanted to cook something for Papa. (He had actually eaten all of the toffee, although it had turned out rather soft, but we were eager to prove ourselves capable of higher achievements.)

All the dolls' crockery-ware, saucepans, and frying pans were taken over to the Haus; we did not receive grownup replacements for over a year. The greatest drawback of the Bauernhaus was that it had no water in or near it. We had to fetch water ourselves or send a footman the long way to the palace for it.

In the beginning, the court lackeys were strictly forbidden to set foot in the Bauernhaus; their liveries would have been out of place in the peasant environment. After a while, however, the duties of fire-lighting and water-carrying, initially performed with enthusiasm by the Princess and her playmates, became irksome, and the two footmen, who had had a dull time hiding in the nearest shrubbery, were permitted to share our domestic labors.

Ebert, the footman of the Princess, would, with his knife, shave splinters from a piece of wood, leaving them unsevered at one end. Then the bit of wood, with its shavings attached, was lit and placed in the stove with the other logs around it. Soon there was a crackling fire in the little tiled stove.

The first time we undertook an orgy of cooking, Sissy, wishing to play the part properly, put on an embroidered peasant's dress. On the way to the garden we encountered the Home Guard. They were nonplussed when they caught sight of her in this costume and were not sure if it really was the Princess or not. They finally decided to render her the customary honors, but Sissy, having thrown herself entirely into the part of a *Bauernfrau*, was extremely annoyed at the bowing and saluting and presenting of arms that was being conducted in defiance of her theatrical intention. She never wore the costume again; however, this was more due to the fact that she found it tight and hot and impractical for beating eggs, than it was to the attentions of the guard.

Joining Sissy's excitement on the first day were dear cousin Max of Hesse and his brother Fritz, Prince Sigismund, and Princess May. They carried flour, eggs, butter, milk, and other materials, all of which had been commandeered from the royal kitchens.

The stoutest heart would have quailed at the enterprise I had undertaken. To cook—or rather to teach a lot of riotous children to cook—on a stove whose capacities were not yet known, in a kitchen supplied chiefly with doll utensils, and to present the results of these efforts a short time later in a sort of combined tea and supper to the Emperor and Empress of Germany! And goodness only knew how many other people had been hospitably, but recklessly, invited.

It was very hot. Mosquitoes swarmed everywhere. The chimney smoked relentlessly till one of the footmen discovered a damper. The wood was wet. There was no water, no knives and forks, and we had forgotten the salt; but the affair had to be a success, and we persevered.

The Princess had decided that we would have pancakes for tea, the usual English kind made with eggs and milk, and the five children were accordingly sent outside on the veranda to beat eggs while I tried to review my resources and collect my thoughts. It was a dreadful business with a swarm of children asking questions in the loud-mouthed

German way, running up to show their eggs or spilling them on the floor.

By some miraculous means we managed to make a cake and ice it with chocolate, a sheer *tour de force* of inventive genius on my part, for I had never done such a thing before in my life. We cut quantities of thin bread and butter. And the much-beaten eggs duly mixed with flour and milk made excellent pancakes. Each child tasted them liberally and pronounced them *Grossartig!*

All too soon the Emperor and Empress were seen wending their way in our direction, accompanied, to the Princess's indignation, by two adjutants. "I never invited the gentlemen," she said. "There won't be half enough pancakes to go around."

I remained discreetly in the background, concentrating on frying. The tea was good because it was freshly made, and the pancakes for the same reason, hot from the fire and spared the usual long journey down the tunnel from the palace kitchens located across the Mopke from the dining rooms.

Their Majesties were, of course, served on dolls' plates; nevertheless, the Emperor ate with hearty appetite and appreciation, praising Sissy's cooking and obviously believing, in the usual facile masculine way, that she had suddenly acquired this difficult art. From my post at the frying pan, I heard her holding forth on the necessity of beating the eggs severely for ten minutes—she did not mention those that had escaped from the basin to the ground—and talking with the air of a person who had plumbed the depths of culinary challenges. "Yes, of course, they stick to the pan if you don't put in lots of butter—lots and lots." We had indeed used several pounds.

I think His Majesty accounted for four pancakes and then concentrated on chocolate cake and bread and butter. In time, the Empress noticed my absence, and I was compelled to appear, red-faced and greasy, and accept the imperial congratulations. Room was made for me to sit down with Their Majesties, and the chocolate cake was recommended.

"Fancy an Englishwoman knowing how to cook," the Emperor laughed. I firmly pointed out that not a single German lady inhabiting the palace had any culinary knowledge whatsoever, that their ideas were hazy and vague in the extreme, and that no one had helped in that afternoon's work. The Emperor's eyes twinkled. "Ah, ah!" he laughed, "the British Dreadnought again to the fore."

That was his name for me. Although as a rule only one of the three ladies of the Princess—Fräulein von Thadden, Mademoiselle Lauru, or myself—would accompany her to the Mittagessen, on one occasion we were all invited. As we followed her into the dining room, an adjutant remarked within the Emperor's hearing that the *Geschwader der Prinzessin*—the Princess's Squadron—had arrived.

This epithet to our trio amused His Majesty, and he tried during the meal to fit us with appropriate nautical names. Fräulein von Thadden, although she was tall and thin, was called the "tug," and Mademoiselle, the "torpedo-boat." He decided that "Dreadnought" was the term that best applied to me. The other ladies escaped any further reference to their supposed prototypes, but I was not so fortunate. Dreadnought—the construction of which in England was of obsessive interest to the Emperor—stuck to me. When I would appear in a new hat or dress, His

Majesty would say, "Here comes the Dreadnought in a new coat of paint."

It was at the same Mittagessen that we ladies for the first and only time had the privilege of taking wine with the Emperor. Usually on birthdays and anniversaries of various kinds, it was a custom at court to stand up and clink glasses together before drinking, but this was not often done with the Emperor present, although he sometimes drank wine with a particular gentleman whom he wished to humor. I had never seen a lady invited to take wine with His Majesty and believed it to be a privilege reserved for the sterner sex, but while I was chatting with Count Blumenthal at table, an officer on the other side touched my arm and whispered, "His Majesty wishes to drink wine with you. *Aufgestanden und Ausgetrunken!*—stand up and bottoms up!" The Emperor was smiling in my direction, glass in hand, so I stood up at once with my champagne glass filled to the brim, and was able to toss it off creditably, thanks to the adjutant's kindly hint and the comparative innocuousness of the beverage.

The Bauernhaus remained for several years a center of joyous-hearted hospitality and reckless and extravagant cookery. Once, a cousin of the Princess, Prince Leopold, came over to help prepare supper, accompanied by a French governess and an elegantly attired tutor in a top hat and frockcoat. There was not a place in our cookery scheme into which the tutor fitted, so we sent him and the French lady to walk about the gardens together, while the children sat down to peel potatoes for an Irish stew. Prince Leopold insisted, in spite of advice to the contrary, in also trying to peel the onions, but after weeping copious tears over the first one, he allowed me to finish. Besides the stew, we had chops, poached eggs, pancakes, and lemonade.

The Empress, wearing a light and lovely toilette, arrived at an acute stage of activity, when every child was running, shrieking, clattering glasses, or spilling water, while the sputter of chops and pancakes and the reek of frying filled the small kitchen. The Empress often came, and sometimes the Emperor with his suite of four gentlemen. It was the pancakes for tea that they liked, hot and crisp out of the pan—as did everyone in the palace who used to stroll down to the Bauern-Haus to see how the cooking was getting on. Count Blumenthal, especially, displayed, as did the Emperor, a shameless appetite for pancakes. To be both cook and hostess to so many guests is a strenuous business, and the Princess always abandoned the cooking as soon as her parents arrived, leaving me to carry on.

It was Ebert, the footman, who came out splendidly. He made the tea, wiped up the awful messes of eggs and milk that were spilled everywhere. By magic he brought order out of chaos and achieved what was never achieved even in the palace—hot plates for the pancakes. He was a patient, cheerful, helpful person, rushing breathlessly in the wake of the Princess with her raincoat over his arm. He constantly longed to go to Berlin to see his wife and his children in the evenings, and something always happened that prevented him from going. They had hard lives, those personal attendants on royalty. With the other footmen, Ebert was later conscripted into the Great War, and, from the other side, I thought of him often and prayed for his safety.

A heavy thunderstorm once threatened at the moment when the supper had reached the point of perfection. We

had fried our pancakes—they were always on the menu—
to the accompaniment of thunder and blue flashes of
lightning, but the Princess ignored the gathering storm,
absorbed in the mixing of her batter and the smoothness of
her potato purée. I emerged in a heated state from the
kitchen, to find Ebert protesting, standing on the veranda
pointing to the darkened heavens, and the Princess, with a
fork in her hand, flourished toward the sky like another Ajax
defying the lightning, emphatically refusing to return to the
palace before the supper was eaten.

"Our beautiful supper," she cried. "I won't go in. The
storm's nothing. It's going over."

A harassed Fräulein von Thadden appeared round the
bushes and commanded our instant return to the palace. In
the several minutes of heated discussion that followed, the
storm did pass over, and we ate our supper to the sound of
its rumbling retreat toward the river.

The Obergouvernante had disliked being beaten at
cooking by a mere Englishwoman, and she tried, after
watching our initial efforts, to make pancakes, too, when
it was her turn for service in the afternoon. All might
have gone well if they had not forgotten the butter. As
it was, I returned from shopping in Potsdam to a dis-
tressing odor of burnt flour floating down the staircase.
"What a horrid smell!" I exclaimed as I entered the dining
room. I knew well what it was, and I did not feel sorry about
it either.

"Yes, we burnt the pancakes. They were horrid. Why
was it?" the Princess moaned. Von Thadden looked
annoyed.

"I expect you forgot the butter," I said ostentatiously. "You must fry things in butter or lard or else they will burn."

Von Thadden groaned. "That was it, Sissy. We forgot the fat. And all our lovely eggs are wasted."

After this mishap, von Thadden did not venture on anything beyond potatoes roasted in the embers of a fire made in the garden by Ebert. Sissy used to bring me two grubby specimens, and I would eat them in my fingers while she watched me admiringly. Sometimes she wanted to send a burnt potato to Papa, but I advised against it. He was a willing eater of everything his daughter brought him, with the exception of the chocolate sausage that she made once with von Thadden. Of this masterpiece, he made derisive remarks, and not even the pink ribbon they tied around it could reconcile him to its edibility.

Another time, we ventured to make vanilla-ice and sent to the kitchen for the ice machine. As we were mixing the milk and eggs and vanilla flavoring, four white-capped cooks in their spotless livery came along dragging some sort of wheeled vehicle on which sat the heavy ice machine—which we found to our astonishment to be as large as a piano. Two cooks managed to lift it down, and we took turns at the handle with such diligence that the ice custard developed a rock-like consistency, and we had to thaw it before it was fit to eat.

*

Fräulein von Thadden's health had finally proved inadequate to the strenuous duties of her position. It was a mystery to me, in view of the medical certificates required from those of us who took up duties at court, that she had ever been selected for a post needing extraordinary powers of endurance. She had been given a long holiday of over six months, during which time she had undergone a severe internal operation.

Month after month, I had waited for her return, doing her work as well as my own and unable to have my yearly leave to England. But after the operation, by order of the Empress, two of the court physicians—one, von Thadden's nemesis, Dr. Zunker—were asked to judge, on the report of the doctor who was attending her, the probability of Fräulein von Thadden ever becoming fit for duty.

Both doctors were of the opinion that her health was liable to break down at any time, so the post of *Äbtissin*—directress—of an aristocratic girls' school—was found for her, and she was dismissed with a large *douceur* and ample provision for her future. During the time of her absence, she had been drawing her salary, of course, and all the expenses of her illness were paid by the Empress.

Unfortunately, the lady refused to retire gracefully. In spite of her long illness and its chronic nature, she professed no confidence in the impartiality of the two doctors and wrote furious letters to both physicians accusing them of favoritism and personal spite against her, an accusation which, at least in the case of one of the doctors, was absurd. Both gentlemen were incensed at her impugnment of their good faith.

Not content with this, the misguided woman repeated these accusations in a letter to the Empress and to several of the court ladies, who were much distressed to find that their paragon—they had always regarded von Thadden as the epitome of all the virtues—should show herself to be, as Countess Keller mournfully remarked, "so very small in mind."

The storm swept the court. Dr. Zunker said, "The late Obergouvernante was not a fit person to have the charge of our Princess," and Fräulein von Gersdorff said she was "surprised and disappointed" with her ingratitude. I, too, was surprised. I had always believed her when she called the ceremonies of court life "shams and absurdities" and understood them to be repellent to her. I had thought she would welcome the opportunity of being released from their contemplation.

She came to the palace once or twice later to visit the ladies, who—Countess Keller especially—had been most kind and considerate to her during her long illness, but she wore an air of suffering martyrdom which withered everyone's sympathy. "I am sent away," she said to me. "You see I am sent away. There have been lies—lies told about me. It is not the truth; I am well, quite well." She became vindictive and prophesied misfortune on those who had sent her away. She said that the Emperor had treated her abominably in allowing her to be dismissed; she maintained that she ought to have had a pension (after two years' service, one of which was consumed in sick leave!). The ladies were aghast.

Von Thadden was an extremely clever woman in many ways, but narrow in her outlook, bigoted in matters of religion, and, although she exercised a queer, hypnotic power over them, had no real understanding of children. Of their physical and mental needs she was appallingly ignorant.

In view of the Cassandra-like prophecies which she uttered on that last occasion of her visit to Berlin Schloss, it is highly probable that she eventually attributed all the misfortunes that were to befall the Hohenzollern family to the workings of a divine retribution, a celestial manifestation of displeasure at her dismissal from a post whose duties she was incapable of fulfilling.

The new Obergouvernante, Fräulein von Saldern, was a vague, confused, impulsive, good-natured little person, a complete contrast to von Thadden. Von Saldern had no lofty ideals, no special talents, no particular qualifications for the position she undertook, but she was likeable and friendly, and often rather foolish. Even that was a pleasant change from the universal propriety of conduct at court. I was truly glad at her coming, glad that it was no longer necessary for me to go down every day to those stately luncheons and dinners. My attendance was now necessary only twice a week; otherwise, I had my meals comfortably alone in my room with a book propped up in front and a friendly dachshund on the sofa.

*

The Princess had always revelled in birthday anniversaries and their preparations, and, when she was small, was fond of sprinkling the dinner table with flowers—taken out of any vases that happened to be standing nearby. The result of her efforts was to make the tablecloth very damp. The round dining table in her room had a festive appearance when she finished with it, and if one had difficulty in finding the bread or replacing a wine glass after drinking, these were small inconveniences to pay for the happy look of satisfaction in the young child opposite. Still, it was often difficult, on these special occasions, to keep the bunches of greenery out of one's soup, so thickly was the ornamentation spread.

As her birthday was on September 13, a time when the Emperor and Empress were away at the great autumn maneuvers, Sissy usually celebrated without the presence of any other family members, a fact that never troubled her at all. She had the whole of the palace to herself on that day, at her command—which she exercised to the fullest degree.

On the occasion of her thirteenth birthday, the Princess invited the pupils of one of the aristocratic girls' schools of which the Empress was a patroness, to have tea and games with her in the Wildpark, close to the New Palace. I was asked to draw up a program of sports for the day, as the games usually played on former birthdays were stigmatized by Sissy as *kindisch und albern*—childish and silly.

A list of various obstacle and flat races was arranged, as well as potato, egg-and-spoon, and sack races (which, I admit, I hesitated to introduce, fearing they were hardly fitting for the amusement of female German aristocracy, but I gave in under pressure from the honoree).

A delightfully smooth grassy spot surrounded by fir trees was the place chosen for the revels. The day was ideal for a September picnic—one of those warm, mellow autumn afternoons with magic melting blue distances, when departing summer seems to put on her loveliest attire and most attractive mood before saying her final farewell. All the mosquitoes—that plague of Potsdam in summer—had departed; the trees distilled their resinous balm in the sunshine; the beeches were beginning to turn tawny yellow; there was a sparkle in the air, exhilarating to the spirits.

Four *Kremserwagen*—enormous wagonettes much in request on fête days in Germany—brought smiling loads of happy young girls, dressed in neat white-linen uniform dresses and sailor hats. There were seventy or eighty of them, and six teachers. The proceedings began with tea. As soon as it was finished, the crowd of girls, reinforced by some of the young princes and princesses who came accompanied by their tutors—two young men wearing orthodox top hats and frockcoats and a general air of funereal respectability—began to play tag, drop the handkerchief, and other games which they confidently expected as the usual form of diversion.

We stopped them, and Sissy informed her celebrants that a totally new and superior form of entertainment had been provided for them, founded on English principles, of which I was to be the organizer and exponent. Nervous apprehension took possession of my soul, and I wended my way anxiously to our *Sportplatz*. Here the hurdles, corn-sacks, and other material had been brought from the palace stables by two grooms who had hoped to witness English sports from a suitable distance but were remorselessly sent away.

The ropes, red flags, buckets, eggs, spoons, and other things were regarded with excited anticipation and wonderment—especially the basket containing the prizes which, I may as well mention, cost individually not more than twopence each, collectively just eighteen shillings—a sum afterwards refunded to me by Her Majesty, who thought it "extremely cheap for so much joy," providing as it did, more than ninety prizes.

By a subtly arranged system of handicapping and consolation races, each girl, whatever her athletic abilities, won one of the coveted prizes, presented by the Princess herself, who, an ardent devotée of sport, competed with success in many of the races but waived her right to a prize.

This excursion into the unknown turned out a brilliant success: the teachers, who had been formed into a Sports Committee, with feminine intuition immediately grasped their duties, which they carried out with the greatest intelligence and impartiality; the girls were the keenest and most enthusiastic I ever met; their achievements in the sack race—won by the young Baroness Irma von Kramm—must have been seen to be believed ("Is this a usual English sport for ladies?" asked the headmistress, as they hopped screaming past the winning post). The only rift within the lute was the attitude of the tutors, which to say the least, was decidedly chilly. Perhaps they felt uncomfortable in the middle of that vortex of feminity, or they may have been offended at not being on the Committee or that they were not invited in their manly capacity to take direction of affairs. Be that as it may, they remained austere and aloof, only occasionally interfering when someone fell down or seemed likely to get overheated.

One of more genial mood than his fellows had stood near the hurdle in the obstacle race and on its being knocked over, proposed to substitute in its place a rope which, as he pointed out, "could be easily lowered as each girl jumped it," but his suggestion met with general derision—it was making a mockery of the competition—and the tutor retired from further participation.

*

One spring morning I was awakened by the agitated voice of Countess von Brockdorff. I got up quickly, wondering what could have brought that dignified lady up two flights of stairs to my top bedroom. It was to ask me if I felt capable of riding with the Emperor and Empress at quarter-past seven the next morning, as both the younger ladies-in-waiting, Fräulein von Gersdorff and Countess Stolberg, were suffering from colds.

Countess von Brockdorff was apologetic about asking me, but I wouldn't have missed it for anything. I had ridden several times with the Empress but never when she rode with her husband. To ride behind Wilhelm, with the clods his horse would kick up flying into my face, was one of those privileges I had never hoped would be mine.

I assured the Countess she might depend on me if only one of the ladies would take charge of the Princess in my absence, and she, much relieved, went downstairs again and sent her footman to tell the Kammerdiener of the Empress of the absence of the lady-in-waiting and that I would be able to take her place.

It was one of the laws of the palace that the Empress should never ride without an accompanying lady. If no lady had been available, she would have had to give up her ride. As to me, the hours I spent in the saddle were the most agreeable of the twenty-four. I was always ready to take the place of a lady who for any reason was not able to ride— and none of them was an enthusiastic horsewoman.

The next morning, feeling a trifle nervous and excited, I walked down the big staircase in my habit. The Sandhof was filled with beautiful horses and officers in uniform, Sattelmeister, grooms, and a dragoon detailed from one of the regiments.

The Sattelmeister were in full-dress uniforms of cocked hats and laced coats and with jack-boots. I bowed to those of the gentlemen I knew, and they looked at me askance. They knew it was not part of my job to ride with Their

Majesties. I ought to have been sitting at breakfast with the Princess. They were very jealous if they saw any attempt on the part of a subordinate to usurp the functions of a superior official. I thought it best to explain the situation to Herr von Mirbach, who was riding as a gentleman-in-waiting to the Empress. Then I got on my horse, for we all had to be in the saddle ready to start as soon as the Emperor and Empress were mounted.

Harlequin, a phlegmatic skewbald, was waiting by the steps. Finally, the Emperor, in Hussar uniform, came onto the terrace through one of the glass doors, and got on the lazy steed. The Empress issued from another door, mounted, and everybody fell into line behind them. The Master of the Horse, Herr Plintzer, rode with an eyeglass in his eye, which remained firmly in its place through the hardest gallops.

The sandy cart paths of the fields and villages made excellent places for galloping, and Their Majesties set their horses into long, swinging canters almost as soon as we were outside the palace gates. It was a lovely morning in May, the most beautiful month of the year in the Mark Brandenburg. The apple and cherry trees were in full blossom, the green corn was springing, larks were carolling, and I had an excellent, well-trained horse beneath me.

The Emperor had a good seat in the saddle; his bright red cap moved swiftly through the avenues of trees. Batteries of artillery came dragging their guns along the sandy roads. We were smothered in the dust they raised. They saluted and called out "Good Morning, Majesty," at the word of command. Then we were on the big *Exerzierplatz*, where Ulanen and infantry were exercising. We galloped right on over the plain, the Emperor saluting as he rode but never drawing rein until we got to the entrance to the gardens of Sans Souci, through which the cavalcade slowly returned homeward.

I hastened to my neglected Princess, who had been left in the charge of Marie, her maid. "You've been riding with Papa," she cried, "and I had to go to lessons! It's a shame!"

She certainly knew how to get round Papa. A few days later, I was again awakened from slumber and received the command to ride with Their Majesties "and the Princess." The ladies of the court would, I knew, consider it wrong of Their Majesties to take Victoria Louise out in the early morning when she was supposed to be at lessons, but I was helpless in the matter. I was, after all, not expected to be "firm" with the Emperor. That morning he was going to inspect one of the detachments of soldiers that was being sent off to Südwestafrika to replace the men lost in the Herero War.

In one slaughter of a German detachment ambushed by natives, the only son of the captain of the Emperor's river-steamer was killed. The grief-stricken father refused to believe the news. "My son was a doctor," he said repeatedly. "He was not a soldier. How could he be killed? Doctors are not in the fighting line. They're at the rear of the troops."

Often, the young officers who had volunteered for service in Südwestafrika were invited to luncheon at the palace. They were strong, handsome men, full of courage. The Princess would sigh and wish that she, too, could go to war and fight.

On this day, the detachment was drawn up on the Exerzierplatz. They had doffed their handsome uniforms and were in khaki, with slouched hats, and loose, workman-like jackets and breeches that separated them already from the comrades who would remain behind. The Princess was subdued. Never before had she seen men stripped of the superfluities of the barrackroom, out of their gay, expensive, impractical uniforms and prepared simply for the grim realities of war in a faraway country.

The Emperor gave a short, conventional speech telling them they were fighting for the glory of the Fatherland. But the speech fell flat. The Herero War had lasted too long; enthusiasm had waned. The war had added nothing to the military glory of Germany and had taught the Germans a great deal about the difficulties of skirmishing in an uninhabited country where none of the rules of war in which they had been trained seemed to apply. One could feel that the Emperor himself was sick to death of such a profitless venture.

We galloped home to meet a severe-faced tutor, Herr Gern. "Where were you, Princess?" he demanded—ignoring me completely; was I not an accomplice in this crime?—"I have been waiting here an hour for you to come to your lessons."

"The Kaiser commanded me to ride with him," said the Princess, using that awful name as a shield. "I couldn't help it."

That afternoon the Princess suggested that we should make a chocolate cake in the Bauernhaus and give it to Herr Gern. I recognized immediately that the child had an insight into the nature of men that would most likely prove far more valuable than the missed lesson in Euclid.

*

After their marriage, the Crown Prince and Princess Cecilia lived at the Marmor Palace; here, all of their children were born. The arrival of the first little boy, Prince Wilhelm, was an exciting day for all of Germany. The great event happened about eight o'clock in the morning, and by eleven o'clock, picture postcards were on sale in which the Crown Princess, naively represented in evening dress, was depicted holding in her arms one of those dreadful abominations called a *Steckkissen*, a sort of flat pillow much used in the Fatherland, on which lay a solid-looking infant purporting to be the newly born Prince.

This same child on the same Steckkissen was also on another postcard, lying on the knees of the Emperor, who was smiling into the middle distance. It bore the inscription, "The First Grandchild." As His Majesty was cruising off Kiel on the *Hohenzollern* at the time, he didn't see his first grandchild until six weeks after he was born, but manu facturers of postcards are not disturbed by minor details of this nature.

Later on, the Emperor mentioned at table that, owing to the forgetfulness of the young officer charged with the forwarding on board of his mail, the telegrams informing him of the happy event did not reach him for a good many hours after they arrived in Kiel; and it was from a con gratulatory message handed on board from the Sultan of Turkey that His Majesty first heard that he was a grandfather.

The fact that the Empress was a grandmother and she herself an aunt made the Princess very thoughtful for a time. She indulged for some time in long fits of silence, pondering this new development. The christening was of great interest to her, because the youngest Hohenzollern princess was always chosen to carry the infant to the font. She practiced this ceremony a few times with a white cushion to which was pinned a long tablecloth to represent the white satin train which Hohenzollern babies wore at the ceremony. The train was embroidered with the name of every prince and princess who had worn it, and a new string had to be added for every christening, so that the imagination refused to consider the length to which it might have inevitably extended in the course of ages. The train was carried by four ladies of noble birth and was fastened, not to the infant himself, but to the white satin cushion.

Royal christenings were celebrated in the long Jasper Gallery in the New Palace, a magnificent apartment, which, owing to its length, was also the favorite scene of indoor sports for the Princess and her friends when wet weather prevented their indulgence outside. Only the week after the christening, seventy-five girls from the Augustastift were invited to the palace, but the afternoon had turned out hopelessly wet, so the gymkhana that had been planned had to take place indoors or not at all. The Jasper Gallery proved itself an excellent place for egg-and-spoon races as well as for the needle-threading and bun-eating contests. The mirrors which had lately reflected the stately tread, the brilliant uniforms, and the trailing dresses of the courtiers, now duplicated and reduplicated a seemingly endless procession of wildly hopping maidens with jerking pigtails, who, shrieking with laughter and accompanied by many tumbles, bumped along over the marble pavement to the goal.

A few rooms near the gallery had once been occupied by Frederick the Great. One of them still contained his harpsichord, and in another, row upon row, were left the books he loved—all in French, not a single German one among them.

Sometimes, the children would storm violently through these older rooms, where all was left as much as possible undisturbed. The faded green silk curtains waved and trembled as the girls passed boisterously onward. Once, I saw the yellow parchment label bearing the old King's handwriting drop from the back of a book in the glass case, shaken from its precarious hold by the rush of active young feet.

Those were eerie places, where one did not care to linger long alone when the shadows of night were falling. It was easy to imagine a bent old figure in a crushed-looking cocked hat, rusty knee-boots, and a blue-lapelled riding coat peering round the corner to see who was disturbing the silence, watching the flight of that impetuous child of his house as her laugh echoed back toward the deserted rooms, where, for a few moments, the air, awakened from the stifled atmosphere of the shut-up apartment, was startled into movement by her footsteps on the polished floor.

The foresters at Rominten hold up antlers for the Emperor's inspection. Note how many lay on the ground: numbers were the sole aim of the hunt. One year, after three days of hunting, the Emperor boasted that he and his guests had bagged over sixteen hundred head of game. (Photo by Anne Topham.)

THE HUNTING LODGE

The Emperor's favorite shooting domain, Rominten, was far away in East Prussia on the Russian frontier. Every autumn, huge loads of antlers labelled *"Rominterheide"* would arrive at the New Palace—the most recent trophies of His Majesty's gun.

One midsummer day the Princess announced, to the consternation of Countess Keller, that Papa was building a new wing to the *Jagdhaus* so that Mamma and she might join him there. "Won't it be lovely," she said, and danced about the room.

"When you are grown up and done with lessons, Princess," suggested Keller.

"Not a bit when I am grown up. This autumn. Papa says so—the house will be ready by September."

If Papa said a thing would happen, it usually did, let who might disapprove. So a few weeks later, the Princess, in her new hunting dress, accompanied by a blackboard, a desk, a large chest of schoolbooks, Herr Porger, and I, went off to join Their Majesties' special train at Berlin.

The Emperor and Empress were waiting for us in the train, and there was a very large suite with them, including Prince Philip von Eulenburg, a frequent companion of the Emperor and the most beloved of his friends.

The Empress was attended only by Countess Stolberg, who would be on duty the whole time. But in Rominten, there were no ceremonious occasions and no constant changes of costume—one of the chief burdens of court life—so the duties were comparatively light.

The Emperor was in a hilarious mood, his face crinkled with laughter. He told one small anecdote after another, some of them almost childish, but irresistibly comic when accompanied by his infectious laugh. One was of a child at a *Volksschule* who wrote an essay on the lion as follows: "The lion is a fearful beast with four legs and a tail. He has a still more terrible wife called the tiger."

The royal hunt uniform, which is worn only by those in the royal service and those to whom the Emperor grants permission, was picturesque, a soft olive-green, with high tanned-leather boots and a belt around the waist from which was suspended the *Hirschfänger*—hunting knife. In the soft green hat, turned up at both sides, was generally fastened either the tail-feathers of the capercailzie or the beard of a gemsbok, which stuck up like a shaving brush at the back.

At supper on the train, everybody was wearing ordinary clothes, but they assembled at breakfast in complete hunting-dress, even to the footmen. Although I possessed no uniform, I was unwilling to be a jarring note in the hunting harmony and so had provided myself with a suitable green *Sportskostüm*, while the Princess had a regulation green *Letevka*—Norfolk jacket.

The train passed through the Cadinen station—the farthest in the Empire I had been to at that time—and it was a further journey of eight hours to reach Gross-Rominten, a village that was still seven or eight miles from the hunting lodge itself.

Formerly, the village where the Emperor had built himself a house was called *Teerbude*—Tarbooth. It was a poor place, inhabited by people who made a spare living by distilling tar from the pine trees. Although the 90,000-acre forest belonged to the Crown, it had not been properly developed and was in a neglected condition.

A stream called the Rominte ran through the district, so the Emperor changed the name of the place to Rominten and as usual set himself to build and improve. His frequent visits to Norway had given him a love for the houses there, built of pine logs; and having the necessary material at hand, he built in the Norwegian style of architecture.

The road to the Jagdschloss lay through long vistas of pines which grew to an enormous height, though a few years before, the devastations of the caterpillar called *die Nonne*—the nun—destroyed the trees and made a fearful havoc. The road wound past places where whole plantations had perished and all the young trees were "in mourning" —they each had bands of tar-smeared paper round their trunks to prevent inroads of the insidious enemy. The Emperor tried to persuade me that the black bands had been put on the trees because an *Oberförster* was dead, but being of a sceptical turn of mind and knowing a little about forestry, I accepted the imperial explanation with some reserve.

At the village of Rominten, cut young pine trees were set at intervals along the road and triumphal garlands of pine branches stretched across it. Before the entrance to the Schloss ranged lines of sturdy woodmen and foresters in their smart uniforms, holding torches in their hands: night fell early in this region, and the immense trees growing so close to the house intercepted a good deal of light. In the inner gravelled space between the two parts of the Schloss were waiting the Oberförster, gentlemen of education and culture, who were trained for years in the excellent German schools of forestry.

Also there to meet Their Majesties was Baron Speck von Sternburg, whose brother was at that time the German ambassador in Washington. Von Sternburg was the head administrator of the whole forest; he lived and moved throughout it from year to year and knew every stag that roamed its solitudes. He was responsible for the Emperor's sport and made all arrangements. Von Sternburg knew by heart the habits—almost the thoughts—of the deer and could tell at what particular moment they would come out to browse on the open meadows that were dotted about like small green islands in the vast ocean of trees.

All of the houses of the Oberförsters were in telephonic communication with the Schloss, so that they could send word at once of any animal paying an unexpected visit, as sometimes wolves and elk were known to wander over the Russian frontier.

The Emperor was barely descended from his carriage before he began the hunting talk with Herr von Sternburg.

In the meanwhile, the Empress and the Princess entered the house to explore.

The Schloss was really two houses, built entirely of pine logs, and connected by an overhead gallery supported on massive pine stems as thick as the masts of a ship. In every room, the walls consisted of the bare logs, which had been trimmed into slightly oval form and laid one on top of the other, the whole then smoothly varnished. Tables and chairs were made of the same wood, and the green carpets with a moss-like pattern carried on the woodland theme.

The roof was deep and low, and the upper story had a gallery running its length which overshadowed the windows of the lower rooms, making them rather dark. The fireplace and chimneys were made of unglazed red brick, and the fire of logs was built on a wide, flat hearth, raised a little above the floor level. All was simple, solidly, ruggedly built. The log walls had one drawback: smells and sounds penetrated their crevices easily. If the footman in the basement indulged in a cigar, the Empress in her sitting room upstairs was instantly aware of it.

The dining room, which was in the part of the house occupied by the Emperor, was a fine room with a high-pitched roof of massive beams, from which hung many trophies of the chase, fallen to His Majesty's gun. There was a long, wide window to the left, two large brick fireplaces at the end, a sideboard with a buttery-hatch into the kitchen, and wooden chairs surrounding the massive table which were penitential in their hardness. Since His Majesty sat on them with no cushions, no one dared complain.

The Emperor once overheard some comment of mine relative to the chairs' unyieldiness. "What's the matter with the chairs?" he asked sharply, bulging his eyes at me. "Don't you like them?"

"Yes, Your Majesty," I replied, "they are beautiful chairs, but somewhat—er—harsh on first acquaintance."

"Harsh?" he laughed derisively. "I hope they are! Time you came here and learned to do without cushions. Here, we live hardily." He asked every day thereafter if the chairs were getting a little softer.

Certain friends of His Majesty came every year with him to Rominten. First and foremost among them was Prince von Eulenburg, who was a pale, gray-haired, somewhat weary-looking man with a pallid, fleeting smile, something of a visionary, with a nature attracted to music and art, as well as toward all that was strange or unusual in life.

Prince von Eulenburg was a born raconteur, like the Emperor, but he told his tales in a quiet, soft, subtle voice, with a grave face and a certain fascinating charm. One could easily understand how the robust personality of the Emperor, so frank, so open, was attracted to the somewhat reserved, mysterious, gentle nature of this brilliant man, who yearly entertained His Majesty at his own home, Schloss Leibenberg, accompanied the Emperor on his Norwegian cruises, and was the repository of His Majesty's thoughts and aspirations.

Only a year or two after my first visit to Rominten, however, Prince von Eulenburg disappeared in disgrace, and Rominten knew him no more. Yet probably no one was ever more missed than he, whose name was never again mentioned. I can still see his pale face emerge from behind the red curtains of the gallery when he came to the tea table of the Empress and sat down to entertain us with his store of literary and artistic reminiscences. He had the look, even then, of an ill man, a man whose nerves are not in the best condition, who is pursued by some haunting specter, some fear from which he cannot escape.

A man of a different type who also came yearly was Prince Dohna of Schlobitten, a tall, elderly gentleman who was a mighty hunter. We were much indebted to him for instruction in the proper terms of venery, for, as the Princess impressed on us, it was impossible when at Rominten to speak of any part of an animal by its usual name. "Nose, eyes, ears, and tail" were shocking to the ear and were changed into something technical and sporting. The "ears" of hare, for example, had to be called its "spoons," and the feet of the deer became "runners"—I think—but it may have been something else.

*

In spite of his belief in the special mission of the Hohenzollern family to carry out divine purposes—an idea not corroborated by the course of history—the Emperor was in every respect more democratic than his court. The magic *von* had, under his influence, lost some of its prestige, and he bestowed the coveted syllable on certain people whom he desired to see at court, and invited to his table many men not enjoying the prepositional advantage. One of them, Herr Ballin, the head of the Hamburg-American line of steamships, was a Jewish entrepreneur. Ballin was even asked to Rominten, where only the elect expected to meet each other. Not only that, a rare privilege was conceded to him: he was allowed to go stag hunting and, worse still, bagged three fine specimens, one of them a stag-royal.

What made this more galling to the blue-blooded

entourage was that a special friend and adjutant of the Emperor, the Princes' tutor at Plön, charming old General von Gontard, had been accorded a similar favor, but came back time and time again without the coveted spray of oak leaves in the back of his hat.

A universal groan would go up from the lingerers in the courtyard as the yellow *Jagdwagen* appeared in sight and still no *Spruch* was visible. "There, the General has again had no luck!" they would sigh. It became monotonous to see the General depart, all smiles in his green uniform, amid a chorus of *Weidmanns Heil*, and watch him return sadly at dusk.

*

One notable visitor came once to Rominten for a short stay of an hour or two on his way back to Russia from America—a rather stern, silent, harassed-looking man, with an air of abstraction beside the Emperor as they walked up and down on the Sand-Hof before the Jagdhaus. It was Herr Witte, the Russian statesman soon to become Count Witte, on his way home after negotiating terms of peace between his country and Japan. At table, he sat eating soup somewhat nervously, with the air of a man in a dream, listening politely to the Emperor's talk, replying in monosyllables, but conversing with no one else. He was tired and apprehensive. Soon after dinner we saw his carriage departing for the station. He was in Russia before nightfall.

*

Our table conversation at Rominten was more stimulating than elsewhere. The Emperor—never reserved—spoke with even more abandon and was always in good spirits. It was at the Rominten dinner table that he talked a good deal about Russia, partly because of the recent Russo-Japanese War, and also perhaps because Russia lay only a few miles away. The officer in command of the frontier Russian garrison was invited to lunch during the Emperor's three-week stay. He was a tall, bullet-headed man, still young, and his chest was covered with decorations. When I once expressed to Count Blumenthal my surprise that one so young should possess such a number of distinctions, the governor answered with contempt, "Those are only *Bahnsteigdekorationen*—railway platform decorations. He has to form a guard of honor at the first Russian station whenever a royalty travels through, and they all send him something to add to his collection."

The Emperor, too, was indignant on the subject of the Russian fondness for decorations and the unblushing way in which they begged for them. On the occasion of the Emperor's visit to the Czar in St. Petersburg, one Russian officer was asked on what grounds he considered himself deserving of a decoration, and he answered that he had been in the room several times when the Emperor had passed through.

The Emperor also held some strong opinions on the Japanese, with whom, to his great disgust, England had just concluded a treaty. "You people make a treaty with such people!" he exclaimed, turning to me and speaking angrily and, as usual, holding me responsible. He proceeded to relate anecdotes all turning on the supposed treachery and cunning of the Japanese. One was of an English naval captain who had had a Japanese cook serving in the galley of his ship. Two years later, this same captain, on visiting a Japanese battleship, discovered that his former "cook" was, in reality, one of the superior officers of the battleship.

Another tale was to the effect that, during the war, a Russian ship, having seized and taken a Japanese passenger steamer, discovered in the luggage of some of the men on board, papers setting forth, among other things, the number of native regiments in India, the names of their British officers, and copious notes as to the possibility, if trouble arose, of their loyalty or disaffection to the British Raj.

He addressed these stories, which I believed to be quite well authenticated, across the table to me, speaking in English. When he reached the culminating point, revealing Japanese duplicity, he repeated his former remarks, thumping his clenched fist on the table. "And with people like these you form an alliance!"

"It proves at any rate, Your Majesty," I said, "that the Japanese are not at all behind Europe in their secret service organization." I do not know, to this day, if the Emperor really believed that military espionage was an activity peculiar to the Japanese.

*

At the time of the Russo-Japanese War in 1904, the feeling of the German public was entirely on the side of the Orientals, but the Emperor's sympathies—and those of his family—were wholeheartedly on the side of Russia. "If they"—the Russians—"do not sweep back the Japanese, we shall have to do it some day," the Emperor would often remark.

Sissy, a great enthusiast for any cause she undertook, asked every child who came in to play with her in which direction lay her sympathies: Japanese or Russian. If a child hesitated, she was treated with scorn as a person of intellectual weakness. Sissy was grieved, however, to discover that every time she pursued the inquiry to the bitter end, it was a partisan of Japan that was revealed.

At that point, she would count on her fingers the reasons for her hope of Japan's ultimate defeat. "First of all, because they are heathen," she would say. "And secondly, because of Tante Alix [the Czarina], and thirdly, because we shall have to beat them if the Russians don't."

*

Every morning in the early darkness, sometime between five and six, or perhaps even earlier, the panting of a motorcar could be heard outside, and presently it would depart, bearing away the Emperor and his loader to some remote corner of the forest where a lordly stag had been marked as coming in the early mornings to *nasch*.

At eight, the Princess and I breakfasted alone in the corridors outside Her Majesty's sitting room. Often, we made ourselves buttered toast at the big fire which blazed on the hearth. One morning, the Princess, who had a feminine instinct for that sort of thing, took a succulent plateful of this delicacy down to His Majesty, who happened for a wonder to be at home for breakfast at the appointed hour. (Rominten was the only place where Their Majesties breakfasted with the suite; usually, it was a meal taken *en famille* and at a very rapid pace.)

The Emperor appreciated the Princess's buttered toast so much that the Empress directed that some should be sent down every morning. Now, buttered toast is quite unknown in the Fatherland, excepting perhaps in large fashionable hotels where international customs prevail. Rather leathery dry toast is served at tea. When the royal command for buttered toast reached the kitchen through the medium of the footman, it created nothing short of consternation. A flurried lackey came hastening up to me, begging for some slight hints as to how it should be made. I foresaw that any instructions I might give, when they reached the cook distilled through the mind of the footman, would be vague and unsatisfactory. I did my best, but the Empress told me later that the toast was inedible, a result that gratified the Princess, who believed she was the only person capable of making toast for Papa.

Lessons with Herr Porger lasted until twelve o'clock, when a short walk with the Empress was taken, weather permitting. After luncheon, if the stag or stags slain by the Emperor had arrived, we were all assembled under the dining-room window for the ceremony of the *Strecke*. The stags were laid on the small lawn beneath the windows, and three of the Jäger blew the *Ha-la-li* on the hunting horns, instruments strongly reminiscent of cornets. Those hunting calls, instituted and partly composed by Louis XV, always reminded me—I don't know why—of the Last Post.

Between three and four in the afternoon, the Emperor in his hunting cart would start off again to shoot, the Empress and the suite shouting *Weidmanns Heil!* as he drove away. Then the rest of us, including the Empress and the Princess, would climb into the yellow-varnished hunting carts and drive in the opposite direction to try to get a glimpse of stags browsing.

Our conversation had to be rather suppressed for fear of alarming the deer in their sylvan silence, and we descended from the carts to walk to one of the numerous pulpits, as they were called—small raised platforms screened by a frame of pine twigs, from which the Emperor sometimes shot, although as a rule they were used for observation only, and the shooting was done from behind another screen below.

It was tantalizing going to see the deer feed, because often they didn't appear. The stairs up to the pulpits creaked and groaned as anyone weighty went up them, and the rest regarded the guilty one with annoyed looks and said, "Shshsh." When the stags did appear, stepping out proudly from the dark shadows of the trees, it was a fine sight. The deer on the Rominterheide were remarkable for their splendid antlers. There are few things more graceful than the manner in which a stag carries his wide-spreading ornaments, especially when running with the speed of the wind in the forest.

One day, when the Empress had been with the Princess in the village visiting some of the cottages, we were met at the gate of the Schloss by an excited footman, who said that an *Elch*—which I took to mean a moose or an elk—had been seen by the Baroness von Sternburg in the forest, and that the Emperor had ordered out all the automobiles and carriages and that every available person was to serve as a beater, Her Majesty and the Princess and we ladies of the suite included.

Everyone flew in and out of the Schloss fetching walking sticks and cloaks, and in a few seconds the first automobile, containing the Emperor and Empress, the Princess, Countess Stolberg and I, and the Emperor's loader, with the heavy sporting rifles being outside with the chauffeur, started off in pursuit of this animal which, not having a proper sense of political boundaries, had wandered over from Russia in the night. We hoped it had not wandered back again, but I had a sneaking sort of feeling down in my heart that I should be almost glad if it had done so.

The car flew along, the Emperor talking wildly about the Elch and its habits and his hopes of slaying the trusting creature, and at last we were deposited eight miles from home on a marshy piece of ground. There we were met by Baron von Sternburg and commanded to follow him in perfect silence, the Emperor meantime going on in the car in a different direction.

After a long, damp walk, we were posted at intervals of about a hundred yards along a thick alley of pines, with whispered instruction to stay where we were and prevent the quarry from breaking through, although we all had grave doubts as to our ability to prevent any animal as large as a moose from doing anything it felt inclined. I went up to the gentleman on my left and whisperedly asked what methods I must employ supposing the mighty beast suddenly appeared in front of me, and he indicated a feeble waggling of the hands as being likely to turn it back in the direction of the Emperor's gun.

I cannot say if we should have been able to intimidate the moose by means of the maneuver; we were not put to the test, for after waiting for nearly two hours and growing minute by minute more ravenously hungry, while the water penetrated our boot soles, it became evident that the sagacious animal must have returned to his native wilds. We returned sadly to our long-delayed, over-cooked dinner, where we found the unfortunate Herr Porger in a typical pique—he had been waiting for his food without any of the alleviating excitement of the chase.

*

At Rominten, the court indulged in freshwater crayfish—almost the size of small lobsters—which were handed around in a kind of silver fish-kettle from which we extricated them with long, curved, silver forks. Though delicious, they were tiresome things to eat, as one had to dissect them thoroughly to get at the best morsels, which always lurked in the more inaccessible parts. Most of the gentlemen took them bodily in their hands and sucked them. In whatever way one chose to eat them, the water in which they had been boiled ran down one's sleeve and onto one's knees. We always wore our oldest evening dresses when *Krebs* appeared on the menu.

*

During one visit to Rominten, an inspection of the officers at the nearest German garrison took place. The Emperor—as was the custom of all Hohenzollern sovereigns —went around the ranks of soldiers asking questions and testing their general knowledge. The Empress, the Princess, and the ladies of the court were sitting in a gallery overlooking the courtyard, and we could see and hear distinctly all that went on below. One remark I heard as the Emperor stopped directly underneath the gallery. "What is a grenadier?"

"A soldier," was the reply.

"Yes, but what kind of soldier? What does he do?"

I caught sight of the face of the young lieutenant in command of this platoon and never saw groping perplexity written more large on any man's face.

The Emperor, not getting a satisfactory answer from the young soldier, proceeded to instruct him in the function of a grenadier as primarily a thrower of hand grenades, explaining in detail how first of all a few grenadiers were attached to each regiment of soldiers, how later on whole companies of them were formed, and when the fashion of throwing bombs by hand went out, the name was retained. "But it is quite possible," the Emperor said, "that with the new explosives that have been discovered, hand grenades will again be used in modern warfare with practical effect. And the name 'grenadier' will mean what it originally did."

*

Once, on our way from Rominten back to Berlin, we had a disagreeable adventure in Königsberg, where the Emperor stayed for a few hours to dine at the officers' mess of one of the grenadier regiments stationed there.

We had started from Rominten very early in the morning, and the Princess, rather unluckily as it turned out, was still wearing her green hunting uniform, although the rest of us had reverted to ordinary costumes. The Emperor and his suite were to stop at Königsberg, while the Empress, Sissy, the ladies, Prince von Eulenburg, and the gentleman-in-waiting, Count Karmer, after a short wait of half an hour to let the express to Berlin pass before us, would proceed to Cadinen, there to await the arrival of His Majesty toward evening.

We had all descended onto the red-carpeted platform to witness the reception of the Emperor and had seen him drive away amidst the cheers of an immense crowd, when the Princess begged her mother to fill up the intervening twenty minutes left to us by a "short walk." She was tired

of being in the train. The Empress agreed, although someone suggested that moving about in such a crowd would
be difficult.

We walked across the space in front of the station
which had been kept clear by the police, in full view of the
enormous mass of people gathered there; the Princess in her
green uniform was a very conspicuous object. A pleasant
elderly officer was to escort us on what the Empress called
"our little stroll through the town." Full of apprehension,
we walked over the empty space, the Empress chatting to
the officer, while the rest of us looked at each other, trying
to think that what we foresaw must happen would perhaps
not be so inevitable. Most of the extra policemen drafted
into the town had been placed on the streets along the route
where the Emperor would pass, and, as we had directed our
steps to a more secluded thoroughfare, there were none to
be seen anywhere.

The people began to cheer wildly as soon as they
realized that the Empress was before them, for her name
naturally had not been included in the program of the day's
ceremonies. The crowd broke up at once with a yelp of
astonished joy and flung itself with blind ardor upon our
small group. It was a wonder to see the orderly, apparently
disciplined crowd of a moment before, which had waited
peacefully for the Emperor's return, suddenly disintegrate
into a wildly running horde, to watch the policemen,
excited and nonplussed at the unexpected turn of events, be
swept like leaves before the wind. Their shouts and blows
were powerless to stem that torrent of humanity.

"Let's get back to the station," implored the Empress.
We all wanted to return to the station, but a glance behind

showed its impossibility. All we could do was keep on, an officer pointing out a sidestreet which he thought led back to the station in another direction. The officer kept shouting vain appeals to the crowd, which became every moment denser, ruder, and dirtier. It was the hour when the workshops and factories vomited forth their occupants for Mittagessen, so that it soon became a crowd of Socialists and Jewish Poles. Unfortunately, our road led through some of the worst quarters of the town.

The cheering and hurrahing soon ceased, but the shouting and yelling went on: we were the center of a frowzy mob which smelled abominably and treated our small group as though we were a show of some kind out for their amusement. The officer again appealed to the better feelings of the people, and begged the dirty children to remember what they had been taught in school, but they only laughed and darted in and out and laid their filthy hands on the dress of the Empress.

In my younger days, I had learned from a schoolboy brother a certain sudden grip at the back of the neck, which we often employed in any slight dispute. As these horrible children grew bolder and more repulsive, I found this old "choker," as we had called it, very useful in intercepting them. As a yelling boy bumped along, he was suddenly brought up short in mid-career and, by a grip at the nape of his neck, flung back among his comrades. Although it was warm work for such a hot day, I continued unweariedly, with a certain sporting pleasure which struck me at the time as amusing, to capture one filthy youngster after another and fling him violently back into the roadway. The officer still shouted after policemen, and, presently, one was walking beside me, also aiding in the good work of chucking out.

Gradually, a few more policemen were picked up and we got into a rather more respectable neighborhood, but the crowd was still frightfully dense and the policemen banged and thrust unmercifully. Sometimes quite innocent, unsuspecting people just coming out of their own doorways were taken by the shoulders and whirled back into their homes again. At last we came again in view of the station, and a mass of policemen took us in charge, still very nervous—the policemen, I mean—and very irritated with the crowd, and perhaps a little with us.

The time for the train was overdue. We scrambled in hurriedly, but the Empress wished to show the officer some recognition of the strenuous activity he had displayed on her behalf. The gentleman-in-waiting hastily produced a case full of those royal monogrammed scarfpins, studs, and brooches which are part of the travelling equipment of every court. The officer received a tie-pin, thrust into his hands almost as the train moved off, and we were left to review and discuss the experiences of the last half hour.

"Never, no, never in the course of my experience," declared the Empress, "was I in such a fearful crowd. I began to think that we never should emerge alive. It was too horrible." She shuddered. The Princess was unusually pale and subdued.

In the next morning's *Königsberg er Nachrichten Times*, there was a paragraph in the news column to the effect that the Empress and the Princess, with a small following, had walked *ungezwungen*—freely—through the town for a short time. Obviously, the reporter had not been in the thick of the crowd.

*

Another time, returning from Rominten, we stopped at Marienburg, the town where in former days there had been a castle of Teutonic Knights, that ancient fighting order of monks whose task it was to Christianize by sword the heathen Croats and Poles—and Prussians, but the Emperor did not mention them—who lived between the Vistula and the Memel.

The ancient fortress of these old Crusaders had fallen into ruins, its stones removed to build other houses; one of its few remaining buildings was used for storing grain. The Emperor had set about recreating the medieval fortress-monastery. Upon the ancient ruins, he had rebuilt new magnificent constructions of red brick, the building medium which is universal along that coast of the Baltic. There was a splendidly restored chapel, and on the sunny Sunday that we stopped morning service was held.

We descended from the royal train and walked to the huge buildings which overshadowed the quiet little town. There, we were conducted through the great door of the citadel into a courtyard and thence along new red-brick Gothic cloisters into the chapel, which, though beautifully fitted with stained-glass windows and replicas of the ancient furniture, somehow failed to touch the imagination. All was too new and lacked the crumbling touch of time, the glamour of the past. Only one thing was dramatic: the entry of the Emperor.

We were all standing, the Empress and the Princess before two Gothic chairs placed opposite the altar. Between them was another chair of rather different style. All the ladies and gentlemen of the suite and certain officials were ranged on each side. The body of the church was filled with a congregation who had been invited to attend, neighboring landowners with their families.

There was a dead silence. The empty throne seemed to be waiting. Then I was aware of the Emperor in his long, gray military cloak, helmet in hand, coming slowly, very slowly, with a queer kind of strut, up the center of the chapel. He was alone.

He stepped into the chancel with a dramatic air. His face was stern and tragic, as it was apt to be in public. He was obviously full of the sense of the part that he was playing— the part of a hero of romance. One knew that he saw himself as one of those ancient knights, that he felt that he, too, would with his sword preach the gospel—the gospel of his own power.

The Emperor, tired of waiting for von Zeppelin's LZ-5 airships, reclines in the arms of his daughter. Prince Oskar is sitting next to her. The rest of the Emperor's entourage "lingers in the background." (Photo by Anne Topham.)

POLITICAL INTIMATIONS

One wet evening while the court was staying in Berlin, a rather wheezy, whining music could be heard emanating from the salon of the Princess. Its tunes rose and fell, presently increasing in volume, and becoming every moment more insistent. Suddenly, the door of my sitting room, where I was trying to write letters, burst open, and though at first I could see no explanation of this phenomenon, soon around the table crawled the Princess herself, on all fours, dragging beside her the instrument of torture—a miniature barrel organ. The music, of an appallingly strident nature, was ground out relentlessly by the Princess, playing the parts of both the street organ-grinder and—doubtless from the intimate knowledge gathered during visits to the Berlin Zoo—his monkey, as well.

When the music at last blessedly subsided, a blue muffin-cap belonging to Prince Joachim was thrust toward me, and in broken German-Italian I was requested to donate something toward the support of the musician and the monkey. Already a few nickel Pfennigs lay there, indicating that other members of the court had been solicited. I presented a few pfennigs, and the musician-monkey scampered away.

Later on, I saw Sissy, while dressing for dinner, counting up her gains. "What shall you do with all that money?" I asked.

"I shall give it to the Navy League," she said seriously, and began to count it over again. I went out, laughing to myself to think that I had contributed the sum of one half-penny to the German Navy League, the avowed instrument of the "blue water" party in Germany, which was so bitterly hostile to England.

A few days later I saw, for the first time, the great inspirer of modern German naval policy and of the Navy League, *Grossadmiral* von Tirpitz, who lunched at the royal table, where he became a fairly frequent guest. Von Tirpitz was good looking, of a tall, straight figure, bald-headed, and wore an exceptionally long, thin beard. His face was fine featured and pale, and his eyes were seldom engaged with the immediate surroundings. He was a quiet man who smiled rarely and fleetingly at the Emperor's quips and sallies. Before lunch was served, he did not enter into conversation with any of the suite, but after grave and formal greetings, stood apart, wrapped in his own thoughts. His place at table was beside the Emperor, and, from mine near the end, I would often glance up from my plate and catch the concentrated look of his brown eyes musingly fixed on me. I wondered if he were looking through me absently at something beyond, or if I reminded him of the

British Empire and the many things in our British policy that are an eternal puzzle to the German mind.

Of all the men who came to court, von Tirpitz seemed to me the most able and sagacious, perhaps because he was so silent. He never gave an opinion, he never revealed his thoughts in public, he was always coldly polite, formal, and dignified.

The building of the first English Dreadnought formed at that time the chief topic of conversation among the upper social circles of Berlin. No one ever heard von Tirpitz air his views on them in society, but he began building German equivalents without any delay, wringing the money from a public which he had educated into a frenzied desire to have them.

The following year in September, I went for three weeks to Plön, where the young Princes were educated. Being so near to Kiel, I thought it would be a pity not to go and see the famous harbor and the German fleet. Kindly escorted by an amiable young German lieutenant with whose wife I was friendly, I went to Kiel and saw a part of the German war fleet anchored in the landlocked harbor—ten warships lying like flat-irons on the water. The lieutenant was possessed with a childlike desire that I should be impressed by the majesty and sufficiency of German naval preparedness, and took me around the harbor in a small steamer. "They are fine, are they not?" he said, waving his hand at the distant warships.

"Very fine," I replied. "Nearly as fine as ours at home." He winced. It is one of the drawbacks of German education that it does not prepare a man for light badinage on subjects which touch his national pride.

"Nearly as fine!" he said angrily. "You wait awhile. You will see if our navy is 'nearly as fine'. We intend to have the best navy in the world. You just wait a little longer."

"All your warships burn Welsh coal, don't they? at least if they want to get up their best speed?" He reluctantly admitted that it was so. "That shows how idiotic we are in England, doesn't it?" I suggested. "We sell to your navy our best Welsh coal, while we keep on having to increase our naval expenditure enormously. Yet if we stopped the supply of coal, your fleet would be hopelessly crippled, wouldn't it? Because the best German coal isn't nearly as good as ours."

When I returned to the New Palace from my visit to Plön, I told the Princess that I had seen the German fleet at Kiel. She was annoyed. "That isn't the German fleet," she said hotly. "That's only a tiny part of it. Don't think you've seen the German fleet; why, we've lots and lots more ships than that." I assured her that I was quite prepared to believe it.

"We shall soon have a much bigger fleet than you in England," she continued. "We are going to keep on building and building."

I couldn't resist teasing her a little. "Oh, well, in England, we shan't be just sitting still and doing nothing, I hope. We shall be building, too." Hereupon, she became very angry, and I was glad an interruption put an end to our talk.

But Sissy must have told the Emperor something of our conversation, for a day or two later he came up to me after dinner and said in his usual jocular manner, "So you saw some of our German ships at Kiel, I hear. What did you think of them, eh?"

I replied that I admired them exceedingly. "England

must not look to her own laurels," I concluded laughingly. "I see we must keep on building. No reduction yet possible in the navy estimate."

"But it's nonsense," burst out the Emperor, "to talk as if the German Navy were even approximately near the British Navy in size. We are a long, long way behind. I can't understand all this protest in England against Germany building ships. We naturally have our trade interests to safeguard, our colonies to protect. How are we to do it without an efficient navy? Here you are building Dreadnoughts by the dozen, and if we build one or two there is a tremendous outcry in your press."

I said that I thought it foolish of the English to expect any nation to stop building battleships if it chose to do so. "It seems to me," I said, "that we ought to keep quiet and say nothing, but keep on building, too. Only it's rather an expensive business."

It was a trait of the Emperor's character never to consider the expense of any scheme. It irritated him; it was to him petty-minded to be trammelled by financial considerations. The money had to be found somehow. He left it to others to discover how.

*

Early in January 1908, the Socialists threatened to be troublesome, and preparations were made for their reception at the gloomy Berlin Schloss. The Princess went onto the roof of the palace and stayed for several hours at the windows, hoping that they would come and entertain her by having their heads broken where she could see it all, but the square below remained unusually peaceful. Carriages were not allowed out.

Nobody worried anymore about the Socialists. It was, generally speaking, Berlin policemen who were most to be feared on these occasions. They panicked, and smote unoffending citizens on the heads with their truncheons. Once they hit two English journalists; another time they tried to arrest me for crossing the Schloss square on my way home from shopping.

"But I live in the royal Schloss," I protested. It was most uncomfortable to feel a policeman's grip on my arm.

Fortunately, I had my Einlaskarte with me, the orange one supplied to ladies-in-waiting and *hohe Herrschaften*, so the policeman let go and apologized when I showed it. I told him he was a fool, and he apologized more humbly than before. German policemen are not like English policemen. I do not think they ever will be.

On this occasion, the *Sozialdemokraten* had announced their intention of holding an immense mass meeting, marching to the Schloss, and demanding an audience with the Emperor so they might lay before him their grievances. The Emperor had batteries of artillery brought into the yard of the Schloss and riding stables, and the garrison was augmented. All day from my window, I watched the soldiers pour in and wondered what would happen—our rooms seemed to be directly in the line of fire—if things came to a crisis and people began shooting. This was all day Saturday, and we had been warned not to leave the Schloss.

But on the Sunday afternoon no Sozialdemokraten had appeared, and I had grown tired of being imprisoned. Without saying anything to anyone, I put on my outdoor things and went out. The gloomy Schloss was unendurable.

If there was any shooting in the streets, I had settled in my own mind that I would lie down flat on the ground till it was over.

There were several manservants passing in and out as I walked from the courtyard into the street, where everything was unusually quiet. Nobody in the square, a few policemen guarding the bridge. I went into a sidestreet, avoiding Unter den Linden, where a respectable-looking, ordinary Sunday crowd was promenading.

The only disturbers of the peace I could see were the Berlin mounted police, who galloped madly and aimlessly up and down sidestreets in an excited manner. I wondered why they were so flurried. Nothing seemed to be happening, the people were as orderly as it is possible for a crowd to be, but the clatter of the hoofs of police horses as they galloped over the granite setts of the streets was somewhat terrifying.

As a matter of fact, the threatened march to the Schloss had been a feint on the part of the Socialists, whose huge demonstration took place in a totally different spot out by the *Tempelhoferfeld*. The police galloped their horses for nothing. The guns were taken out of the Schloss the next day, back to Potsdam, the soldiers returned to their barracks, and all the papers echoed with laughter. The Socialists had scored again.

*

One day in the autumn of 1909, a telephone message came from Prince Oskar in Berlin, saying that Orville Wright was flying on the Feld. Without delay, two autos were ordered by Her Majesty—one for herself, Princess Feodora, and the Princess; the other for the suite. The palace buzzed like a hive while footmen fell about summoning the ladies to get ready at once. The two professors, Herr Gern and Herr Porger, employed to instruct the Princess in history and literature, were sent away in a carriage to the scene of the action, a proceeding suggested by the Princess, who never failed to display diplomatic tact. Mademoiselle Lauru and I huddled on our outdoor things and tied motorveils with trembling fingers. It was *de rigueur* to get excited over flying, and nothing annoyed the Princess more than an attitude of philosophic calm.

We picked up Prince Au-Wi and Prince George of Greece on the way, and sped onward to the big cavalry exercise ground, over which the cars bumped at a furious pace. When we arrived, there was no sign of Mr. Wright. A gentleman appeared who announced with a pronounced American accent that all flying was finished for that day. The police had gone home, and there was no one to keep the crowd from straying onto the grounds.

But Princess Feo was leaving the same evening, and Her Majesty particularly wished her to see a flight. There was some discussion as to whether soldiers should be attached from the adjacent barracks to keep the course. The American gentleman seemed to think that would make no difference to Mr. Wright. At last, a man was sent to Wright's tent to announce Her Majesty's arrival, and presently Wright came along, buttoning up his leather jacket as he walked, a taciturn man who spoke in a soft, gentle voice when he spoke at all, which was not often.

Some policemen on bicycles had materialized out of the surrounding landscape, and drove the crowd back to the road, where they were kept penned up by the arm of the law while we stood in the middle of the field to watch the flight.

It would never do that we ladies of the court had witnessed so auspicious an event alone. A few days later, the Emperor himself went with the Empress and the Princess to see Wright fly. It was the middle of October, and the days were getting short. There had been some delay in starting, so that as the cars tore onto the Feld, the sun was setting in great clouds of scarlet and purple and night was fast approaching.

Wright was waiting beside his machine. After a word with the Emperor, he put on his jacket and goggles, and in a few seconds the motor began to hum steadily. The propellers whizzed round, and the huge machine moved along smoothly and swiftly up into the darkening heavens. Its widespread planes showed blackly for a moment against the intense sunset, and then it went droning in immense space, rising higher and higher toward the stars. For nearly half an hour, above our heads, the aeroplane circled and dived and dove and rose again, humming smoothly and sleepily in the distance, then coming near with a threatening murmur, to rise and disappear again in the darkness, reappearing presently like a gigantic moth. Finally, it descended, dropping lightly within a few feet of us. The people on the edge of the field cheered heartily.

The Emperor and Empress congratulated Wright, and there was a long explanation of "how it was done," though most of the officers could not understand the American accent. Presently, a signed photograph of the Emperor, which one of the adjutants had been carrying, was produced and given to Wright by His Majesty. Then a lady who had been modestly hovering in the background—Miss Katherine Wright, the aeronaut's sister—was called up. She took charge of the photograph and made delightful American remarks about it.

By this time, it was absolutely dark, but the powerful acetylene lights of the three cars illuminated the scene. The Emperor could not tear himself away from the aeroplane; while he was still asking questions, I talked with Miss Wright, an extremely charming woman, who said that this was probably her brother's last flight on German soil. They had already stayed a day longer than intended so that he might fly before the Emperor, before they departed for Paris and London en route for America.

Although this was the first aeroplane the Emperor had ever seen, we had had for a long time in Germany entertained a preoccupation in the popular imagination with airships: Zeppelins. Once, in the earlier years of Count von Zeppelin's monster creation, a message had come to the court that von Zeppelin was flying from Frankfurt to Berlin and would arrive about five o'clock in the afternoon. There was the usual hurrying to and fro. The Emperor, Empress, Princess, and we of the suite hurled ourselves into motorcars and rushed to Berlin, but after waiting several hours on the Tempelhofer Feld, with nothing to eat and not much to do, we returned without a glimpse. The rumors of the airship's arrival had been entirely unfounded.

But the royal appetite was whetted. A few months later, von Zeppelin himself announced his intention to bring his airship to Berlin. On the day set, all the shops closed at noon, and the whole population of Berlin turned out and walked up and down the street with their eyes fixed heavenward.

Every lady and gentleman of the court was invited by ticket to the Tempelhoferfeld, at which the airship was to descend, or the roof of the Schloss, as the Zeppelin was to maneuver around the building. But, just as all the excursion trains from the country had brought in the surrounding inhabitants to swell the already dense crowd of sky-gazers, a special edition of the newspapers was issued announcing an injury to the airship which prevented further flight. Everyone went sadly home.

The next day, Sunday, news came that the defect had been repaired, and the airship, with Count von Zeppelin on board, would appear at noon. This change of plans was inconvenient, for there was a newly restored church to be dedicated in the presence of the Emperor and the Empress and the chief military authorities. Baron von Mirbach said later that he had never seen such an obviously distracted congregation. The drawn-out service, the long-winded address—German sermons usually lasted at least an hour— were listened to with barely concealed impatience and lack of interest. The clergy themselves seemed to keep one ear turned toward that heaven to which they were directing their audience, in apprehension of hearing the mighty droning that would proclaim von Zeppelin's arrival.

From the windows of the Schloss, overlooking the courtyard, it was common to see the adjutants who accompanied His Majesty descend from their cars with dignity, salute the guard with grave courtesy and deliberation, and then retire without undue haste from the public view. But on this occasion, they tumbled out of the cars and rushed up the steps like schoolboys, colliding as they ran with the footmen and *Burschen* who came running with their flat undress caps to exchange for the spiked headgear they had worn in church.

It is a popular myth that the German is phlegmatic. He is nothing of the kind. He is extraordinarily excitable. He gets out of temper, shouts and wrings his hands in moments of stress, and sheds tears easily. His feelings are on the surface. His military calm is acquired. He abandons it and becomes almost hysterical when something touches his heart and imagination.

The advent of Count von Zeppelin in his airship was the culminating act of a great national triumph. The indomitable old man who had worked so long and so pluckily at his herculean task, was at last to receive some of the homage due to his tenacity and self-sacrifice. People thronged the streets and crowded the housetops.

The fashionable crowd ascended to the roof of the Schloss by devious ways, through little dark sculleries, up queer steep steps and ladders, past funny little apartments smelling strongly of cheese and garlic where the families of some of the servants lived tucked away in a corner of the big building, out onto the copper-colored roof along narrow plank paths, made primarily for the use of sentries who nightly patrolled these upper regions—some of them had inscribed verses on the walls, conveying discontent at the atmospheric conditions prevailing there on winter nights.

On this day, the sky was gloriously blue, and as far as the eye could reach, on every one of the many flat roofs in the vicinity were masses of people—not, as was usually the case, a mere fringe of daring spirits leaning over the parapets, but throngs spread over the whole surface. Every man, woman, and child held a fluttering flag. One could almost see the palpitating heartbeat of the nation.

For weeks, the picture-postcard shops had been filled with every kind of card, many of a coarse nature, depicting an entire country obsessed with the possibility of airships: drawings of a bridegroom at the church door rushing away from his bride, the mourners at a funeral flying down the street, a mother leaving her crying child, a hungry man leaving his dinner—all crying *"Zeppelin kommt."* Absurd as these comic attempts were, they did not exaggerate the attitude of the people.

After an hour or two of waiting, an electric thrill ran through the elevated crowd. Someone had caught sight of the airship. By degrees everyone found it—a tiny, cigar-shaped speck, hardly visible against the deep blue distance. A wave of cheering swelled and ebbed. The speck grew gradually larger. Cheers in the distant part of the city reached us in ever-increasing volume. The droning of the engines was audible. Presently, the dirigible could be seen over the Brandenburgertor. Still more frantic cheers arose from the streets, the packed windows and roofs. The great machine swung steadily up Unter den Linden and sailed magnificently round and round the Schloss, while the waves of cheering were crested with a fluttering of white hand-kerchiefs like a storm-tossed sea. Again and again the Zeppelin made its stately circuit of the royal castle, then slowly turned and headed for Tempelhoferfeld, where the Emperor and Empress with their families and all the greatest men in Germany were waiting to congratulate the splendid old veteran.

A few days after von Zeppelin's triumph in Berlin, there came, anticlimactically, the fall and destruction of the great machine. But by that time, the German people had taken Zeppelins firmly to their hearts, and no disasters, not even those later ones involving horrible deaths by burning and drowning, could dampen their delight in this newest war machine, this huge air-monster which Germany had produced and brought to such perfection.

I confess that to me the first sight of the wonderful air-machine was thrilling. As the elongated bulk loomed overhead, the streets below took on an unfamiliar aspect, turning pink with the uplifted faces of the huge gathering. It was a beautiful, windless day, and it strikes me now with a strange ruefulness that I, an alien in the land, should have felt something of the same enthusiasm as the people around me, even though the regretful thought forced itself into my mind that this triumph of human ingenuity and skill would inevitably be used for military purposes with the object of destroying human life and human happiness.

Still, as an Englishwoman who had lived in Germany for a length of time, and who had consorted with Germans and gained a measure of insight into their mode of thought and their manner of viewing things, I knew what to avoid and what line to take in dealing with anything so hypersensitive, so open to attack, so highly strung as the German national consciousness. The sensitive Englishwoman—or Englishman—does not go blundering along, making a fatuous example of herself and betraying at every step her complete indifference and ignorance of all matters which Germans hold most dear. She does not trample unnecessarily with a blithe unconsciousness of harm on all their national prejudices. But, too frequently, this is what our British representatives did—men fresh from England and with no knowledge of Germany and its ways.

Once there was a group of English and Germans intent on creating an Anglo-German equivalent of an *entente cordiale*. A steamer-load of cheerful British gentlemen crossed the North Sea, visited various German towns, made speeches, ate quantities of German food, visited *Denkmals*, museums, and *Biergärtens*, and were entertained and feted in the hearty German manner. Their triumphant path was strewn with flowers and Rhine wine, and the German eagle and the British lion appeared to be fraternizing in an agreeable if somewhat physiologically unnatural manner. The pacifists were more than hopeful; they were content.

When the British delegates arrived in Berlin, the Emperor invited them to the New Palace, and, though not personally present, he gave them a luncheon there and deputed officials to see that they received every possible attention. I watched from my window in the angle of the palace the horde of gentlemen emerge from the palace doors, flowing in a black-coated flood over the terrace and breaking up and reforming into constantly converging pools, finally carefully shepherded into imperial carriages and driven off to see Sans Souci and the Potsdam palace.

Before the delegates left Berlin they managed to deliver a severe blow to my national pride. An informal supper had been arranged at which Germans and English would meet and socialize, swear eternal friendship, and pledge themselves to work together for a better understanding of each other, a goal with which I was heartfully in accord. Accompanied by a German friend, a professor at one of the universities, I wended my way to the big hall where the reception was being held and found it already in full swing. The people were scattered about at little tables listening to music; there was a representative gathering of Germans and Englishmen seated on the platform above the audience. Flags were lovingly entwined in a wealth of evergreens.

When the music was finished and the applause had died down, the headmaster of one of the government schools in Berlin rose and made a speech in English—a clear, well-enunciated speech—for every German, as a child, is painstakingly trained to express himself, not only in well-chosen language, but in tones which will make no excessive demands on the aural capacities of the hearer: mumbling is not permitted. A shouting declamatory style is encouraged in announcing even the smallest incident. The German's speech had nothing of the shamefaced modesty which often characterizes English orators and makes them appear anxious to conceal rather than reveal their ideas, and his content was no less good than his delivery. It was lucid and convincing, pointing out the patent benefits of an Anglo-German alliance; it was full of practical common sense but touched with appealing sentiment. The speech alluded to the mutual indebtedness of German and English literature and contained apposite quotations from Shakespeare which, most likely, many of the Englishmen present failed to recognize. In all, it was, from every point of view, an admirable and excellent address.

He was followed by an English gentleman, newly arrived in Germany, who stepped from among the group on the platform, and in the well-known English parliamentary manner, in a breezy, electioneering style, his thumbs in the armholes of his waistcoat—an attitude which to a German is exceedingly strange and undignified—he proceeded in an easy, jaunty way to harangue that serious cultivated audience of expectant Germans.

I can never forget the acute agony which I suffered during those minutes. If, at the risk of broken bones, a trap-door in the floor had opened and swallowed me up so that I had been spared the frightful exhibition that that gentle-man made of himself, I should have been forever grateful. I still wince at the shame of it: his fatuous smiles and wriggles, his feeble, labored, quite incomprehensible witticisms, and his childish appeals and assertions that if the people there assembled would only continue to drink tea together for a few months longer, England and Germany would be welded into an abiding friendship which no diplomatic blunders could assail. He appeared to have nothing what-soever to say and eked out the paucity of his ideas by a multiplicity of words. The peroration was an attempt to lisp out a German sentence which he evidently had painfully acquired a few hours previously and had subsequently forgotten. He had only retained in his memory some broken fragments and chippings of a once-noble sentiment.

After he had jerked and wriggled himself to the puerile conclusion, I, stricken with humiliation, escaped into the night to ponder, as the train carried me back to the New Palace, our strange English methods of doing things, our choice of men, our neglect of those who can and patronage of those who can't. I wondered if all nations were guilty of these mistakes or if it were an English monopoly.

The Emperor, of course, was not himself the most skill-ful diplomat, and on more than one occasion his candor proved an embarrassment to his ministers. Only once, however, do I recall his natural exuberance invoking a sense of shame among the German people. The event came to be known as the "*Daily Telegraph* incident."

On one of the Emperor's visits to England, he gave a newspaper interview that appeared—without a clear source—a year later in the *Daily Telegraph*. The remarks by the Emperor, and particularly his revelations that he had aided the British during the Boer War, created nothing short of consternation in Germany. The publication of the interview shook the faith of the German people in their ruler as never before.

It may be difficult to realize how firm in those days was the absolute belief of the Germans in their Emperor, how great their blind faith in his infallibility. They accepted his doctrine of divine right; their Kaiser was a beneficent being who worked day and night for the good of Germany and who saw eye to eye with the people, who, more or less willingly, bore the increasing burdens of taxation which he thrust upon them.

In the matter of the Boers, their feelings had been deeply aroused. Only the summer before, two Boer generals had visited Berlin and were acclaimed as popular heroes; cheering crowds collected each day outside the hotel where they were staying. The German people had altogether approved of the Kruger telegram—in which the Emperor sent his good wishes as to the outcome of the Boer War to South Africa's President Kruger—even if the gesture was unwise in regard to Germany's relationship with England. It was the futile illusion of many stay-at-home Englishmen in those days that they were admired and beloved in

Germany. They were nothing of the kind. They were looked upon with suspicion and hatred as possible rivals, and often with contempt as belonging to a nation whose glory was in decline.

With the immediate translation of the *Daily Telegraph* interview into all the German papers, what shrieks and denunciations arose on all sides! How sad and bitter, how deeply wounded was the entire German press and the people that their Emperor should have confessed to trying to aid the hated British to beat the Boers, that he should have sent them plans of campaign!

I first read the outburst in the *Tägliche Rundschau* and took the paper into the room of the Obergouvernante.

"Whatever has your Kaiser been doing now?" I said tactlessly. I wanted to discuss the whole thing with her, but realized quickly that I had made a mistake, so I retired with my newspaper and studied it by myself. The ladies of the court were not political, only patriotic.

It was strange what an atmosphere of gloom fell on the palace in a few hours. As a rule, when the Emperor was at the New Palace, everybody was in a state of suppressed excitement waiting for the next thing to happen. Shall I ever forget the ghastliness of the dreadful luncheons of the next few days, partaken of in silence in that gaily painted room, where the nude gods and goddesses everlastingly disported themselves upon the walls enwreathed in garlands of flowers? The silence that prevailed was terrifying. The Emperor sat in a kind of stony stupor, eating and drinking in a mechanical way, as though he did not heed what he was doing.

I myself had a guilty sense of blame in the matter, being

of the nation that had exposed the Emperor to this painful and humiliating position; I wanted to keep out of the way, to make myself inconspicuous. In the days that followed, the Emperor did nothing but brood over this rift between himself and his people. It was a totally new experience. Not since he had ascended the throne had there been raised such a chorus of disapproval. His ears were accustomed to a very different song.

The wounded Emperor cancelled all engagements. Sometimes he paced up and down the Sandhof without speaking a word to the attendant gentlemen, who, scared and dismayed, at last fell behind him, walking also in complete and unfamiliar silence. It was peculiarly characteristic of the man that at a time when a cloud had obscured his popularity with his people, when he was smarting under the sense of having, with the best intentions in the world, brought a storm of resentment and criticism upon his own head, at the moment when, if ever, a man needed to be alone with his thoughts, he had not saw fit to dispense with the attendance of his gentlemen and had chosen a very conspicuous part of the palace grounds in which to air the heaviness and depression from which he was suffering.

The Empress was always in tears. The Emperor moved about in a mournful silence, speaking seldom and then in an undertone, as though someone he loved were dead. Everybody else talked in whispers, not daring to make any effort to break the ghastly silence. Adalbert, Oskar, and Au-Wi made short, hurried visits home.

If the Emperor and court took so much to heart, the people themselves were hardly less grieved. I called to see some friends in Potsdam, an ordinary German household of the professional class, and they were plunged into almost as deep a depression, absolutely brokenhearted. A children's party which they had intended to give two days after the newspapers' revelations was cancelled at the last moment, the parents declaring themselves utterly incapable of indulging in any festivities—even children's festivities—at such a sad time for Germany.

Strangely enough, the Emperor, who spoke to so few in those days, talked many times to me on trivial subjects— about horses and books. His soul seemed unable to bear contact with his own people. His continued gloom, which lasted several days, terrified everyone. There was something unnatural, inexplicable, in this harsh silence of the voluble ruler. Rumors ran through the palace.

One afternoon I was ordered to ride with Their Majesties and their children, who were accompanied by the usual large suite. For two hours we galloped down the sandy lanes, through the fields and over the cavalry exercise ground, along the lakeside and through the thinning woods—a gallop that tried horses and men severely. Throughout its duration, the Emperor said nothing, but continued to gallop. At last, Baron von Mirbach spoke softly to the Emperor and said, "I think this is a little too much for Her Majesty." The Emperor looked up like a man waking from a dream and fell into a walk which continued all the way home. The Empress smiled rather wanly at him as she descended from her horse.

A few days later, I happened to be at the Wildpark station when Prince von Bülow, the Chancellor, wearing full dress uniform, appeared at the New Palace to exact from the Emperor the pledge that never in the future would he grant an interview to anyone for publication without first submitting the text to his ministers.

It was a tense time that followed the arrival of the Chancellor, for everyone knew that unless the Emperor acceded to the expressed wishes of the Reichstag and promised to put the necessary curb on the exuberance of speech which was one of his chief characteristics, Prince von Bülow would have no alternative but to resign his post as Chancellor, with perhaps serious results to the Empire.

Von Bülow was a polite, courteous, handsome, and dignified man. He and his wife, a charming Italian woman, had dined frequently at the royal table. Princess von Bülow was small and lively and wore diaphanous artistic gowns, somewhat scandalizing the court ladies, who were invariably clad in sober silks and satins. Once, when Italian royalty was visiting the Prussian Court—it was in a time of slit dresses, very tight around the ankles and no undies to speak of— Fräulein von Gersdorff was so distressed at the revealed lower limbs of the Italian women that she seriously proposed—and was with some difficulty restrained— sending to each woman's room an appropriate petticoat borrowed from the housemaids.

Outside the palace, a crowd waited for von Bülow's return. "Still Chancellor?" murmured Baron von Mirbach when, after two hours, von Bülow stepped from his carriage. The Prince smiled. The Emperor had given his assurance: he would practice the utmost prudence; he would put his signature to nothing which his ministers did not formally approve.

And so the cloud between sovereign and people passed. The Emperor recovered his spirits, cracked his usual jokes at the table, and was hilariously delighted to have the incident pushed into the background.

Within a few days, the Emperor was telling, in his usual emphatic manner, a story of the time when his sons were young and first began to study under a German tutor. In their infancy, they heard and spoke more English than German, so knew comparably little of the latter language, much to the indignation of many good German patriots. One day, the tutor asked Prince Adalbert if he could tell him what was the emblem of Germany, and received the English word "eagle" in reply. The tutor, who knew no English, shrank back in horror, hardly believing his ears: for the German word *Igel*—hedgehog—is pronounced in exactly the same way, and the thought that a son of the Kaiser could possibly believe that this ignoble animal represented the German Empire was naturally very painful and repellent to the good professor.

The Emperor told the anecdote, speaking in German, and gave the English translation of *Igel* as "porcupine." He repeated the mistake several times, and the adjutants and ladies sitting in his immediate vicinity all recognized the error—Count Blumenthal turned to me in a whisper and said, "But isn't 'porcupine' *Stachelschwein* in German?"— but no one made any remarks, tacitly agreeing to let the mistake pass unnoticed. I, however, rushing in where aides-de-camp feared to tread and moved by the pedagogic instinct which prompted the correction of other people's lapses, called out when I next heard the offending word: "Hedgehog, not porcupine, Your Majesty."

The Emperor stared at me with frowning eyes for a moment—not angry, but merely concentrated in thought—

and then immediately recognized his mistake. "What? Hedgehog? Why, yes, of course it is. Hedgehog, not porcupine. Both rather prickly, though—eh?" And he went off into a loud roar of laughter at his own joke. The period of mourning had clearly passed.

Princess Victoria Louise in her Totenkopf—Death's Head—uniform on October 22, 1909, the day the Emperor made her the colonel of the Second Hussars stationed at Danzig. "She will ride at the head of the first regiment that invades England," the Emperor said gaily to me. (Photo by Anne Topham.)

CHAPTER THIRTEEN

COMING OF AGE

One of the Emperor's characteristics was that he could explain everything to everybody—with one exception: the suffragists. He was never able to explain them. They baffled him entirely. At first he thought they were just disappointed spinsters, but in view of the number of married women in their ranks, he was obliged to abandon this idea. He then groped in vain for a satisfactory solution.

Some of the suffragists were once on board the *Hohenzollern*—not uninvited ones, of course, but a few of the charming English and American women who came to Kiel for the yacht-racing, and who sat on his decks and drank his tea, and shocked His Majesty by revealing themselves as sympathizers with the feminist suffrage movement. The Emperor became inarticulate at such moments. He wanted to know, "What in heaven do women want with a vote?"

"We are coming to Germany soon, Your Majesty," smiled one fair lady with the intrepidity of her sex. "We are going to help with the movement here."

"Here? There is no movement here, and if you begin burning houses and horsewhipping people in Germany, what do you think the police will do? They won't send you flowers and newspapers and let you go free two days afterwards. We deal with people differently here, I can tell you."

It was of no use to explain to His Majesty the difference between militant and non-militant suffragists. This was a distinction too subtle for his mind; he saw them all tarred with the same brush, a menace to the peace of mankind, a clamorous nuisance, and a disturber of settled convictions and ideas. "Women should stay at home and look after their children," was his last word on the subject. And if someone were to point out the flaws in this remedy, as for instance, the thousands of women who had no children either of their own or someone else's to see after, he took refuge in ridicule. He was quite sure that a vote was a desperately bad thing for women.

However, he allowed women to be colonels—honorary colonels—in his army. The Empress, the Crown Princess, the Princess Fritz, the Princess August-Wilhelm, and Princess Victoria Louise each had her regiment, at the head of which on parade days she rode in full uniform—though a long riding skirt is perhaps the least practical military garment that can be imagined.

The young Princess received her colonelcy when she was only seventeen, a few days after her confirmation, which was the formal ending of her schooldays—the days when German girlhood of whatever class renounces its childhood forever.

"Confirmation!" grumped Baron von Mirbach. "What does confirmation mean? For the boys it means permission to smoke cigarettes; for the girls, freedom to go to balls and parties. That's what confirmation means in Germany."

At the Prussian Court, it signified something strenuous, and all Hohenzollern princes and princesses were strictly prepared for it some months beforehand by the court chaplain. It was considered a solemn moment of their lives, and at the ceremony each of them had to read aloud before the assembled congregation a *Glaubensbekenntnis*—confession of faith—a declaration of their religious beliefs, written by themselves, and explicating their views of what that belief implied as to the guidance of their future lives. It was an impressive, almost painful ceremony, this effort of unformed boys and girls to give expression to their ideas of how to shape their futures worthily. The day before the confirmation, the candidate was examined in religious knowledge by the chaplain; the Emperor and Empress were the only other people present.

All the near relatives came to the confirmation, including the Princess's godmother, the venerable widow Grand-Duchess Louise of Baden, "Aunty Baden," a daughter of the old emperor, Wilhelm I, and the mother of the Queen of Sweden. Aunty Baden was a gray-haired, straight-backed old lady, a true Hohenzollern in character: decidedly opinionated and with a restless, energetic mind. She had no pity for modern nerves and modern fatigue. She belonged to the old school, to an age of tough fiber.

At the opening of the Kaiser Frederick Museum, when a statue to the Emperor Frederick, her brother, was unveiled, the indomitable old lady examined everything with a vital curiosity, insisted on penetrating into every room and studying the remotest Greco-Assyrian sculptures with the liveliest interest. Hardly a scarab escaped her notice. When the Empress suggested softly that it was getting late and that the suite was tired and hungry, Aunty Baden only turned with renewed zest to an adjoining gallery, "Oh, here are many beautiful things! We must look at these before we go! See how interesting!" Everyone else was bored to extinction and fainting for lack of sustenance, but the old lady continually made new discoveries, and it was only with the greatest difficulty that at last the Emperor induced her to return to the Schloss.

On confirmation day, the Grand-Duchess arrived in the *Friedenskirche*—the Church of Peace, built in the gardens of Sans Souci, where the Emperor and Empress Frederick were buried—leaning on the arm of her nephew, Emperor Wilhelm, who always treated her with great devotion. She had laid aside the black dress she usually wore and appeared in creamy white, a long white veil falling behind almost to the hem of her dress.

All the old teachers and servants who had ever been connected in the slightest degree with the Princess were invited to the church. Herr Kaspar, long retired from service, who first placed her on her pony; her former tutors, Herr Gern and Herr Porger; her former governesses, including the unrepentent Äbtissin Fräulein von Thadden; and young girls from the nearby school, grown up now and forever through with wearing black uniforms and tight hair.

The Lutheran service was simple. The chaplain's address and the reading of the confession occupied the chief part of the time. In an hour it was over. The Emperor was extremely pleased with the way in which Sissy acquitted herself. "She is a chip off the old block, isn't she?" he said, talking about the way in which she read her Glaubensbekenntnis. "It was like a *Kavallerieattacke*"— the military comparison did not appear to strike him as out of place—"so direct and forcible, couldn't have been better."

Perhaps the Emperor's martial comment was caused by his knowledge that in four days he proposed to make his daughter colonel of the Second Hussars stationed at Danzig, the regiment of which his mother, the Empress Frederick had also been colonel. On the birthday of the Empress, October 22, the news was announced.

A rumor of the event had taken wind, but the strictest secrecy was enjoined. The necessary saddlery and—still more important—the feminine uniform had been prepared in advance, the latter without any trying on. It took three maids, several ladies, and at the last moment, the patient ministrations and advice of the Emperor's *Liebjäger* to get the Princess satisfactorily into her uniform. It was fearfully tight under the arms and round the neck, and the new patent leather boots pinched horribly, so that the radiant glow of satisfaction in the glory and honor of wearing it was tinctured with some pain and discomfort. The day was unusually warm, almost oppressive, and the heavy cloth loaded with astrakhan, the hot fur cap with its skull and crossbones —the emblem which gives the regiment its name, the *Totenkopf* or Death's Head Hussars— combined with the cumbersome habit skirt, weighted the Princess almost beyond endurance.

All the officers of the regiment had travelled from distant Danzig, a twelve-hour journey, to be presented to their new colonel, and the Empress's birthday table—with the usual dozen new hats—hardly received any attention at all, everyone being absorbed in the new recruit to His Majesty's forces.

"She will ride at the head of the first regiment that invades England," said the Emperor gaily to me.

"Yes, I hope so. Then we shall be delighted to see it," was the only possible answer I could find.

"Oh, yes! You will receive her with open arms, no doubt." He laughed, but looked as though he were not quite sure of the matter.

With the celebration of the confirmation, the education of the Princess was ended; my tenure was over. Indeed, Mademoiselle Lauru had left the court already, and the departure of Obergouvernante Fräulein von Saldern was imminent. I returned to England before Christmas.

*

After a passage of three years, in 1912, the Empress invited me to return to Germany for a visit at the Prussian Court. The Emperor, of whom I saw a great deal during that time—for a wonder, he was at home!—was very affable and greeted me with the well-remembered title I had been christened with. "Ah! Here is our British Dreadnought again," he said, shaking hands.

We discussed, among other things, the *Titanic* disaster, which had recently occurred while I was visiting in Canada, and I referred to "the silence" of two minutes by which the railways and churches had honored the memory of the Canadians who had perished. The Emperor had not heard about the silence and questioned me closely after I casually referred to it.

"What a very queer idea" he said, "keeping absolutely quiet for two minutes. What's the good of it?"

"Just a pause in life to give a thought to those who were gone, I suppose," I answered. I did not then know how significant, in just a few years, this rite of silence was to become.

*

I was invited to Berlin once again for the marriage of my pupil to the young Ernst August, Prince of Cumberland. One thing that amused my Princess enormously over this marriage was that King George of England's formal permission for it to take place had to be asked. "Fancy asking the King of England if Pol and I can marry each other!" she said, bridling at the idea. (The name by which the bridegroom was known in his family, Leopold, was shortened to "Pol.")

Of all possible marriages, this one was the last anyone would have dared to prophesy, so utterly improbable did it seem. The Duke of Cumberland, father of the bridegroom, was the disinherited heir to the vanished throne of Hanover, and had, from childhood, been the implacable enemy of the Prussian royal house and government. All attempts by the Emperor to bring about a reconciliation had failed.

With almost monotonous regularity, the newspapers would announce an approaching meeting of the Emperor with the Duke, and with equal certainty a paragraph would appear the next day announcing the latter's departure from the scene of the proposed rendezvous "a few hours before His Majesty's arrival." The name "the Vanishing Duke" became peculiarly appropriate, and the feud settled into a hopeless state where every effort at resolution had been exhausted and nothing remained to be done. Many brilliant statesmen and crowned heads had to concede defeat after praiseworthy but ineffective efforts. At last those two great factors in the affairs of the world, death and love, intervened.

The Duke's eldest son was travelling in his motorcar through Germany on his way to the funeral of his uncle, the King of Denmark, when he met his death by accident in a lonely part of the road. He lay for a time unrecognized, and then, his identity discovered, the Emperor immediately dispatched two of his sons to render all possible help. For two nights, the body of the young Cumberland remained in the little village chapel near the place where the accident happened, guarded by Prussian soldiers and Prince Fritz and the Crown Prince. Later, the Princes escorted the coffin on its way to the burial.

A few weeks afterward, Ernst August, the second son of the Duke, who, by his brother's death, had become heir to the family rank as well as the family feud, came on behalf of his father to thank Emperor Wilhelm for his sympathy and aid in their sorrow. For the first time, he and the Emperor's daughter met, and they spent an hour or so in each other's company. A new element had been introduced into the quarrel: so strong was the mutual attraction felt by the young people for each other that, in spite of the short time of their meeting and the tremendous old prejudices, they conquered the accumulated hate of the years and within a few months announced their engagement.

It was a betrothal which filled the German people with joy and a sense of relief, but some of the ladies of the court had the brilliant idea of instructing the young Princess on the particular events that had led up to this long-existing feud between Guelph and Hohenzollern. A distinguished professor from Berlin University was invited to the Schloss to give her a lecture on the subject. But when it was tactfully broken to the Princess that such a lecture was in contemplation, she refused to come and listen to it. "Pol says he does not wish me to hear anything about it. He says it is far too sad a story. He will tell me himself what he wishes me to know of it." The ladies and the professor withdrew their plans.

On the evening of May 24, 1913, following the wedding ceremony, I stood among the crowd of ladies and officers in the gallery of the beautiful Weissersaal in the Berlin Schloss and watched the scene below, one of marvelous beauty, full of sparkle and color. A regimental band, that of the Garde du Corps, was stationed in the Saal. At a signal from an official, the music began: slow, stately marches were played, old-world tunes that were an echo of past times. The royal ladies were seated with their multicolored trains spread out in front of them, while rows of red-clad pages stood behind their chairs waiting to advance when the time arrived.

From the side entrance of the Saal, stepping in time to the music, came Prince von Fürstenburg, the Marshal of the Court, carrying his wand of office and preceded by a double row of twenty-four pages who bore large torches. In rhythm, they moved once around the room. When the Marshal stopped and bowed to the bride and the bridegroom, the couple at once descended from the slightly raised platform where they sat, and hand in hand, preceded by the torch bearers and with four ladies carrying the bride's train, they moved around the hall in time to the music. I had seen this ceremony three times before—at the weddings of the Crown Prince, Prince Fritz, and Prince Au-Wi, and I cannot express its wonderful fascination, its mixture of poetry and romance. There was a lulling monotony of sound, the flicker and smoke of the torches, the dignified movement of the dancers, the crowd of seated royalties opposite a standing group of courtiers. It had a fairy-tale quality, an aspect of Cinderella.

The bride and bridegroom, having made a tour of the room once alone, now took the hands of their parents: The bride offered her left hand to the Duke of Cumberland, her new father-in-law, the unseated head of the house of Hanover, and her right hand to her father, the Emperor, the head of the house of Hohenzollern. At the same time, the bridegroom was making the stately walk with his mother, the Duchess of Cumberland, and his mother-in-law, the Empress. Again, they slowly marched around the room.

Every woman at court was wearing her hair in an old fashion, combed straight up off the forehead and rolled over a wire frame, a style which we in England had discarded some time before. Each lady's train was carried by four pages; the trains of the bride and the Empress, sweeping the floor in white and silver, were carried by four ladies-in-waiting, who themselves wore trains of rose. Round and round the bride and bridegroom marched and returned, each time giving their hands to additional royal guests.

King George and Queen Mary of England were walking for the first—and last—time of their lives in the historic dance, while Nicholas II, Czar of all the Russias, cousin of the Emperor and the British sovereign, took his part also in the ceremony with a grave smile on his face. In the third round, the Princess reached out to him and gave him her right hand, while on her left was the British sovereign, King George. (An hour or two later, the Czar departed for Russia; it was the last time he was to see the Kaiser before the war. King George and Queen Mary remained two days longer in Berlin to attend a special performance at the opera of *Corcyra*, a work written on imperial command about the dances of the peasants of Corfu.)

Round they paced each in their turn, until at last the younger princes and princesses—there were so many of them in Germany—came on in threes and fours; otherwise, the dance might have stretched until midnight—and moved in a chain of smiling youth down the polished floor.

Peeping over the marble rail of the gallery were two young lieutenants in uniform whom I had seen only four years before in sailor suits. They were the cousins and former playfellows of Sissy, the Princes Max and Freddy of Hesse. Dear, sweet Max, who gallantly rid us of the Unkenruf at Cadinen, who indignantly set the rules of hide-and-seek, who so seriously flipped the pancakes and roasted the potatoes. They preferred to watch, still awed children, from the gallery. Their parents, the Prince and Princess Frederick Charles of Hesse, came down from the dais and took their part in the moving picture below. All round the hall, in the gallery, and on the wide stairs leading up to it, a crowd of courtiers looked and whispered.

Everybody was charmed and in good humor. It looked as though universal peace had settled upon the nations. At no former Prussian wedding—not even that of the Crown Prince—had there been two crowned heads among the guests and those, moreover, of Russia and Great Britain, the countries of whom Germany was most suspicious. It was, everyone agreed, a happy augury, and not less so because of the apparent ending of the quarrel between the Emperor and the Duke of Cumberland. Never before had there been such a delightful sense of peace and harmony, of genuine delight, of a belief that the future would be better than the past.

When the ceremony ended and the bride and bridegroom had at last finished their task, when the last guest had returned to the dais, the Emperor gave a signal, and the line of red pages, still carrying their torches, turned toward the wide exit. The bride and bridegroom followed them hand in hand, then the Emperor and the Czar, the Empress and the Czarina, King George, Queen Mary, and the rest of the royal guests, walking in stately procession, and slowly disappearing from view.

In the gallery above, the music became fainter and the moving panorama of color below gradually dissolved as though it had never been—if we who watched had only known that we were beholding the close of an era, the sunset of the world's friendship.

The bridal procession vanished from the Weissersaal, the music died away, and the lights were extinguished one by one, leaving only the corridors illuminated, down which the stream of guests outside the royal circle was returning. I found myself walking with the decorous crowd of ladies with their trains over their arms, with gorgeous chamberlains in their coats stiff with gold embroidery, wearing the gold key emblematic of their office, and officers of the army and navy. There was no crush, no overcrowding the spacious galleries, time for greetings and talk with old acquaintances.

But when we passed through the ponderous doors at the end, opened and shut by royal lackeys, we came upon a scene of strange disorder and confusion. Everyone appeared to be pushing and struggling and thrusting at each other. Somebody cannoned against me with such irresistible force that I was cast bodily onto the capacious chest of a dignified—at least he would have been dignified if circumstances had allowed it—gold-laced official. I still remember the scratchy feeling of the gold lace as it scraped my arms and face. I rebounded from him into the arms of a Kammerherr, an old friend, as it happened, who received my sudden onslaught charmingly and declared himself delighted to see me—a proof, I thought, on his part of splendid presence of mind and good humor.

We had no time to say more, for to our horror we suddenly found ourselves being roughly thrust upon certain royalties, those whom only a half hour before we had seen passing with so much stateliness down the hall. Here they were in some mysterious manner in the vortex of a very badly behaved crowd.

Everyone could at last see that the commotion was caused by the rough byplay of a group of young officers who appeared to think it good fun to push and charge into the guests from the outskirts. A few of the older men and the court officials did their best to protect the ladies, but the young lieutenants hustled and thrust regardless of the consequences and seemed to have lost any sense of decent behavior. Some of those near me apologized profusely but all the time did their best to increase the confusion and acted ill manneredly.

The situation was frightening and chaotic. The ladies'

veils and dresses were torn and jerked, they were flung backwards and forwards, and shouts and screams could be heard, adding to the joy of the hooligans. But when the various royalties who were trying to pass through the room to their apartments began, too, to be tossed and hustled violently back and forth, matters were immediately perceived to be serious, and Prince von Fürstenburg, the master of ceremonies, who half an hour before had been leading the pages in the Torch Dance with pomp and grace, seized his long wand of office, struck it angrily against the floor, and harangued the mob—for it could be called nothing less—restoring order in a few minutes.

The cause of the concentration of the crowd in that room had been to obtain one of the white silk ribbons bearing the cipher of the bride and the date of her wedding—the bride's garter, which was being distributed by Countess von Brockdorff, the Mistress of the Robes. The Countess, unnerved by the mob which forced its way upon her and handicapped by her long white gloves, which stuck to the fringes of the ribbons and prevented her from handing them out speedily, fumbled over her task and was so slow that the worst elements of the crowd—and there is no gathering quite so ruthless and selfish as a well-dressed one—got restive.

The Emperor was extremely angry and decreed that at no future wedding should there be any garter distribution, that they would be delivered by post. It was to be an unnecessary ruling. The only other weddings—of Oskar and Joachim—took place hastily, during the war, with none of the accustomed ceremonies. The Torch Dance was never again performed in the Prussian Court.

*

The day after the wedding, the court returned to the
New Palace, and the Empress invited me there for dinner.
It was like old times except for the absence of the Princess.
The Empress talked to me affectionately of her daughter.
"The poor child did nothing but cry after she was engaged,"
said the Empress. "She was imagining that war would break
out—extraordinary, isn't it?—thinking that poor Pol would
have to go away and fight and they would never meet again.
She was continually crying when he was away, and grew so
thin and miserable—always fretting and unhappy."

The Empress smiled indulgently at the memory of her
daughter's folly, while some of the ladies commented on the
peculiar obsession of the Princess. They also told me how
old Dr. Zunker, anxious to encourage the disconsolate
fiancee, had jokingly assured her that even if war did break
out in the Balkans, she would have no reason for special
uneasiness. "It will be a campaign of just six weeks or so,
and princes are sent to the front packed in cotton wool,"
laughed Dr. Zunker. "They are only unpacked when they
get home again."

The Princess had laughed—"I was born on a Friday and
on the thirteenth of the month, but my luck hasn't been so
very bad, has it?"—but she continued to be anxious. She had
always had a surer instinct than those who surrounded her.
She knew that the ladies and gentlemen of the court were
often curiously ignorant of the political eddies that ebbed
and flowed around them. They were accustomed to daily,
wild rumors; they had heard them often. They were sure
that trouble would be avoided by tactful diplomacy. They
dismissed the possibility of the tactful diplomat not being

forthcoming, that some time the reins might be in the hands of a well-meaning blunderer.

The Emperor, on this day after the wedding, was curiously unlike himself. Although no other guests were present at dinner at the New Palace—only the usual suite—he took absolutely no notice of me beyond a rather gruff and perfunctory greeting, talking all the time with one or other of the gentlemen.

After dinner, I sat with the Empress and her ladies at the table where a couple of oil lamps stood, and we glanced at the papers and talked of the events of the past week and of the future of the Princess. The light shone on the beautiful soft white hair of the Empress. Her kindly face—which I was never to see again—looked a little weary. She kept glancing anxiously from time to time at her husband, who remained aloof, moving nervously on one leg, as was his manner, talking all the time in his rather thick nasal voice to his *Flügeladjudant*.

The usual glasses of fruit juice with beer were handed around, and we sipped and talked while the Empress worked at her crochet. She disliked to sit with idle hands. Toward ten o'clock, she rose and departed, and the ladies, beginning with the Excellencies, Countess von Brockdorff and Countess Keller, and ending with the young Countesses, passed after her through the doorway, each one turning as she passed to make the customary *Knicks* to the Emperor.

I, of course, was, as in old days, at the tail of the procession, and when I came to the door prepared to make my curtsy, the Emperor most unaccountably turned his back and talked volubly, apparently quite oblivious of my presence. All the same, I knew it was studied rudeness on his part. He had deliberately ignored me all evening. "He is annoyed with something our government has done," was my thought. I left my *Knicks* unperformed and followed the Empress to say farewell. In the morning, I left for England.

*

Over the years that have since passed, one event that occurred during my stay at the Prussian Court, an event seemingly minor and routine when it transpired, has come into focus in my memory in all its painful, ironic detail.

It was in the autumn of 1909, shortly before the confirmation of the Princess and the end of my tenure. The Austrian Archduke Franz Ferdinand and his morganatic—commoner—wife, the former Sophie Chotek and then the Duchess of Hohenberg, visited the Emperor and Empress at the New Palace. The Archduke was a stout, truculent-looking individual of no pronounced qualities of mind. His wife appeared to be decidedly the better half, and she made a fond impression upon the Empress and the ladies of the court during the several days we spent together while the Emperor and the Archduke went hunting.

After the Austrian couple departed, frequent and heated discussions took place, particularly between Fräulein von Gersdorff and Countess Stolberg, with regard to the position of the Duchess when it should transpire that her husband would become emperor, especially in view of the complicated situation arising from the fact that though by the constitution she could never succeed to the throne of Austria, barricaded as it was by stringent laws of succession, there was no reason she should not ascend to that of Hungary. The Duchess was popular among the clergy of the Roman Catholic church, and it was believed by many that the church would have thrown the whole weight of its influence into the attempt to get her acknowledged as reigning empress. On the other hand, it was maintained that neither the old aristocracy of Austria, so tenacious of its rights, nor the next heir to the throne after Franz Ferdinand, would be likely to tolerate the granting of imperial rights to a line whose claims were patently unlawful.

Just over a year after the wedding of the Princess, an assassin's bullet settled this question for all time.

As I look back and think of that Duchess, that graceful woman—not beautiful, but intelligent—with her uninteresting spouse to whom she was deeply devoted, and of the fact that their assassination at Sarajevo was the pretext and signal for the outbreak of the most dreadful war that has ever been chronicled—when I consider that the fate of those two people, insignificant in personality and of no intrinsic value to the world, should have been the means of setting alight the flame that has devastated Europe, I wonder at the sublime gullibility of nations, at their willingness to slay and be slain for a cause which is hid from them, at the waste of so much splendid valor and precious human life for a thing of so infinitely little worth: the prestige of a vain and futile monarchy, and the ambition and pride that lie at the root of every war that has ever been.

The engagement portrait of the Prince of Cumberland, Ernst August ("Pol") and the Princess Victoria Louise ("Sissy"), spring 1913.

EPILOGUE

On June 28, 1914, the Austrian Archduke Franz Ferdinand and his wife were assassinated in the Serbian town of Sarajevo, precipitating the series of events that led to the outbreak of World War I—the Great War—on August 4, 1914. The Great War cost Germany the lives of 1,773,700 of its subjects. Among the earliest casualties were the Princes Max and Freddy of Hesse—the Emperor's nephews and the Princess's cousins and playmates —killed in the first months of the war. Prince Sigismund, another cousin of the Princess and a frequent visitor to the Bauern-Haus, was also killed before the war was over.

A few days before the end of the war, in November 1918, the Kaiser agreed to abdicate as Emperor of Germany but refused to abdicate as King of Prussia. However, Prince Max von Baden (Aunty Baden's son and cousin of the Kaiser), well aware that the Kaiser had no more support in the military or in the Reichstag, deliberately announced that Wilhelm had renounced both thrones and that the Crown Prince had renounced the succession. The ex-Emperor and the ex-Empress, as well as a number of the members of their suites, including General von Gontard, Countess Keller, and Countess von Brockdorff, fled to exile in Holland and lived in the Amerongen Castle.

The Crown Prince, commander of the Fifth Army in the Great War, returned to Germany in 1923, and, although he remained married to Cecile, gained the reputation of a playboy and, according to one historian, "frittered away his life on a succession of mistresses." In 1933, he joined the Nazi party. His oldest son, the Emperor's first grandchild, was killed in 1940 in the German invasion of France. His second son, Louis Ferdinand Hohenzollern, lives in Germany and is a modern pretender to the throne of the German Empire. Crown Prince Wilhelm died in 1951.

Prince Eitel-Frederick commanded the First Foot-Guards Regiment in the Great War. He was later an early supporter of the Nazis and was conspicuous at Berlin social events sponsored by Nazi leaders. He divorced his wife, Sophie of Oldenburg; they had no children. Prince Fritz died in 1942 in Potsdam, and, as the Hohenzollerns had been implicated in an earlier plot to assassinate Hitler, the *Führer* decreed that Fritz's burial should take place without military honors. His friends from the *Wehrmacht* attended in civilian clothes.

Prince Adalbert, an officer on board the battleship *Luitpold* in the Great War, was the only prince to join the navy (he was the namesake of a cousin of King Frederick Wilhelm IV, founder of the Prussian Admiralty). He never married; the Emperor's attempt to arrange a marriage between him and a daughter of Czar Nicholas II was rebuffed. For many years, Adalbert lived in La Tour de Peilz in Switzerland, where he died in 1948.

Prince August-Wilhelm spent the war as a staff officer. He was married unhappily to his first cousin, Princess Alexandra Victoria of Schleswig-Holstein-Saxe-Gotha. In the early 1930s, he became an active Nazi; in the 1934 purge, he was stripped of his brown-shirt uniform and expelled from the Storm Troops because he had been "too intimate" with Karl Ernst, the Storm Troops leader. In 1939, he gave a press interview denying reports that he and other members of the Hohenzollern family had been arrested, or that they had had any connection with the attempt to assassinate Hitler in Munich. In World War II, his only son was an officer in the *Luftwaffe*. Au-Wi died in 1949, according to his sister's memoir, of "ailments he had sustained in...[Allied] internment camps."

Prince Oskar, in the Great War, commanded the Liegnitz King's Grenadiers. He later was a member of the governing board of the Nazi party until Hitler dissolved it on assuming power. His oldest son, Oskar, was killed in the 1939 invasion of Poland. Oskar died in Munich in 1958.

Prince Joachim, a cavalry officer during the Great War, married the seventeen-year-old Princess Marie August of Anholt before the war ended. According to the memoirs of Princess Victoria Louise, the marriage was "unfortunate." For no recorded reasons, Joachim committed suicide while visiting Au-Wi's Potsdam home in 1920. He was survived by a son.

The Empress Augusta, in weakening health for several years, never recovered from the death of Joachim, although to spare her greater sadness, she was told he died in an accident. She died only a year later, in 1921. In 1923, the Emperor remarried; his second wife was a widow, Princess Hermine von Schonaich-Carolath.

The Emperor lived in a house in Doorn, Holland, for twenty-one years. The Dutch government refused to hand him over to the Allies for a trial, and he spent the final years of his life as a country gentleman: he grew a beard, chopped wood, formed a local literary society, and wrote scientific and historical papers. He died in Doorn in 1941 and was buried there. While the other members of his family were buried near the Berlin Schloss, the Emperor stated that his remains were never to be removed to German soil until the monarchy was restored.

Princess Victoria Louise, who became, upon her marriage, the Duchess of Brunswick of Blankenberg in Braunschweig, died in 1980. Her husband, Ernst August, the former Prince of Cumberland, and later, the Duke of Brunswick, died in 1953. They had five children: Ernst August, Georg Wilhelm, Friederike, Christian, and Heinrich.

—W.R.C.

ABOUT THE AUTHOR

Anne Topham was born in 1864 on the Old Farm in Spondon, Derbyshire, England, the first child of what was to be a large family. Her father, Thomas Topham, was a farmer on the Mundy Estate at Mackworth and was also a local butcher.

Anne was educated at the Moravian School at Ockbrook and, upon graduating, worked as a governess to girls of prominent families. A local newspaper account of her, published upon her death, noted, "She was known as a bright and entertaining companion amongst all sorts and conditions of people."

She first visited Germany with a friend in 1896, a three weeks' tour of the Rhine country, and recorded her observations, which she published in 1916 as *Memories of the Fatherland*.

Her associations and reputation as a governess served her well; in 1902, when she was thirty-eight years old, she received an invitation to join the court of Kaiser Wilhelm II of Germany as the English governess to his seventh child and only daughter, the nine-year-old Princess Victoria Louise. Miss Topham—who became known at court as "Topsy"—served in that post for seven years, leaving in 1909 after the confirmation of the Princess.

Anne Topham returned to her home at Spondon, and, as her obituary reported, continued to "cultivate the literary gifts she had discovered she possessed during her sojourn in Germany." Indeed, she had already written many magazine articles on features of the court life, and a novel, *Daphne in the Fatherland*. She now worked to compile her experiences into what was to become her most successful book: *Memories of the Kaiser's Court*.

On August 4, 1914, a state of war was declared between Great Britain and Germany, and on this day, according to press accounts, "by a supreme stroke of good fortune, Miss Topham was able to announce [her book] for publication." *The Daily Mail* hailed *Memories of the Kaiser's Court* as "the book of the year," and it became an immense success in both Great Britain and the United States.

The financial success of the book allowed Miss Topham to concentrate on a full-time writing career, completing, before her death, five additional novels and two more works of nonfiction. She also made forays into politics from the point of view of High Toryism, wrote continually for the London papers, served in several civic posts in her parish, and grew prize-winning primroses.

Nevertheless, she was in continuous poor health, and on December 12, 1927, she died at the age of sixty-three. Her funeral was attended by "a large concourse of friends and relatives," who sang "Light at Eventide" and "Abide with Me" as farewell to a woman who had enjoyed "a career of unique and outstanding interest."

The first son of Victoria Louise, the Duchess of Brunswick, was named Ernst August. He was born in March 1914, and was delivered by the court physician, old Dr. Zunker, who had presided at the birth of the Princess twenty-two years earlier.

CHAPTER NOTES

Chapter One

14: Abd-al-Hamid II (1842–1918) was the Sultan of the Ottoman Empire from 1876 to 1909.

14: Sophie was the next-to-youngest sister of the Emperor; her husband, Constantine, became the Duke of Sparta and, later, King Constantine I of Greece (1913–1917, 1920–1922). Constantine and Sophie had three sons: George, who became George II of Greece (1922–1923, 1935–1947); Alexander, who ruled in 1917–1920 after his father's first deposition; and Paul. Alexander died in 1920 as the result of a monkey bite.

16: The Kaiser was away from his family, wherever they happened to be staying, for about thirty weeks a year. (*Kaiser Wilhelm II*, Emil Ludwig, G. P. Putnam & Sons.)

Chapter Two

24: Also called the South African War (1899–1902), the Boer War was fought between the German-supported Dutch *Boers*—Dutch for "farmers"—and the British. Gold was discovered in the Transvaal plateau in 1886, and British immigrants, who had settled primarily in the southern Cape of Good Hope, swarmed in to mine. Attempting to stem the tide and to keep their autonomy, the South African Republic and the Orange Free State taxed the immigrants heavily and denied them citizenship. The two Dutch states united in 1896, and the British sent troops to protect its commercial mining interests, which the Boers interpreted as an attempt to seize the Transvaal.

Equipped by Kaiser Wilhelm II, the Boers, backed by local tribes, went on the offensive. But reinforcements and naval superiority turned the tide in favor of the British. The Treaty of Vereeniging in 1902 sealed the British victory and embarrassed the Kaiser. (*Spectrum American Encyclopedia*, ed. by Michael D. Harkavy, American Booksellers Association/Spectrum Database Publishing; *Concise Columbia Encyclopedia*, ed. by Judith Levey and Agnes Greenhall, Avon.)

26: Kaiser Wilhelm II was born January 27, 1859. His mother, Princess Victoria, suffered through a long and painful breach delivery without anesthetic. Forceps were used clumsily in the delivery and crushed the infant's left arm, which was pulled almost completely out of the socket. Three days later, it was noticed that the muscles were crushed and the arm was paralyzed. Neither the hand nor the arm recovered, despite constant treatment. (*Dreadnought*, Robert Massie, Random House.)

30: The Emperor frequently changed his clothes as often as twelve times a day. (Eulenburg, quoted in Ludwig.)

35: The actual title was *Life of Frederick the Great* (1860). Thomas Carlyle was known for his admiration of autocratic and dynamic leaders and his disdain for democracy. (*Benét's Reader's Encyclopedia*, Harper & Row.)

35: King Frederick Wilhelm I (1688–1740), father of Frederick the Great and a strong and rigid ruler, was responsible for creating the famed disciplined Prussian army. (*Chambers' Biographical Dictionary*, J.O. Thorne and T.O. Colloctt, W.R. Chambers Ltd.)

Chapter Three

42: The Emperor owned seventy-three castles and country estates. (Ludwig.)

56: On one of the few quiet winter evenings at the New Palace there were no guests, only two ladies and four gentlemen present. The

Empress was sewing; the Emperor was reading dispatches or newspaper cuttings, occasionally aloud; and the others were turning over illustrated journals at the big table till close on eleven o'clock. The Emperor suddenly said to the Empress: "Do you intend to stop here all night?" "No, William, but I didn't like to disturb you, as you were so busy reading all evening." "Well, what else can I do, when this place is so frightfully boring!" (Zedlitz, quoted in Ludwig.)

61: Count Robert von Zedlitz-Trutzschler was the author of the book, *Twelve Years at the German Court* (New York: Doran, 1924.)

62: George III of Great Britain and Ireland, third Hanoverian king (later called Windsor), used soldiers from neighboring Hesse-Cassel, called Hessians, to fight American colonists during the American Revolution. (Spectrum.)

Chapter Four

71: Under Kaiser Wilhelm II, the stables were kept busy: while the court was in Berlin and Potsdam, they prepared over two hundred teams a day. (Ludwig.)

82: The King of Norway was Haakon VII (1872–1957), second son of King Frederick VIII of Denmark. His wife, Maud (1869–1938), was his cousin, daughter of his aunt Alexandra and her husband, King Edward VII of Britain and Ireland. Their son, Olaf V (1903–1991), personally led the Norwegian forces against the Nazis in 1944 and succeeded his father in 1957. This trip had to have taken place sometime in 1906. (Chambers; *Spectrum*.)

Chapter Five

90: The Cuirassiers were cavalrymen who wore a leather breastplate, called a cuirass.

Chapter Six

116: After an attempted flirtation with the Princess Cantacuzene, Crown Prince Wilhelm sent "each 1st of January, a telegram of greeting, or some souvenir: a small painting of himself on horseback, a photograph of him with his fiancee, three or four watercolors showing the ancient uniforms his regiments had worn, a picture of his eldest son." (*My Life Here and There*, Princess Cantacuzene, the Countess Speransky, Charles Scribner's Sons.)

117: *Hohenzollern*, the Emperor's imperial yacht, cost 4.5 million marks to build, and was of the design of military battleships. It was made into a pleasure boat, much to the consternation of the Reichstag. The white ship was decked with decorative armament and named for the Emperor's family, the dynasty that rose to prominence in the late twelfth century. (Ludwig.)

Chapter Seven

121: Elbing, now known as Elblag, is in Poland and is twenty-five miles from the southern Lithuanian border, where it overlaps Poland to the north. It is about ten miles south of the Gulf of Danzig in the Baltic Sea, twenty-five miles west of Gdansk-Danzig.

136: Lord Reginald Brett Esher was appointed by Prime Minister Balfour in 1903 to be chairman of the royal commission to investigate charges of incompetence and corruption in the British army in the wake of charges after the Boer War. (Massie.)

Chapter Eight

139: The Life Guards were two regiments of cavalry that acted as a body guard for the Emperor and Empress.

140: The Herero War was one of a series of colonial wars that pitted European powers against idigenous African peoples. The Germans fought a series of "savage" wars against the Hereros in Southwest Africa (now known as Namibia), annexed as a "protectorate" by Germany in 1884, as well as the Maji-Maji in Tanganyika. The Herero Wars were fought between 1905–1908 when the final Herero and Nama rebellions were crushed. A total of 84,000 Africans— three-quarters of the population—were killed by direct German military action. (*Columbia History of the World*, ed. by John Garraty and Peter Gay, Harper & Row; *Concise Columbia*; *The African Experience*, Roland Oliver, Harper Collins.)

140: Elsass-Lothringen is one of several names for the Alsace, Lorraine, regions that form some of the borders between north-western Germany, France, Luxembourg, Belgium, and Netherlands, which had been under constant dispute between Germany and France since annexed by Lothair I in the ninth century. (*Concise Columbia*.)

140: Prince Otto Edward Leopold von Bismarck (1815–1898), Duke of Lauenburg, was known as the Iron Chancellor and is considered the father of the modern German state. He provoked France into the Franco-Prussian War (1870–1871), which resulted in the unification of the Prussian and German states and the crowning of Wilhelm I, grandfather of Kaiser Wilhelm II, as the first German emperor. Bismarck was forced to resign in 1890 by Wilhelm II. (*Concise Columbia*.)

140: Karl von Clausewitz (1780–1831), Prussian general and revolutionary military theorist, was chief of the Prussian army after the Napoleonic Wars. He wrote the influential military work, *On War*, which expounded the doctrine of total war and war as a political act. (Chambers.)

141: France declared war on Prussia on July 19, 1870. Other German states leaped to Prussia's defense. Napoleon III was captured and deposed September 1, 1870, ending the second French Empire. Paris surrendered in January 1871, after a long siege, and ceded Alsace Lorraine. On January 18, 1871, Wilhelm I was declared emperor of the new German Empire.

149: Albert (1819–1861) was the younger of the two sons of Ernest I, the Duke of Saxe-Coburg-Gotha, who caught the attention of and married an infatuated Queen Victoria in February 1840. He was made consort in 1840 and Prince Consort in 1957. (Chambers.)

153: The first Socialist workers party was founded in 1863 in Germany by Ferdinand Lassalle. Socialists, led by German and mostly Jewish intellectuals, believed in collective government ownership and management of production and distribution of goods; the response was government-fostered anti-Semitism. (*Concise Columbia*.)

154: In 1806, Prussia joined the Third Coalition of Britain, Austria, Russia, and Sweden to fight Napoleon I, but was defeated at Jena on October 14. However, after Napoleon's retreat from Moscow in 1812, a coalition of Prussia, Britain, Sweden, and Austria defeated the emperor at Leipzig in October 1813. (*Concise Columbia*.)

154: Frederick Wilhelm III (1770–1840), grandnephew of Frederick the Great, was at first neutral to Napoleon. Incensed Prussians forced him, via his strong-willed wife, Queen Louise, to join the Third Coalition. (Chambers.)

154: Gerhard Johann David von Scharnhorst (1755–1813) was a German general, who, in 1807, reorganized the Prussian army and restored morale, leading to the decisive defeat of Napoleon at Leipzig. (Chambers.)

154: Heinrich Friedrich Carl, Baron von Stein (1757–1831), was a German nationalist, Secretary of Trade and Reform, who supported Scharnhorst's army reforms and was instrumental in building the coalition against Napoleon in 1812. (Chambers.)

155: Ulanen were mounted cavalry who carried a lance in the old German armies; this style was later adopted by the Polish army.

00: The political philosophies of Welt Politik and Wasser Politik—global politics and water politics—were outgrowths of Weltmacht—world power—the concept of German nationalism, colonial imperialism, and manifest destiny, fostered by Bismarck and embraced by Kaiser Wilhelm II and his chief admiral, Alfred von Tirpitz. The Kaiser discovered that no large battleships had been built in the five years previous to his ascension to the throne in June 1988, and he embarked on a massive building program to rival the British efforts. In 1891, at Stettin, he noted that "Our future is on the water," accelerating the battleship race with Britain. He battled with the Reichstag for naval appropriations every few years from 1898 until the war. (Massie.)

Chapter Nine

161: Schleswig-Holstein is a principality wedged between Prussia and Denmark at the base of the Jutland peninsula. The territory was annexed by Denmark in November 1863, in violation of international treaties. In response, the duchies were conquered by Prussian and Austrian troops under Bismarck in the war of 1864 that awakened German nationalism, and annexed in 1866. (*Spectrum.*)

Chapter Ten

193: The H.M.S. *Dreadnought* was the most influential navy vessel ever built: its primary design was used by every nation in the world and can be seen in the *Wisconsin*-class battleship still in use by the U.S. Navy. The exact ship in question was the largest battleship ever built (18,000 tons), and nothing afloat could match its speed (21 knots) or firepower (ten 12-inch guns). It was launched February 10, 1906, accepted into His Majesty's Navy on December 11, 1906, and made flagship the following spring. By the start of the war, Britain had nine *Dreadnought*-class battleships. (*Spectrum*; Massie.)

205: "Mark" refers to divisions of Brandenburg, which formed the nucleus of Prussia.

Chapter Eleven

214: Prince Philip von Eulenburg (1847–1921) was an influential confident of the Emperor until vengeful and politically motivated rumors of homosexuality resulted in a scandal and ruined him in 1907.

215: "The 100,000 acres of primeval forest had been transformed under orders from the Kaiser into a sort of sportsman's chess-board. An army of foresters attended the shooters on bicycles, in carts, on horse. . .so that actually every. . .point was under the keenest observation from first to last." (Zedlitz, quoted in Ludwig.) "The shoots were horrible. This massacre of unfortunate creatures, utterly unable to escape from their fate of destruction, is no kingly recreation." (Eulenburg, quoted in Ludwig.)

216: Of the Kaiser's hunting at Rominten: "He is much incommoded by his paralyzed left arm. His loader has to lean his right arm on a long pole, thus serving the Prince as a support for the rifle. Not every buck will put up with this!" (Eulenburg, quoted in Ludwig.)

220: Topham's impressions of Witte were shared by the Princess Cantacuzene: "At a dinner table, [Witte] was taciturn to a degree. Many women who were his partners thought he meant to insult them, and they said that to hear him eat his soup was agony. One person told me he had watched him pick a chicken leg and throw the bone under the table! The great man was ugly, but with deep, fine eyes and capable hands. . . . I found him rather attractive." (Speransky.)

223: The anecdote of the buttered toast is reminiscent of the A.A. Milne poem, "The King's Breakfast," which was published in 1924 by Methuen, also Topham's original (1914, 1916) publisher.

Chapter Twelve

245: The airship accident during an attempt to fly nonstop from the floating sheds on the Bodensee to Berlin. "The man at the elevator wheel had been flying the airship nose-down because she was light. The man on the rudder wheel could see nothing in front of him because the lowered nose obstructed his view. It was a comical misfortune that the airship should collide with a solitary pear tree on the flat, bare landscape." (*Airshipwreck*, Len Deighton and Arnold Schwartzman, Holt, Rinehart & Winston.)

252: In 1896, the Kaiser sent a telegram to President Kruger of South Africa that said, in part, "I express sincere congratulations . . . that you have succeeded against armed bands which invaded your country as disturbers of the peace. . . ." The telegram was seen as the beginning of serious hostility between Great Britain and Germany. (Massie.)

252: In the fall of 1907, while the Kaiser was on an extended visit to England, he had lengthy, relaxed conversations with Colonel Stuart-Wortley, to whom he later gave permission to publish the information exchanged therein. The Kaiser's remarks appeared in the London *Daily Telegraph* in October 1908 and immediately caused an international uproar. Among other revelations and boasts, the Kaiser claimed to have given England the strategies to win the Boer War; he made ominous military threats against Japan and the Far East; and he referred to a Russian-French coalition against the British during the Boer War. Everyone was horrified, including the German people, who had supported the Boers during their war against the British and who were dismayed to learn that the Kaiser had taken the side of the British. (Massie.)

256: According to Princess Victoria Louise, "Bülow tried to cheat his way out of the whole business by publishing a declaration that he had never known about the controversial article, and, had he known, it would never have been published. . . .This from a man who had not only read the article twice, but who had personally decided on its exact form and content for publication. . . .At the Foreign Office no one doubted that Bülow had played false, and that he had knowingly played false because he himself was a perfidious man." (*The Kaiser's Daughter*, Princess Viktoria Luise of Prussia, Prentice Hall.)

Chapter Thirteen

267: "The Duke and Duchess of Cumberland possessed great wealth. . .[the old Duke] was the eldest son of the blind old King of Hanover, whom Bismarck had dethroned. . . .His sons had never used the title of king, but had taken his father's second title, which was

English. He. . .was phenomenally ugly, and about fifty, cultivated and amiable." (Speransky.)

270: "Auguste [sic] Wilhelm and [his] wife [were] both fat and deadly dull." (Speransky.)

GLOSSARY

Abiturien Examen — final examination

Äbtissin — directress, abbess

allerunterthänigst (alleruntertänigst) — most humble, most obedient

Apollosaal — hall of Apollo

aufgestanden und ausgetrunken — stand up and bottoms up

Augen rechts, Augen links, Paradeschritt, Präsentiert das Gewehr —
    Eyes right, eyes left, goose step, present arms

Augusta Stift — Augusta foundation

ausfallen — be cancelled, not take place

Ausflüge und Landpartien — excursions and picnics

Ausgang — exit

Aussichtspunkt — place with a view, observation point

Badeort — spa

Bahn — track, menage, arena

Bahnsteigdekorationen — railway platform decorations

Bauersfrau — peasant woman, farmer's wife

Bauernhaus — peasant cottage

bekommen — to get

Bernstein — amber

Bescherung — presentation of Christmas gifts

Biedermeier — homely or early Victorian style (in Germany, from 1820–48)

Biergärten — beer-gardens

Biergläser — beer glasses

Bildergalerie — picture gallery

Blutwurst — black-pudding

Brotpudding — bread pudding

Bornstedter Gut — Bornstedter estate, Bornstedter farm

Brandenburger Tor — Brandenburg Gate

Brautpaar — bridal couple

Burg — fortress

Bürgermeister — Lord Mayor

Bürgersfrau — citizeness, middleclass woman

Burschen — here: student (member of Burschenschaft; i.e. student's
association)

Cadiner Fabrik — factory at Cadinen

Cercle — social gathering of distinguished individuals

Christbaumengel — angel for Christmas tree

Communs — barracks

Coupé — compartment

Cour — reception

Denkmals — monuments, memorials

die kalte Pracht — the cold splendor

Die Prinzessin! Die kleine Prinzessin! Ach wie niedlich — The princess,
the little princess, oh how cute.

Dienerschaft — servants

Dienst — service, employment, duty

Dienstmann — porter, doorman

Droschke — carriage

dumm — stupid, ignorant

dumme Kerle — ignorant fellows, stupid guys

ebenbürtig — equal in birth

Ehrensteuer — tax of honor

Eiersuchen — egg-hunt

Eingang — entrance

Einlasskarte — admission ticket; here, "building pass"

Eisenbahn — railway

Elch — moose, elk

Elsass Lothringen — Alsace Lorraine

Er ist doch der Kaiser! — But he is the Emperor.

Erfrischung — refreshment

Exzellenz — Excellency

Exerzierplatz — parade ground, drill yard, barrack square

Feld — field

Ferien — vacation

Fest — party

Flügeladjudant — aide-de-camp

Fräulein — Miss

Friedenskirche — Church of Peace

Frisches Haff — strip of land forming a lagoon from the Baltic Sea;
　　"fresh lagoon"

Frühstückstafel — breakfast table

Gartenrestaurant — garden restaurant, open air restaurant

Gendarm — rural policeman, constable

Geschwader der Prinzessin — the Princess's squadron

Glaubensbekenntnis — confession of faith

gnädiges Fräulein — Miss, Madam

Grüss Gott! — God greet you!

Gott bewahre! — God forbid!

Gott sei Dank! — God be thanked!

Gottesdienst — church service

grässlich — horrible, awful

Gratulationscour — formal ceremony to congratulate a high ranking
　　personality

grossartig — wonderful, marvelous

Guten Tag! — Good day!

Haff — lagoon

Halloren — guild of Saxonian salt-workers

Hamburger Kücken — Hamburg chicken

Haus — house

Hausfrau — housewife

Ha-la-li — mort, kill, death (hunting)

Heil dir im Siegerkranz — "Hail you in the victor's crown" (German national anthem, early twentieth century)

heisser Wunsch — ardent/burning desire

Herlich! Wunderschön! Prachtvoll! — marvelous, lovely, magnificent

Herrschaften — persons of rank

Hirschfänger — hunting knife, bowie knife

Hoch lebe der Kaiser! — Long live the Emperor!

Hochs — cheers

höchst demokratisch — highly democratic

Hof — court

Hoffourrier (Hoffurier) — quartermaster sergeant at court

Hofprediger — court chaplain

hohe Herrschaften — people of high rank

Hühnerfrau — woman in charge of chicken

Igel — hedgehog

im Freien — outdoors

Inspektor — inspector

Ja, ja für die Kaiserin — Yes, yes for the Empress

Jagdhaus — shooting lodge

Jagdschloss — hunting lodge

Jagdwagen — hunting car

Jäger — rifleman, fusiliers

Jägerhut — huntsman's hat

Kabinettshaus — "house of cabinets"

Kadettenschule — officer's training school, cadet college

Kaiser — emperor

kalte Schnitzel — cold veal cutlets

Kammerdiener — valet, groom, personal servant

Kammerherr — chamberlain

Kastellan — castellan, steward

Kavallerieattacke — attack of the cavalry

kein Wagen — no carriage

Kieler Woche — "Week of Kiel" annual boat show and regatta held in Kiel

Kinderfest — children's party

Kinderheim — home for children

Kinderschaft — children

kindisch und albern — childish and silly

Knicks — curtsy

kolossal — colossal (coll.: extremely, immensely)

Kommissbrot — army bread, soldier's bread

Konfekt — candy, here: chocolate rings

königliches Schloss — royal palace, royal castle

Königsberger Nachrichten — Königsberg News

Korso — procession of carriages

Krönungstag — anniversary of accession

Kur — course of baths, taking the waters

Kurhaus — spa hotel

Lampier — person in charge of lamps

Landadel — country nobility, gentry

Landgraf — landgrave; German prince

Landgräfin — landgravine; German Princess

Landrat (pl. Landräte) — chairman of rural district council, district administrator

langgestreckt — long-drawn-out

Leberwurst — liver sausage

Leibjäger — chasseur

Letevka — Norfolk jacket

Louisenstrasse — Louisenstreet (name of street)

Lustgarten — pleasure gardens

Mädchen — girl(s)

Marmorsaal — marble hall

Mittagessen — lunch

Mopke — court

Muschelsaal — hall of shells

Musterkinder — model children

nasch(en) — to nibble

natürlich — of course, naturally

Neuer Garten — "New Garden"

Neues Palais — "New Palace"

nicht hinauslehnen — do not lean out

die Nonne — the nun

Oberförster — head forester, head game-keeper, head forest ranger

Obergouvernante — head governess

Oberhofmeisterin — Mistress of the Robes

Ofen — stove, oven

Onkel — uncle

Ostsee — Baltic Sea

Paradeschritt — goose step

Parkett — stalls

Pfannkuchen — pancake; the Berlin variety to which she is referring is
    like a jelly doughnut

Pfefferkuchen — gingerbread

Pfennig — penny

Pfingsten — Whitsuntide

Pickelhaube — spiked helmet

prachtvoll — magnificent

praktisch — practical

Prinzenwohnung — apartment of the princes

Prinzenvilla — villa/house of the princes

Prinzipienreiter — stickler for rules, pedant, dogmatist

Quatsch — nonsense

Reitbahn — riding school

Rominter Heide — Heath of Rominten

Saal — hall

Sandhof — gravelled courtyard

Sattelmeister — stable master, saddle master

Schafskopf — block head

Scherkel (Ferkel) — piglet

Schildersaal — hall of shields, hall of coat of arms

Schloss — palace

schnell — quick

Schrippen (Brötchen) — breakfast rolls, rolls

sehr modern — very modern, very progressive

sehr nett — very nice

so ein Kerl — such a fellow, such a guy

Sozialdemokraten — Social Democrats (one of the main two parties in
    Germany)

Speisekarte — menu

Sportkostüm — casual/comfortable suit for sports; "sports suit"

Sportplatz — sports ground, playing field

Spruch — here: award (hunting)

Stachelschwein — porcupine

Steckkissen — baby's pillow

Stiftskinder — students on scholarships

Stille Nacht — Silent Night (Christmas carol)

Strecke — bag (hunting)

Südwestafrika — South West Africa (now: Namibia)

Tägliche Rundschau — Daily Review (name of newspaper)

Tante — aunt

Tanzproben — dance practice

Teerbude — tar booth

Tiergarten — park in Berlin's center ("zoological gardens")

Tor — gate

Totenkopf — death's head, skull

Truchsess — Lord High Steward

Tugendbund — association/club of virtue

Turnsaal — gymnasium

Ulan (pl. Ulanen) — lancer

ungezwungen — freely

Unke (pl. Unken) — orange speckled toad

Unkenruf — cry of the Unke, fig. for "bad prediction"

"Unsere Zukunft liegt auf dem Wasser!" — "Our future lies on the water!"

Unter den Linden — formerly the main boulevard in Berlin ("Under the
    Lime-trees"); Linden Avenue

Verein — club, association

Verstecken — hide-and-seek

Volksschule — elementary school

Warenhaus Wertheim — Wertheim's Department Store

Wartesaal — waiting room

Wasserpolitik — "water politics"

"Weidmanns Heil!" — "Good hunting!" (Greeting among hunters)

Weihnachtsabend (Heilig Abend) — Christmas Eve

Weihnachtsgeschichte — Christmas story

Weisser Saal — white hall

Weltpolitik — world politics

Wildpark — deer park, game preserve

Wohnung der Prinzessin — apartment of the Princess

zanken — quarrel, wrangle

Zeppelin — blimp

Zeppelin kommt — the blimp comes

Ziegelei — brick-works, brickyard

Zwieback — rusk, "twice-baked" biscuit

I N D E X